*The Honor Plays
of Lope de Vega*

The Honor Plays
of Lope de Vega

Donald R. Larson

Harvard University Press
Cambridge, Massachusetts
and London, England
1977

Y / 144 / 52
'1/4
£9·80

Publication of this book has been aided by a grant from the Andrew W.
Mellon Foundation

Library of Congress Cataloging in Publication Data

Larson, Donald R.   1935–
   The honor plays of Lope de Vega.

   Includes index.
   1. Vega Carpio, Lope Félix de, 1562–1635—Criticism and interpretation.   2.   Honor in literature.   I.   Title.
PQ6490.H7L3   862'.3   77–22950
ISBN 0–674–40628–1

For my parents

Preface

THIS book is a study of that group of plays of Lope de Vega known as the honor plays. It differs from other investigations of the same subject in that it attempts to comprehend the entire corpus of Lope's honor plays while at the same time respecting the integrity of the individual work. The latter I regard as of fundamental importance. The monographs of Américo Castro, William L. Fichter, Ramón Menéndez Pidal, Alfonso García Valdecasas, and Antonie Adrianus van Beysterveldt, which, like mine, deal with more than one or two of Lope's plays, are all helpful in their own ways, but for the student of literature they are also somewhat misleading, for they treat the plays primarily as vehicles of ideas, leading one to assume that they are to a large extent interchangeable. The truth is, however, that the honor play was in Lope's hands a very protean form: *El castigo sin venganza* is a work quite different in tone and effect from *Peribáñez y el Comendador de Ocaña*, and neither of them arouses the same response as, say, *El castigo del discreto*.

Given this variation, the validity of any study that examines the honor plays as a group may appropriately be queried. I would respond to the question with two facts. First, because the plays are all shaped from the same basic form, they do offer significant points of similarity as well as points of difference. Second, and more important, the variation that they exhibit follows an identifiable and meaningful pattern. The plays mentioned above derive from different periods of Lope's life, the first being a work of his old age, the second, an effort of his middle years, and the third, a product of his youth; and although they are dissimilar, each is in large measure typical of the honor plays of the period from which it dates. What this implies, clearly, is that there is within the group of Lope's honor plays a development of some sort. It is my aim to chart, and try to understand, that development.

There are undoubtedly a number of valid ways to do this. Another person pursuing the same objective might have elected, for example, to examine chronologically and systematically all, or nearly all, of Lope's honor plays. The result would be a study that was indisputably comprehensive but also, probably, repetitious. The method I have chosen is more selective. I have picked as representatives two or three plays from each period and examined each of them in some detail. Where it seemed helpful, I have referred to other plays as well, especially in cases where such references might tend to modify the characterizations I draw of the early, middle, and late plays.

In speaking of early, middle, and late plays, I am employing generally accepted critical terminology. I do not know who first saw Lope's dramatic output as falling into three distinct periods, but since Menéndez y Pelayo the tripartite division has been traditional in Lopean scholarship. Surprisingly, however, in view of the apparently widespread belief that periodical divisions are valid for Lope's plays, there has been little methodical comparison of the plays of one group with those of another. To be sure, for many years scholars lacked a trustworthy chronology, without which comparative studies of a serious nature were virtually impossible. In 1940, however, S. Griswold Morley and Courtney Bruerton published their *Chronology of Lope de Vega's "Comedias,"* a tool soon recognized as astonishingly reliable in its datings, approximate as some of them had to be, and the decades that have elapsed since its appearance have not seen any appreciable increase in the number of investigations with a chronological orientation. Speaking before the American "Comediantes" in 1949, José F. Montesinos pointed out the need for studies that examine the "development of themes in Lope." That need is today still essentially unfulfilled.

Whatever originality this book may possess, then, lies in its having put the Morley-Bruerton *Chronology* to literary use, something as yet relatively uncommon. Among other things, this "new" approach reveals that the division of Lope's plays into three periods can be supported by close examination of the texts and is, at least insofar as the honor plays are concerned, quite justifiable. Naturally, no one would care to affirm that strict lines of demarcation may be drawn, and scholars have usually defined the limits of the periods rather loosely. I shall here follow that example. In the succeeding pages, therefore, "early play" should be understood as referring to any work written around or before 1600, "late play" as any work written around or after 1620, and "middle-period play" as any work written between those two dates.

Every piece of criticism is directed principally to a certain kind of reader. This one is no exception. It is addressed primarily to those who have some familiarity both with Spanish writing in general and with the Spanish Golden Age theater in particular. I am aware, however, that the appearance of a book in English on a playwright universally acknowledged to be among the greatest in European history may arouse the interest of some who are not, strictly speaking, students of Spanish literature. It is for the benefit of those possible readers that I have included prose translations of all quotations from the plays I discuss. These versions, which are my own unless otherwise indicated, aim to be as literal as possible, consistent with the limits of standard modern English and the need for a clear comprehension of the original Spanish. They are in no sense intended to substitute for the latter.

In conclusion, I would like to make two remarks about methodology. As indicated, this study concentrates on the particular work, and thus much of what is said is necessarily given over to considerations of form. The study is by no means exclusively formalistic, however, for reasons which may be briefly sketched. There is, first of all, the question of understanding. It is axiomatic that literature is composed of words and that words are conditioned by the culture within which they are employed. The necessary corollary of this simple truth is not always, however, even in this age of Newer

New Criticism, sufficiently appreciated. It is that any piece of writing must be perceived within the context of the cultural structure—what Castro has called the "vital dwelling place"—inside of which it was created, or else be comprehended only imperfectly. What is true of all literature is especially true of the *Comedia* of the Spanish Golden Age. For as Stephen Gilman pointed out in the *Bulletin of the Comediantes* (Spring 1960), we are dealing here with a theater in which the audience is "built, as it were, into the play and present by implication in every speech and line." This being the case, any attempt to provide a reading of the plays that is not constantly informed by the specific audience to which they are directed—the people of the late sixteenth and seventeenth centuries in Spain, with all of their prejudices, fears, and aspirations—is doomed to automatic failure.

The second reason that this study has not been limited to formalistic considerations is that such an approach, when exclusive, is inimical to the very purpose for which most of us read. That purpose, I take it, has to do with the search for meaning. We read because in literature we find systems of values with which to enlarge, adjust, or redefine our own. Values, however, are never absolute, but always relative to a particular set of circumstances, and it is as such, surely, that they must be apprehended. The writings of Sophocles, Dante, and Shakespeare were originally dialogues with a certain historical moment: if we would appreciate the importance of their response, therefore, we must first familiarize ourselves with the questions asked. It has been said that great literature is "timeless," not despite but precisely because it was once, and in a sense continues to be, "timebound." In the title chapter of his recent book, *Historicism Once More* (Princeton University Press, 1969), Roy Harvey Pearce has expanded on the truth of this assertion. The value of art, he writes, is that it shows us how it was possible to live in and through the forms, repressive and expressive, of the artist's civilization, thus leading us to an awareness of how it is "possible to live authentically in and through the forms peculiar to *our* civilization."

Preface

The first form of this monograph served as a doctoral dissertation in the Department of Romance Languages and Literatures at Harvard University. To the director of that dissertation, Professor Stephen Gilman, I am profoundly grateful, not only for his guidance and encouragement during the time of its writing, but for many kindnesses in the years both preceding and following that period. I am also grateful to Professor Frank P. Casa, who was the second reader of my dissertation, and to Professors Charles F. Fraker, Joseph H. Silverman, and Edward M. Wilson, all of whom have read one or another draft of this study in its entirety. From each of these I received many helpful suggestions for improvement, as I did also from the consultant for the Harvard University Press and two other readers who must necessarily remain anonymous. Naturally, none of these scholars is responsible for any errors of fact or interpretation that may remain in my text.

I am indebted to the Royal Spanish Academy for permission to quote extensively from their edition of Lope's plays; to the Manchester University Press, for permission to cite from their edition of Calderón's *La vide es sueño;* and to A. David Kossoff and José Amor y Vásquez, editors of the *Homenaje a William L. Fichter* (Madrid, Castalia, 1971), for allowing me to adapt for use here my article appearing in that volume, "*Los Comendadores de Córdoba:* An Early Honor Play."

Special thanks go to my wife, Gail, who suffered the burdens imposed by the writing of this book more than anyone, and always with unfailing patience and good cheer; to three friends and former colleagues, George A. Shipley, Marilyn M. Imes, and Anthony L. Geist, who lent support, both moral and material, when it was most needed; and to my editors at the Harvard University Press, Nancy Clemente and Ann Louise McLaughlin, who gave unstintingly of their interest, tolerance, and expertise.

Contents

1   Introduction: Honor and Honor Plays   1

2   Early Plays: Comic Solutions to the
     Conflict of Honor   17
       Sixteenth-Century Antecedents   17
       El castigo del discreto, La bella malmaridada, and
          Las ferias de Madrid   23

3   Plays of the Middle Period:
     Vengeance Celebrated   38
       Los comendadores de Córdoba   38
       An Excursion into History   54
       Ritual, Myth, and Romance   59
       Peribáñez y el Comendador de Ocaña   65
       Fuenteovejuna   82

4   Late Plays: The Turn toward Tragedy   113
       Tragedy and the *Comedia*   113
       La victoria de la honra and *Porfiar hasta morir*   118
       El castigo sin venganza   131

5   Conclusion   159

Appendix. Tentative Chronology of the Honor Plays of Lope
   de Vega   169
Abbreviations   174
Notes   175
Index   213

1

Introduction: Honor and Honor Plays

EVERY critic who undertakes to reopen the discussion of a topic that has received as much consideration as Lope's honor plays does well to clarify his terminology at the outset. I begin, therefore, with a definition of what I mean by an honor play. As used here, the term "honor play" refers to a particular dramatic structure. It is a play that, in the Aristotelian language employed by Francis Fergusson in his influential *Idea of a Theater*,[1] incarnates an "action" whose object is to regain "honor" that has been lost through an offense of some sort. Generally speaking, the "action" of an honor play is shaped by the interplay between three characters, two men and a woman. The two men are, respectively, the protagonist of the play and his antagonist. The woman's role in the typical honor play is no less important, however, for she is the pivotal character, the person who brings about the antagonism.

It should be understood that not all plays that involve honor are honor plays. Thoughts of honor are never far from the minds of male characters in the Spanish *Comedia*—as indeed they are never far from the minds of a great many males in the French and English theaters of the seventeenth century —and those thoughts are frequently centered on their womenfolk. But the man's thoughts do not result in an honor play unless they turn to actual preoccupation, unless that preoccupation arises from a genuine and serious threat to his reputation involving a woman to whom the man is closely connected, unless that threat leads to active conflict, and unless the

1

conflict constitutes the thematic focus of the play. Clearly, certain works that are sometimes regarded as honor plays do not satisfy these criteria. Consider, for instance, those romantic comedies (*comedias de capa y espada*) in which the honor of an important male character is temporarily threatened. In these plays, of course, the threat is not of an especially serious nature, for it can be, and is, resolved through marriage. Moreover, it does not constitute the true thematic interest of the drama. Love, not honor, is the comic theme, and in concerning themselves primarily with love, these comedies are merely bowing to the dictates of their genre.[2] Another kind of play that is often grouped with the honor plays is the one in which a man wrongly suspects his wife of being unfaithful or of plotting infidelity. However, the "action" in this type of play has as its object not the regaining of lost male honor but the disclosure of female constancy. It thus properly remains outside the range of a discussion of honor plays. There are several other kinds of plays that fall into the same category, all of which are enumerated and described briefly in the Appendix. I have not dealt with them here, preferring to proceed without delay to a consideration of the form of the typical honor play.

Characteristically, the plot of the honor play begins when the principal female character—usually the wife of the protagonist, but on occasion his daughter or sister—attracts the erotic interest of the man who is to be the antagonist. This interest may or may not be reciprocated. In either case, the woman before long finds herself being actively pursued, a situation that sooner or later comes to the attention of the hero. When it does, he invariably concludes that his honor has been critically wounded, and that he has no choice but to seek immediate redress. Depending on the degree of hurt, various kinds of reparation are now open to him. One, however, is not: namely, marriage. That solution, invariably the means of healing wounded honor in the *comedias de capa y espada*, is here impossible, either because the woman concerned is already married or because some disproportion in the social statuses of the woman and her admirer prevents a wedding from taking place. Lacking the solution of a wedding, the aggrieved protagonist nearly always considers the possibility of assassination, and not infrequently he carries it out as well. Sometimes the hero's vengeance falls on the antagonist alone. Sometimes it falls on both the antagonist and the woman he desires (such is the case when the woman is supposed to have encouraged the advances of the male enemy). In either event, the ending of the play is the same. The hero expresses satisfaction that he has fulfilled his obligation to himself and to society, and there is general acknowledgment that his honor has been restored.

Quite obviously, the typical Spanish honor play bears some resemblance to Shakepeare's *Othello,* and there have been efforts to promote an audience for it in the English-speaking countries on the basis of this resemblance.[3] There is, however, an essential difference between the honor plays and Shakespeare's tragedy. The motivating emotion in *Othello* is jealousy, and, like all emotions capable of producing tragedy, it is regarded by Shakespeare as an ambivalent quality, at once heinous and ennobling. In the *Comedia,* on the other hand, jealousy or, more particularly, marital jealousy is thoroughly disesteemed—one need only recall titles like *Celos aun del aire matan* and *El mayor monstruo los celos* to be convinced of this—and if it enters into the honor play, it does so only peripherally.[4] The protagonist's vengeance is induced more or less exclusively by a desire to repair his damaged honor, and, this accomplished, the typical honor play concludes on a note of unequivocal rightness. Of course, the protagonist may experience regret at being placed in a position where revenge appears to be the only alternative, and he may even, on occasion, express that regret openly. Basically, however, he is certain in his own mind that he has little choice but to do what he does. The result is that the final moments of most honor plays contain no feeling of ambivalence, no feeling of ambiguity, no feeling of contradiction—and hence no feeling of tragedy.

If today's readers are to share at all in the assent with which nearly all the honor plays end, they must have some acquaintance with the assumptions on which it is based. Fortunately, there are a number of studies to which one may turn for illumination, most of them competent.[5] I do not propose to summarize here, still less to reproduce, the exhaustive conclusions of those studies. What I shall do, rather, is examine those questions raised most insistently by the concept of honor underpinning the honor plays. That concept, which is basically a reflection of the attitudes held by the vast majority of seventeenth-century Spaniards, is not difficult to understand. But it does call for the apprehension of certain fine distinctions. In focusing attention on those distinctions in the next few pages, I hope to provide a fundamental axiological context for the honor plays, one that will serve as background to the analysis both of individual plays and of general issues in the chapters that follow.

The initial question is, naturally: what does the word "honor" mean, as it is used by the characters of the honor plays and as it was understood by the members of the original audiences of those plays? To avoid later confusion, it may be useful to begin by specifying what exactly the word does *not* mean. It does not mean, first of all, what we in English call "sense of honor." The latter is, of course, conscience or, as Webster puts it, "a nice sense of what is right, just, and true." Although it too, or something akin to it, is encountered in the *Comedia* and in Spanish life, it is, as Salvador de Madariaga among others has pointed out, a quality more characteristic of Anglo-Saxon cultures than Hispanic ones.[6] Its existence, in any case, has traditionally been assumed in Spain to be independent of that of honor itself.[7] To write with scarcely concealed indignation, therefore, as one scholar has done, that "each man [in the Spanish theater] defended his own rights without caring greatly for those of his neighbour,"[8] is to miss the point entirely.[9]

The "honor" of the honor plays, then, is not to be equated with "sense of honor." Neither is it quite the same thing as "fame."[10] To be sure, "fame" and "honor" both imply recognition of personal qualities. But the kind of honor at issue here is something extended by one's contemporaries; more specifically, it is conceded by those with whom one comes in contact in some way, and with a measure of deference. "Fame," on the other hand, at least as that term was understood by the ancients and by most Europeans up until the

Renaissance, is the recognition granted by posterity. It is, in other words, "glory," and because the person who enjoys it is no longer living, it has nothing to do with the relations between people.[11] The distinction between the two concepts has been well expressed by Américo Castro: "The desire for or claim to glory in the Classical and Renaissance worlds sought to fill a present void in polemic with time to come . . . But the honor sentiment which was dramatized in Spain was dramatic precisely because of its social dimension, because it gave rise to conflicts between the individual and society."[12]

Honor, then, is not fame or glory, but simply the esteem and respect of one's peers. Over and over, characters in the *Comedia* make the same point: honor is something external to the individual. A man may have a sense of honor, and his sense of honor may inspire him to acts that earn the deference of others. But no man can grant himself honor, and no man can command honor from his associates if they are unwilling to give it. A famous passage from Lope's *Los comendadores de Córdoba* puts it quite succinctly:[13]

Veinticuatro.	¿Sabes qué es honra?
Rodrigo.	Sé que es una cosa que no la tiene el hombre.
Veinticuatro.	Bien has dicho:

honra es aquella que consiste en otro;
ningún hombre es honrado por sí mismo,
que del otro recibe la honra un hombre;
ser virtuoso hombre y tener méritos,
no es ser honrado; pero dar las causas
para que los que tratan les den honra.
El que quita la gorra cuando pasa
el amigo ó mayor, le da la honra;
el que le da su lado, el que le asienta
en el lugar mayor; de donde es cierto
que la honra está en otro y no en el mismo.

(*Ac.*, XI, 290b–291a)[14]

Veinticuatro. Do you know what honor is? *Rodrigo.* I know that it is something which man does not have in himself. *Veinticuatro.* Well said. Honor is that which is contained in another: no man grants honor to himself; rather, he receives it from others. To be a man of virtue and to have merits is not to be honored, but to give reasons why those who associate with one should honor him. He who removes his hat when he passes a friend or elder honors him; likewise, he who places him at his side, and he who seats him in the place of distinction; from which it is clear that honor resides in another and not in oneself.

There is nothing uniquely Spanish about the definition of honor just given. It was defined in much the same way by the ancient Greeks and by the majority of people in most European countries up until the eighteenth century.[15] Even today, the term nearly everywhere retains, among several possible meanings, the one specified here. Indeed, in those societies that anthropologists call "shame cultures," it has virtually no other.[16] Interestingly, other cultures, those with a profound acquaintance of the idea of guilt, tend to look down on shame cultures precisely because of their undivided loyalty to the notion of honor as reputation, esteem, and deference. They forget that honor conceived in this fashion can function in a very positive manner. It can work, that is, to inculcate and reinforce those values by which a society lives and through which it finds meaning in this world. The process involved is basically a system of rewards and punishments: modes of being that illustrate those qualities prized by the community are recompensed with approval and respect; modes that do not are chastised with disapproval and shame. With his usual cogency, Julian Pitt-Rivers has written of this process:

The ritual and ceremonial aspects of honour . . . serve to establish the consensus of the society with regard to the order of precedence; they demonstrate what is acceptable by reference to what is accepted. If the honour felt by the individual becomes honour paid by the society, it is equally the case that the honour which is paid by the society sets the standards for what the individual should feel. Transactions of honour therefore serve these purposes: they not only provide, on the psychological side, a nexus between the ideals of society and their reproduction in the actions of individuals—honour commits men to act as they should (even if opinions differ as to how they should act)—but, on the social side, between the ideal order and the terrestrial order, validating the realities of power and making the sanctified order of precedence correspond to them.[17]

It goes without saying that the qualities that people choose to recompense with "honor" vary greatly from community to community. Aristotle declared that honor was the reward of "goodness and beneficence,"[18] and his statement no doubt reflects something of the reality of his society. Thomas Hobbes wrote that honor was more likely to be a kind of homage paid to power.[19] Presumably, this says something pertinent about *his* society. In modern Japan, we are told by Ruth Benedict, the value most honored is that of *makoto*, a term which translates as "sincerity," but which really means something like self-abnegation and zealousness in the execution of one's obligations.[20] In Golden Age Spain the situation was somewhat complicated. Aristotle's definition was much quoted, as it was all over Europe during the Renaissance, but in actuality the bases of honor were for most people quite different.[21] What those bases were composes, in essence, the subject of Américo Castro's brilliant *De la edad conflictiva*, and it is to that study that we turn at this point for illumination.

According to Castro, in sixteenth- and seventeenth-century Spain honor was derived both from *who* one was and from *what* one was. In this alone, there is nothing noteworthy. Many societies recognize both immanent honor and adventitious honor or, as one scholar has put it, "vertical honor" and "horizontal honor."[22] What is unusual about the case of Spain is the form taken by the two kinds of honor. For as Castro contends, immanent honor there depended less, or was coming to depend less, on those things that had traditionally been its foundation in Europe—family name, titles, and wealth—and more on the meer quality of *pureza de sangre*, purity of blood;[23] while adventitious honor depended almost exclusively on one condition alone: overt masculinity, or *hombría*.

What is signified by the terms *pureza de sangre* and *hombría* is known, or should be, to all who have some familiarity with what Castro has called the "structure of Spanish history." The values that they imply remain difficult for many to appreciate, however. This is especially true of the first of the two terms. It refers to a lineage unblemished in any way by an admixture of "impure"—which is to say, Jewish or Moorish—blood. But why should a person be "honored" for

7

having only Christian blood in his veins, or to put the matter another way, why should a person be "dishonored" for having some proportion of Semitic blood? The causes, as Castro has shown, are basically historical.[24] During the Middle Ages, the Iberian peninsula was occupied conjointly by Christians, Moors, and Jews. For a time, these three religious groups, or castes, lived together in relative harmony. Gradually, however, an urge toward primacy began to emerge. Each caste struggled to make itself supreme, and the result was a period of intense intrapeninsular conflict. Eventually, of course, the Christians triumphed over the other two castes. Having gained effective control of the peninsula, the Christians then consolidated their "victory" by forcing the subjugated castes either to convert or to emigrate and by identifying themselves ever more completely with their religion, even to the extent of adopting, in complete innocence, the Jewish belief that one's religion determined not simply one's convictions but, in a very real sense, one's "being." One consequence of this belief was that it became possible for the so-called Old Christians to refuse to concede that the New Christians—converted Jews and Moors and their descendants—were Christian in anything but name. They were, in other words, Jews and Moors still, members of the subdued castes and, as such, to be despised, shunned, and harassed.

The paramount importance assumed by *hombría* during the Golden Age is also to be seen, according to Castro, as an outgrowth of the rivalry between castes in the Middle Ages. In the struggle for supremacy, we are told, each of the three castes attempted to assert itself on the basis of an already manifest talent. The Moors had showed themselves to be exceptionally skilled in the arts and crafts, and they founded their claim to preeminence on those skills. The Jews had made notable contributions to business, to the professions, and to learning, and presumed upon that success. The genius of the Christians was their ability to endure the tide of adversity—to endure it and, ultimately, to roll it back. Like the other castes, the Christians were proud of their particular aptitude and assumed that possession of it indicated a natural superiority. They sang of "their" talent in epic poems and ballads, wrote about it, and gradually, as the competition with the Moors and the Jews came to be more intensely felt, convinced themselves that it was not just *a* great value, but, except for their religion, the *only* great value. Thus, by the end of the fifteenth century, the Christians were thoroughly persuaded that money, learning, and artistic skills counted for nothing and that the only way for a man to be truly a man was to exercise to the fullest the masculine attributes of fortitude, bravery, and domination.

In the final analysis, Castro suggests, the two values of *pureza de sangre* and *hombría* were but different aspects of the same basic value. That is to say, the Christian Spaniards emerged from the formative period of the Middle Ages with the conviction that the important thing was "to be": not just to exist, in other words, but, in a world that often seemed to prefer that one not "be," to "be," wholly and completely; to "be more"; to "matter."[25] In the fourteenth century, the Infante Juan Manuel had celebrated this kind of "being" in the person of the "buen omne en si."[26] The "hombre en sí" was the man who lived in and of himself, the man who influenced more than he was influenced, the man who rose triumphant over circumstances by "integrating" them in meaningful fashion into his life. He was, in short, one who possesesed both profoundly and greatly what Castro calls the "imperative dimension of the person." To possess the "imperative dimension," then, was to "be." And to "be" was, in large part, to possess that dimension. *Hombría* was the index of the individual's assertion of the imperative dimension. *Pureza de sangre,* or *limpieza,* was the evidence of its assertion on the part of one's ancestors.

It is, I think, in association with the imperative dimension of the person that one can best understand that most unusual feature of the concept of honor that prevailed in Spain in the seventeenth century, namely, the dependence of the honor of the male on the chastity of the female.[27] Some have attributed the phenomenon to adherence to the biblical teaching that man and woman form in marriage "one flesh."[28] As Francisco Ayala has pointed out, however, this explanation is ultimately unconvincing.[29] For had the Spaniards of the Golden Age truly believed that husband and wife make "one flesh" having a single, indivisible responsibility, then not only the man but also the woman would have suffered dishonor as a result of the infidelity of the mate, and this is not the case. No woman is ever reviled because of the carnal sins of her husband (and, of course, the man himself receives no dishonor from them). Furthermore, it is not only the wife who is able to cast dishonor on the male. A man can be dishonored by any female member of his family who acts in such a way as to cause her chastity to become suspect. Thus, it is quite possible for a father to acquire the shame of his daughter, a brother that of his sister. It is even possible for a son to bear the onus of his mother's disgrace.

These facts, otherwise puzzling, seem logical enough in the light of the connection between honor and the imperative dimension of the person. For if honor depends on the ability to impress one's will on others, it is clear that nothing could be so dishonoring as a man's not being able to exert authority over those whom he is most obliged to control and should most easily control: the women of his family. This holds true whether the man is husband, father, son, or brother.

But this does not explain why Spaniards insisted so zealously on female chastity. To be sure, the Bible is categorical on the subject of adultery, and, as we have seen, Christian Spaniards identified themselves thoroughly with their religion. But the people of other countries, equally Christian, do not regard the loss of chastity as quite so abhorrent or its retention as quite so much a matter of pride. There must be some other reason. Many would contend that the insistence on female chastity was society's way of protecting itself against the depredation of males who had been taught to believe that conquest and domination constituted supreme values; any compromise in this regard, so goes the reasoning, would have opened the way to serious undermining of the institutions of family and matrimony. The argument has much validity. But it seems probable that this insistence is also related to the great importance Spaniards attached to *pureza de sangre*. For if purity of blood was a cause for honor and impurity of blood a cause for dishonor, then all heads of family who believed their lineage to be "clean" would do everything in their power to prevent that lineage from becoming in any way defiled. They would, for example, carefully screen all suitors of the womenfolk in their family and, like the father in Lope's *El galán de la Membrilla,* reject those whose purity was suspect:

Tello.	¿Pues á Ramiro le toca
	algo en la sangre?
Benito.	Tantico.
Tello.	Pues desespere Ramiro
	que jamás mi yerno sea:
	labrador soy, pero crea
	que más por la sangre miro
	que los que suelen nacer
	con grandes obligaciones.
	Vóyle á buscar.

(Ac., IX, 88a)

Tello. There is something suspect about the blood of Ramiro? *Benito.* A little. *Tello.* Then let Ramiro despair of ever becoming my son-in-law. I am a farmer, but he may be certain that I watch over [the purity of] my blood more than those who are born with great obligations. I am going to look for him.

They would also impress on their unmarried daughters or sisters the strict necessity for chastity since, as is intimated in the confrontation between the town elders of *Fuenteovejuna* and the marauding Comendador, a family could be as surely and completely sullied by a casual sexual encounter as it could be by an injudicious marriage:

Regidor.	. . . no es justo
	que nos quitéis el honor.
Comend.	¿Vosotros honor tenéis?
	¡Qué freiles de Calatrava!
Regidor.	Alguno acaso se alaba
	de la cruz que le ponéis,
	que no es de sangre tan limpia.
Comend.	Y, ¿ensúciola yo juntando
	la mía á la vuestra?

Regidor.   Cuando
que el mal mas tiñe que alimpia.[30]
(*Ac.*, X, 542b)

Councilman. . . . it is not right for you to take away our honor.
Comendador. Honor? You have honor? What friars of Calatrava! *Councilman.* There may be some who boast of the cross
[of Calatrava] which you have presented to them whose blood is
not so clean. *Comendador.* And do I dirty yours in joining
mine to it? *Councilman.* Yes, for wrong-doing taints more than
it cleanses.

Fear of contamination, then, would seem to be one reason
that Spaniards were determined that the female not lose her
virginity prior to marriage. It may also be the reason that some
fathers and brothers did not, in the theater at any rate, regard
the shotgun wedding as an automatic solution to abduction
or seduction, for if the man responsible truly was "unclean,"
the tainting that was in seduction merely a possibility would
become through marriage a virtual certainty. Were marriage
in fact impossible—as in the case of an adulterous wife—
then the only means of redress was, generally, vengeance of
some sort. It is difficult for most modern readers to understand
the purpose of this vengeance or, rather, it is difficult for them
to grasp how a man could possibly regain lost honor through
violence alone. The explanation, I think, lies in the fact that
the obvious implication of the dishonoring act is that the
victim of that act does not possess in any effective way the
imperative dimension. The wife who committed adultery
seemed to declare that she was not subject to the rule of her
husband, just as the man with whom she sinned indicated
his belief that he could prey on another man's "possessions"
without fear of reprisal. In acting quickly to eliminate the
enemies of his honor, the cuckolded husband gave the lie to
such suggestions.

It appears to make little difference whether there was
proven adultery or not. At least on the stage, a husband who
only suspected his wife of having been unfaithful resorted to
the same violence as the man who was absolutely certain of
his spouse's guilt. He did so because in the final analysis it

12

was what others thought that counted.[31] And if public opinion held that a man had lost his imperative dimension, and hence his honor, he was absolutely obliged to take steps to show that the loss was, at most, a temporary one.

"Obliged" is here the operative word. For if anything is clear in Golden Age discussions of honor, it is that a man simply must, no matter what his inner inclination, avenge an insult to his reputation. The imperative is undoubtedly a vestige of the customs of an earlier epoch, that period when the absence of strong central authority made the law of talion the indispensable basis of whatever social stability could be said to exist.[32] At the same time, it is a reflection of the notion that no man's honor belongs to him alone. It belongs to the community as well, for the collective honor of the group is nothing more than the sum total of the reputations of all the individual members.[33] Thus, for one person to lose his honor is for society to be hurt in some degree, and for that person to suffer the loss of his honor and make no attempt to regain it is for society to be permanently harmed. This it will not tolerate.[34]

The heroes of the honor plays know this. Over and over they articulate their awareness both of the demands that the community makes on them and of the unhappy situations in which those demands often place them. Those situations can sometimes appear truly racking. Calderón, for example, characteristically forces his heroes to deal with an infidelity that is minimal. Then, as if to compound the difficulty of the protagonist, he is apt to burden him with a lingering affection for the erring mate. What is the hero to do? There is no real choice. A small transgression is still a transgression; the sentiments of one man are less important than the maintenance of society's standards. Calderón's honor plays thus resolve in the expected manner. The hero reasons with himself, puts personal feeling aside, and ends by taking calm vengeance upon those who have called his honor into question. As the drama draws to a close, he receives approbation for having done his duty under trying circumstances.[35]

Before moving on to the plays themselves, it would be well to consider one final matter. Not all contemporary authorities share my view that the concept of honor underpinning the honor plays is basically the same as that to which most Spaniards in the seventeenth century subscribed. The English critic C. A. Jones, for example, has written that "the code of honour in the Spanish drama of the Golden Age is a convention which, although not entirely divorced from reality or from morals, is closely concerned with neither of these things."[36] Others have expressed the same thought in different words.

Those who maintain that the concept of honor displayed by the honor plays is little more than a dramatic convention appear to be preoccupied primarily with the matter of vengeance. They argue that it is inconceivable that in real life instances of infidelity were ordinarily dealt with in the same bloody fashion as on the stage. Granting that numerous documents of the time do record cases of husbands avenging themselves violently on their wives, they maintain that those murders were recorded precisely because they were "sensational," "not normal."[37] Most men, they say, would not have been capable of such an act.

The argument is weakened by its failure to take into account—or to take sufficiently into account—two matters that support a differing point of view. The first is that among the important theological controversies of the time was one that centered on the licitness of vengeance. On one side of this controversy were those theologians and moralists who affirmed that vengeance was never justifiable. On the other side were those who argued that it was justifiable under particular circumstances, among them, adultery.[38] Writers on both sides of the issue spilled a considerable amount of ink, from which one can only deduce that homicide in defense of honor was by no means a rarity; where there is smoke there is fire. Leading one to the same conclusion is the fact that certain documents of the time of a specifically nonsensational character record examples of wife murder in large numbers. One of these is a diary kept by a parish priest in Valencia between 1589 and 1629.[39] The frequency with which acts of homicide appear in the pages of this diary is, as one scholar has written, "astonishing,"[40] and vengeances taken on a wife or rival figure importantly among those acts.

Ultimately, of course, numbers are irrelevant to our concern. The question of whether the concept of honor that informs the honor plays is a reflection of contemporary reality is not to be decided on the basis of how many men in the seventeenth century murdered their wives for reasons of infidelity. Drama does not present a mirror image of existence. What it offers is an interpretation or, if one prefers, an abridgment or distillation. This is as true of the Spanish theater as any other. Years ago the fact was noted by Aubrey F. G. Bell when he wrote that the Golden Age drama "represents not life but a concentration of life, the eternal moments."[41]

What this means with particular regard to the honor plays is that they are true to the existence of their time—and hence far from conventional in the sense in which that word is usually employed—insofar as they incarnate feelings and values with which the members of the audience could sympathize and insofar as they present a dramatic action that strikes the audience as plausible. No one knows how many of the males in the theater public of the seventeenth century had confronted the loss of chastity of a wife, daughter, or sister. Nor does anyone know how many of those who had, had attempted to redeem that loss with an act of violence. What does seem clear is that the vast majority of them could, in their mind's eye, imagine themselves playing the role of the vengeful husband, father, or brother, and that they derived considerable stimulation from doing so. Did not Lope write in the *Arte nuevo de hacer comedias en este tiempo* (1609) that of all possible dramatic plots, those based on threats to honor were the best precisely because of their ability to "move all people"?[42]

Perhaps it would help to think of the honor plays as being an earlier analogue of the modern American Western. Both present an essentially romantic vision of reality, which is to say that they view life as a continuous challenge, but a challenge that men of strength and character are able to meet successfully. The formulation of that vision inevitably involves some distortion of history. It is typical of romantic literature, however, to seek not after historical truth, but rather after "poetic " truth. What it likes best to imitate is not everyday life but life as it sometimes is and always should be. The relation of romantic literature to its audience is thus distinctive; unlike so-called realistic literature, its aim is less to teach or illuminate than to rouse, celebrate, and exalt. Hence its particular concern with values. Those values may not always be consistently put into practice in the lives of the members of the public. But they nevertheless remain goals to be sincerely, if sometimes distantly, pursued.

I shall say more about this aspect of the honor plays later. For the moment, I shall merely observe that much of the confusion over whether or not the honor plays had a substantial basis in reality has resulted from a persistent critical tendency —apparent in the remarks of C. A. Jones quoted earlier[43]— to conceive of honor as a code. Many have been the attempts, for example, to extrapolate from the plays of Lope and Calderón a system of regulations that supposedly govern the lives of the characters in those plays with respect to matters of honor. The inevitable consequence is that the plays are declared untrue to life, for it is apparent that "real" people could not be so punctilious about their reputations. But as Castro has shown in *De la edad conflictiva,* honor functioned, even on the stage, not so much as a code as a sentiment or feeling. It is this feeling, called by Castro the *sentimiento honroso,* that constitutes the strongest link between literature and life in the *Comedia.* For reasons examined later, Lope and those who followed him found it appropriate when celebrating the *sentimiento honroso* to embody it in that particular action which characterizes the honor plays. That that action may not have been as common in real life as on the stage is not particularly important. What is important is that the values that motivate the action were recognized by the great majority of Spaniards, and more than just recognized, passionately affirmed.

2

Early Plays: Comic Solutions to the Conflict of Honor

THERE are still too many gaps in our knowledge of the early Spanish theater for one to feel entirely comfortable when making categorical statements about it. Still, it seems reasonably certain that Lope de Vega was the first to write honor plays of the kind previously described, that is, plays in which the dramatic interest centers on the honor of the protagonist and on his efforts to maintain or recover it. Incidents involving honor are, however, a much older feature of Spanish drama. Indeed, a considerable number of sixteenth-century plays contain honor conflicts, by which I mean clashes arising from an assault, real or imagined, on the chastity of one of the female characters. These plays were long supposed to be a kind of Italianate incrustation upon the Spanish stage.[1] They are, however, perfectly indigenous in their motifs and values. As Ramón Menéndez Pidal has pointed out, the man who avenges himself on an unchaste wife makes his appearance in Spanish literature as early as the *Primera crónica general* (1270–1289);[2] he was also a favorite subject of the late medieval balladeers. In any event, the sixteenth-century plays are of interest today chiefly as the forerunners and progenitors of the later honor plays, and it is their contribution to the development of the later form that concerns us here.

Sixteenth-Century Antecedents

It is generally assumed that the presence of the honor conflict in Spanish drama dates from the *Comedia Ymenea*

17

(1513–1517)[3] of Bartolomé de Torres Naharro. A work that can still be read with a great deal of pleasure, the *Ymenea,* like so many dramatic pieces of the sitxeenth century, owes a considerable debt to the *Celestina:*[4] its hero and heroine, who are called Ymeneo and Phebea, are clearly modeled on Calisto and Melibea, and Ymeneo's two servants, Boreas and Eliso, just as clearly derive from Sempronio and Pármeno. The plot of the *Ymenea,* however, unfolds in a manner quite different from that of its prototype. The play begins with the same headlong fall into passion, and there is later an interlude of nocturnal dalliance, beautifully written, that necessarily brings to mind the scene in Melibea's garden. Unlike Calisto and Melibea, however, Ymeneo and Phebea do not surrender to their carnal desires. Rather, they pledge themselves to each other in a clandestine marriage, and thus when Phebea is confronted by an angry brother threatening vengeance, she is able to defend her conduct and to argue brilliantly and convincingly for the life of Ymeneo. The resolution of the play bears little similarity to that of the *Celestina* or the later honor plays (though it does resemble the ending of the *comedias de capa y espada*): the fury of the brother is calmed, Ymeneo and Phebea are forgiven, and all go off merrily together, singing a *villancico.*

As J. P. W. Crawford has shown in his *Spanish Drama before Lope de Vega,*[5] the *Comedia Ymenea* exercised a notable influence on peninsular drama during the first half of the sixteenth century. This influence is particularly evident in the later theatrical imitations of the *Celestina,* where the weight of Torres Naharro seems at times almost as great as that of Rojas. Honor, in other words, plays a considerable part in several of these works,[6] and in at least two of them there is a real honor conflict. The two plays are the *Comedia Vidriana* (ca. 1535?) of Jayme de Güete and the *Comedia Radiana* (1533–1535) of Agustín Ortiz.

The first of these tells the story of Vidriano and Leriana, two young people of good family who meet and, within a short time, fall in love. For a while, all goes well, but then Lepidano, Leriana's father, attempts to force her into choosing a husband. The result is near disaster. Not having told her parents before of her love for Vidriano, Leriana believes that she cannot do so at this point. She decides that she will enter a convent instead, and is about to go off to her new life when Vidriano dashes on stage, prepared, if need be, to abduct her. Now ensues a scene of great confusion. Finding his honor threatened, and not knowing whom to blame, Lepidano lashes out wildly. First he rounds on Vidriano: "Be more civil, my good man, or here I shall die to protect my reputation and name!" Then he menaces Leriana: "Wicked and faithless girl . . . today you will die by my hand!"[7] His outburst effectively precludes any explanations. Eventually, however, Lepidano's rage passes. Vidriano then steps forward, identifies himself, and offers to marry Leriana. His offer is quickly accepted, and the play draws to a happy close.

The plot of the *Comedia Radiana* is virtually identical. We have the same pair of young lovers, the same *durus pater,* the same attempt at abduction (more properly an elopement in this case), the same threats, and the same reconciliation. Here, however, so that there can be no second thoughts, the marriage is performed immediately and on the spot.

Anyone who reads through a number of the early sixteenth-century imitations of the *Celestina* is inevitably struck by the consistency of their endings. In each of them, there is a sudden swerve toward vengeance and catastrophe followed by an equally sudden pulling away. Why, one wonders, have the authors of these imitations—and I am speaking now specifically of those pieces written for the theater and not of the whole body of works inspired by the *Celestina*—so regularly changed Rojas's somber ending into a happy one? Some would account for the transformation on the basis of what we are accustomed to call "Renaissance optimism." Joseph E. Gillet, for example, attributes the difference between the *Comedia Ymenea* and the *Celestina* to the former's being the product of a "new and more light-hearted age."[8] Another explanation would have us look to the religious background of the playwrights of the first half of the sixteenth century. An astonishing number of those playwrights were *conversos,*[9] and by virtue of their marginal status could be expected to have held ideas on honor and vengeance that differed widely from those of the majority of the people. Each of these lines of argument has its own validity, and each illuminates a particular aspect of the problem. But I wonder if the absence of the catastrophic ending in such plays as the *Comedia Ymenea,* the *Comedia Vidriana,* and the *Comedia Radiana* does not have to do also with certain unwritten laws of the Spanish stage of the early sixteenth century. The theatrical conventions of that era have yet to be studied thoroughly, but it would seem that, whatever audiences were willing to accept in other genres, they were not yet disposed to having a play end in catastrophe. There are, of course, one or two exceptions that prove the rule; Juan del Encina's *Égloga de tres pastores* (1509?), for example, concludes with the suicide of the shepherd Fileno. Such exceptions apart, the dominance of the happy ending was complete. In the early sixteenth century, as in so many other periods, audiences expected to leave a performance feeling uplifted and content.

It is interesting and instructive to note here that two other imitations of the *Celestina,* roughly contemporaneous with the plays just discussed but unlike them never meant to be staged, did actually retain the catastrophic ending of their model. They are the *Tragedia Policiana* (1547) of Sebastián Fernández and the *Tragicomedia de Lisandro y Roselia* (1542) of Sancho de Muñón. Of the two, the first is the less pertinent to this discussion. It does, to be sure, contain a typical *durus pater* who agonizes over his honor: "O fathers, those of you who are to beget daughters of evil inclination ought never to be born. For what goods does a man have who lacks honor? And what honor does a man have who has raised an unchaste daughter? And the man without honor, how will he live in peace?"[10] But the deaths of the two lovers in the piece are essentially unrelated to the honor conflict. Policiano, the hero, dies as the more or less accidental prey of a fierce lion, and Philomena, his mistress, expires from the grief she experiences on finding his body.

The ending of the *Tragicomedia de Lisandro y Roselia* is very different. Here, death follows very much as the result of wounded honor. And it comes with shocking force. Having discovered that his sister Roselia has acquired a lover, Beliseno, a punctilious and hot-blooded young man, determines to take vengeance. He climbs with a crossbow to the roof of his house and there, crouched in hiding, he waits while Roselia receives her friend in the garden below. Then, as the two lovers embrace, he shoots, and with one bolt kills them both.

Whatever the reasons for the absence of catastrophe on the Spanish stage during the first half of the sixteenth century, they ceased to be operative during the second half. This was the period when Spanish drama discovered both Seneca and the Italian *novellisti*,[11] and as the century wore on, blood flowed ever more freely. The motive for the gore was almost always vengeance of some sort, and on occasion vengeance based on considerations of honor. In the *Atila furioso* (1580–1585) of Cristóbal de Virués, for example, Atila puts his wife to death after finding her alone with another man. Likewise, in the same author's *La cruel Casandra* (1580–1585), the Prince kills the Princess because he has been led to believe (falsely) that she was involved in an adulterous relation with a member of the court.

Similar to *La cruel Casandra* is the *Alejandra* (1581–1585?) of Lupercio Leonardo de Argensola, a work that, because of its more extensive treatment of the honor conflict, deserves somewhat greater consideration. The protagonist of the play is Acoreo, King of Egypt. A jealous man, Acoreo harbors from the beginning of the piece the suspicion that Alejandra, his wife, has deceived him with his friend and confidant, Lupercio. When to this suspicion is added the accusation that Alejandra and Lupercio are planning to kill him, he decides to take immediate measures against them. His first act is to have Lupercio publicly drawn and quartered. That done, he calls for Alejandra. When she arrives, he forces her to wash herself in Lupercio's blood (which she believes at the time to be that of a sacrificed bull), reveals to her Lupercio's dismembered body, and then poisons her. It is a moment of great satisfaction for the King:

> Ahora estoy contento, que he quitado
> De mi honra la mancha que tenía,
> Y que en sangre traidora estoy bañado
> De quien pensó bañarse con la mía.[12]

Now I am content, for I have removed from my honor the stain which it held, and I have washed myself in the treacherous blood of the one who thought to bathe in mine.

Acoreo has, however, little time to savor his contentment, for minutes after his brutal murder of Alejandra he is informed that the people have risen against him. By the end of the play, he is dead himself.

It might be supposed that such works as *La cruel Casandra, Atila furioso,* and the *Alejandra* constitute a greater approximation to the later honor plays than do those pieces discussed earlier in the chapter, and in a certain sense that is true. For one thing, the deed of vengeance is in them not simply contemplated but actually carried out. For another, the executor of that deed here occupies the center of interest; the avenger, in other words, is now the dramatic protagonist. These plays are, nevertheless, significantly different from a typical honor play such as Lope's *Los comendadores de Córdoba.* The difference is partially one of proportion: while the honor conflict is in Lope's play the axis on which everything turns, it is in the *Alejandra,* and especially in the plays of Virués, only one complication more in a plot filled with turnings. More important, the distinction is one of values. As we shall see, the vengeance of the Veinticuatro in *Los comendadores de Córdoba* is an act of positive worth, a deed to be celebrated. In the plays of Argensola and Virués, however, as later in the works of the English Jacobean dramatists,[13] vengeance is something to be feared: at once the harvest and the seed of evil. Virués and Argensola have no wish to justify adultery— quite the contrary. But personal vengeance is equally to be shunned, for it, too, is an act of passion, and acts of passion can have none but disastrous consequences.

The fact is that the honor play was not the result of systematic development during the course of the sixteenth

century. It is not even possible to speak of a gradual harden-
ing over the years of the attitude toward adultery. Such
writers as Virués and Argensola may have been less inclined
toward forgiveness than earlier dramatists, but they were not
the only ones who dealt with questions of honor in the latter
part of the century. Indeed, at roughly the same time that
those two writers were heaping corpse upon disgraced corpse,
others were composing *pasos,* or interludes, in the vein of
Lope de Rueda's *Cornudo y contento,* in which the cuckold-
ing of a stupid husband is treated as an entertaining farce.

I conclude, then, that when Lope began seriously to write
plays, sometime in the middle 1580s, neither the form nor
the ethical content of the honor play was predetermined. His
predecessors provided him with a valuable collection of raw
materials; but it seems to have been up to Lope to furnish the
design and the technique. This he did in so inspired a way
that, in this area as others, the products of his imagination
were to be imitated for years to come.

El castigo del discreto, La bella malmaridada, *and* Las ferias de Madrid

An ideally comprehensive discussion of Lope's honor plays
would begin with some consideration of their process of
generation. One would like to know which are the very
earliest honor plays, how these relate to their antecedents and
to each other, how they came to constitute a more or less
fixed structure. Unfortunately, we are not now able to answer
those questions because we lack an adequate chronology of
Lope's early plays. The Morley-Bruerton *Cronología*[14] does
date those works, but the dates assigned are in most cases so
imprecise as to preclude the establishment of that indispensable prerequisite to any study of development in literature, an
order of composition. Speculation about the genesis and early
evolution of the honor play must thus be put off until scholarship has filled in certain gaps in our knowledge of Lope's
theater. In the meantime, it may be useful to attempt not a
history of the early honor plays, but a kind of group portrait
of them.

In the early, pre-1600, period, Lope wrote many plays in which considerations of honor figure peripherally, but only a few fully authentic[15] honor plays—those that concentrate on the recovery or strengthening of the protagonist's honor. These plays do, however, form an aggregation with distinguishable, if not totally delimiting, traits: (1) a tendency to attribute the ultimate responsibility for the protagonist's dishonor to the protagonist himself; (2) a propensity, resulting from the preceding, to regard the actions of the offenders as partially excusable; and (3) a concomitant disinclination to allow the offenders to suffer an extreme form of vengeance, thus permitting them to be rehabilitated at the end of the piece and the play to achieve a happy, or "comic," resolution.

Typical of Lope's early honor plays is *El castigo del discreto,* a work that comes at the very end of this first period (Morley and Bruerton date it September 1598–January 1601). It is based, apparently, on a *novella* of Bandello's,[16] though Lope's plot differs in important details from that of his supposed source and, unlike the latter, is complicated and complemented by a subplot. The play turns on the passion that Casandra, the wife of Ricardo, the protagonist, conceives for an acquaintance of her husband. This passion is, obviously, seriously dishonoring to Ricardo, and when he learns of it, his immediate impulse is to kill her. Upon reflection, however, he realizes that the responsibility for his wife's deviation is largely his: Felisardo, the acquaintance, had rescued Ricardo early in the play from a very difficult situation, and feelings of gratitude had thereafter prompted Ricardo to extol the virtues of his benefactor to Casandra. Eventually, Ricardo decides on a milder form of punishment. He tricks Casandra into believing that he will be away from the city for a time and that, during the interim, Felisardo will pay her a visit. Then, pretending to be Felisardo—who, it should be noted, has remained innocent both of Casandra's love and of Ricardo's stratagem—he slips back into the house, and in the darkness gives his wife a sound beating. The punishment is "discreet" for three reasons: it cures Casandra of her infatuation with Felisardo; it preserves Ricardo's honor (by not exposing his dishonor); and it enables Felisardo later to become engaged to the girl he has loved all along, never having been compromised.

Another early honor play that exemplifies the characteristics of the group is *La bella malmaridada* (1596).[17] Derived loosely from the famous *copla* known by the same title,[18] the work relates the story of Lisbella and her husband, Leonardo. Lisbella is in a state of misery at the beginning of the play, primarily because Leonardo has fallen madly in love with the courtesan Casandra. Leonardo's ardor eventually cools, but before it does, his neglect of his wife has the indirect effect of bringing her to the attention of Cipión, a nobleman of notably amorous inclination. Thus, Lisbella herself becomes the object of an adulterous passion. Fortunately, she, unlike her prototype in the *copla,* does not take revenge on her husband by encouraging that passion, and with the passing of time, Leonardo is convinced of her innocence. But he continues to feel dishonored by Cipión's intentions, and at the end of the play he lures Cipión into his house, intending to murder him. Before he can carry out the planned assassination, however, he is confronted by Lisbella's father, a wise old man who, upon learning of the recent events, decrees that the indiscretions of Leonardo and Cipión alike must be forgiven. All acquiesce in this judgment, and the work concludes with a general reconciliation.

Many readers familiar only with the better-known honor plays of Lope's middle period will find the endings of *El castigo del discreto* and *La bella malmaridada* strange and even, perhaps, unconvincing. One is fairly certain that the harsh vengeance meted out to the malefactors in such later plays as *Peribáñez* and *La contienda de García de Paredes* wins at least some measure of their author's approval. It is thus natural to wonder whether the leniency shown transgressors in the early plays could possibly be a sincere expression of Lope's feelings. We can gain some insight into Lope's views from his short story *La prudente venganza,* published in 1624 and known as one of the four *Novelas a Marcia Leonarda.* The story itself is a kind of *caso de la honra;* it tells of the unfaithfulness of a young wife and of her husband's terrible vengeance. But in a postscript commenting on the husband's action, Lope writes:

Now...although the laws grant this license [vengeance] to husbands because of their just grievance, it is not an example which anyone should imitate, although it is here presented so that it might be one to those women who, with unrestrained desire, risk life and honor for a brief pleasure, in grievous offense of God, their parents, their husbands, and their own reputation. *And I have always been of the opinion that the stain upon the honor of the aggrieved cannot be washed away with the blood of the one who injured him,* because that which was cannot cease to be, and it is folly to think that the offense of the man offended is lifted because the offender has been killed. What happens is that the man injured is left with his injury, and the other dead, thus satisfying the desire for vengeance but not the conditions of honor, which, in order to be perfect, must never be wounded. Who can doubt that objections to this argument are already being raised? In response to those objections, tacit as they may be, I say that dishonor should neither be endured nor punished. What recourse, then, is there? That which a man has when any kind of misfortune has befallen him: to leave the country; to live away from it where no one knows him; and to offer his affliction to God, remembering that the same thing might have happened to him if he had been punished for some of the injuries he had committed. For to want those whom he has offended to tolerate him while he himself tolerates no one does not fall within the bounds of reason.[19]

Lope's position here is clear. He accepts, by implication, the idea that honor is equivalent to reputation or fame, along with the notion that dishonor can result not only from one's own actions but from those of another as well. He refuses to believe, however, that any good whatsoever can come from vengeance, and says that he has always so refused to believe.[20] The statement is arresting. Taken at face value, it lends credibility to the endings of the early honor plays. But by the same token, it would seem to cast doubt on our assumption that Lope countenances the severe punishments of the later plays. Are we mistaken about those plays? Must we now deny their authenticity in order to affirm the authenticity of the early pieces? By no means.

All the evidence of Lope's life and works indicates that he was a man of widely fluctuating ideas and feelings. The loyalties of one year were not necessarily those of the following; what was said on one occasion was often gainsaid on another. That being the case, I see no reason—*pace* the passage just quoted—why we cannot suppose, quite simply, that Lope held at different times, or even at the same time, divergent notions about honor and vengeance. It may be true that his reason told him there was no logic in vengeance. It may also be true that the violent endings of many of the later plays are an indication primarily of a desire to accommodate the tastes of the public. Neither of these conclusions, however, serves to invalidate what has long been evident to many people: that Lope's interest is fully engaged by the plight of the dishonored protagonists of the later honor plays and that the violent solutions to which they have recourse are presented by him in most instances with evident sympathy.

Lope's attitude toward vengeance thus appears to have been complex and vacillating. Clearly capable of appreciating the need for retribution felt by some of his later heroes, he was inclined as a young man to advocate forbearance and understanding in the face of personal dishonor. That this advocacy was not without an element of self-interest goes without saying. A man incapable of exercising discretion in affairs of the heart, Lope on more than one occasion found himself in the situation of Cipión in *La bella malmaridada*.[21] Indeed, it would not be too much, I think, to see a character like Cipión as an alter ego of his creator, a fantasy figure who is able to indulge his erotic impulses without suffering any of the usual consequences.

Indeed, a number of Lope's early-period plays impress one as being little more than thinly disguised wish-fulfillment fantasies. The earliest surviving play, *Los hechos de Garcilaso y moro Tarfe* (1579–1583?), is clearly a projection of the teenage Lope's yearning for military fame and glory. Another kind of adolescent daydream appears to underlie such works as *El hijo venturoso* (1588–1595), *El hijo de Reduán* (1588–

27

1595), and *El nacimiento de Ursón y Valentin* (1588–1595), which tell the stories of young men who grow up believing themselves to be of humble ancestry, only to learn at a critical moment that they are in reality the sons of royalty or nobility.[22] A close identification of author and characters thus is typical of the plays of the early years. In most works, the identification is with the hero of the piece. What is interesting and significant about the first honor plays is that this identification is in all cases partially—and in one case totally—transferred to the man who is the hero's rival.

That rather anomalous work in which Lope's sympathies seem to lie entirely with the antagonist is a very early piece, *Las ferias de Madrid* (1585–1588).[23] Although distinguished by fluent writing and interesting characterization, *Las ferias* is little mentioned in the histories of the Golden Age theater. The reason is fairly obvious. Presented with a work that is in most respects evidently an honor play and yet one that ends unconventionally and in other ways violates the norms of the type, scholars have felt a considerable sense of puzzlement and have preferred silence to an expression of that puzzlement. But *Las ferias de Madrid* is not that perplexing a work if we realize that it is an expression primarily of its author's inner world of needs and desires. I have said that it is somewhat characteristic of the early plays to depict life not so much as it is but as the imagination of a young—and rather immature—man would have it be. In no play, however, is this displacement in the direction of the ideal more apparent than in *Las ferias de Madrid*. Indeed, so powerful is the effect of wish-fulfillment fantasy in this play that the usual oppositions of the honor play are reversed: the man who is the protagonist and nominal hero of the piece is blamed and ridiculed; and the man who is the antagonist and nominal antihero is vindicated and praised. Clearly, then, *Las ferias* is not simply a work that illustrates the characteristics of the early honor plays but one that carries them to the farthest extreme. Here Lope has arrived at—some would say gone beyond—the outermost reaches of the form. The play is thus of unusual interest, and deserves a more extended analysis than that accorded the other early honor plays.

Because *Las ferias de Madrid* is not a play that is widely read, discussion of it may usefully begin with a brief account of the story.[24] The plot centers on the actions of the three principal characters: Patricio, the protagonist; Violante, his wife; and Leandro, the antagonist. From the exposition, we learn that relations between Patricio and Violante are far from satisfactory. Though Violante has apparently been in every respect a loving and dutiful wife, Patricio no longer takes any pleasure in his marriage. Indeed, by the time the play opens, he has virtually abandoned the company of Violante for that of his mistress, Eugenia. As a result of Patricio's desertion, Violante finds herself alone among the crowds at the annual Madrid fair. Here, by chance, she attracts the attention of the handsome Leandro, who immediately begins to court her. At first, Violante responds to Leandro's advances with the utmost discretion. Her interest is also caught, however, and by the end of Act I she and Leandro have fallen in love.

Act II complicates the plot in a manner reminiscent of the *comedias de capa y espada*. Leandro has been summoned to the house of Violante and is standing outside when, suddenly, Patricio appears. Neither man is known to the other, and both are guarded and suspicious. Patricio speaks first. Concealing his identity, he says that he is a recent arrival in Madrid, and attributes his presence in the street to an amorous adventure in which he is engaged. The story is sufficiently plausible that Leandro drops all caution. Forthwith, he launches into an account of his affair with Violante and then, with notable ironic effect, presses his new acquaintance into service as lookout while he, Leandro, speaks to his ladylove at her window.

Once is not enough, however. In Act III, Patricio again finds himself acting as sentinel while Leandro pays court to Violante. This time he means to take advantage of the situation. He will, he thinks, allow Leandro enough time to gain entrance to the house and to urge his suit inside, and then burst in upon the lovers, catching them *in flagrante delicto*. Unfortunately, Patricio is a natural bungler: Leandro escapes and the plan is foiled.

The vengeance must now be replotted. Knowing that

Leandro will shortly reappear, Patricio hurries to the house of Belardo, Violante's father, with the intention of securing aid. He is convinced that he has only to tell Belardo of Violante's transgression for the old man to volunteer to assist in the proposed assassinations. Naturally, he is mistaken. Belardo refuses to believe that his daughter is guilty, and even after he has followed Patricio to his home and there heard from the lips of Leandro himself proof of Violante's infidelity, he cannot bring himself to blame her. Thus, when his son-in-law hands him a sword and demands that he save his honor, he commits a truly startling act, perhaps unique in the Spanish theater: he takes the weapon held out to him and plunges it into Patricio, shouting as he does so:

> ... muera quien hoy deshonra
> hija, suegros, padre y madre.
> Aqueste es hecho de padre
> que sabe de amor y honra.
>
> (*Ac. N.*, V, 622b)

... death to the one who today dishonors daughter, parents-in-law, father and mother. This is the act of a father who knows about love and honor.

At this point the play ends. Belardo having fled, it is assumed by all that Patricio has been killed by a rival for the affections of Eugenia, and attention turns once again toward Leandro and Violante. They come forward, join hands, and vow to wed within the year.

Emilio Cotarelo y Mori thought the ending of *Las ferias de Madrid* "immoral and almost absurd."[25] It is not difficult to imagine why. The sense of the norm is so strong in literature that any work that fails to observe the conventions of that particular type to which we have consigned it—logically or arbitrarily—is bound to seem strange. Northrop Frye notes that *All's Well That Ends Well* has for many years been considered a "problem play" because its ending does not accord with what we have come to expect from comedy.[26] When approached with preconceptions derived from Lope's later honor plays—and surely this is how Cotarelo approached it—*Las ferias de Madrid* seems similarly problematical.

30

whelming in the final moments of the play. He botches one attempt at killing Violante and Leandro, and then tries to force his father-in-law into accepting responsibility for that act, which is his and his alone to perform. Here he shows himself as not just sly but intolerably weak, and furnishes conclusive proof that he is indeed unworthy of his wife. Despite Cotarelo's judgment that the ending of the piece is immoral and almost absurd, there is little doubt that the assassination of such a wretch would have seemed entirely fitting to the audiences of Lope's time.[31]

Few blocking characters, of course, are repudiated in so severe a fashion. Comedy tends to be magnanimous and has no interest in harassing the blocking characters unduly once their opposition has been overcome. Death is by no means an element completely foreign to this form, however. Frye has noted that many comedies contain a "point of ritual death," a particular moment when the shadow of imminent destruction seems to move over one or more of the characters. Such moments are nothing other than vestiges of the literal death that befell the chief actor in the primitive vegetation rites from which, most scholars now agree, comedy derives.[32] In these rites, described so vividly in *The Golden Bough*, a sacrificial victim is offered up, a scapegoat who takes upon his head all the weakness and sin of the old year and thus prepares the way for the purified birth of the new. The cleansing away of the dirt of the past effected in this ritual has its counterpart in comedy when the defeat of the blocking characters appears to facilitate the creation of a new and better order.

The job of establishing the necessity or desirability of such a new and better order often falls in comedy to the subplots or secondary intrigue. Thus it is in *Las ferias de Madrid*. The play contains many episodes that seemingly have little connection with the story of Violante, Patricio, and Leandro, but that in actuality demonstrate the fact that the falsity which characterizes Patricio is a generalized vice to which virtually the entire society of Madrid has succumbed. Thus, the whole of the first act, which is a re-creation of the fair that gives the play its name, can be read as a series of carefully elaborated variations on the typical Renaissance theme of *inganno*. To describe every incident of deception would undoubtedly be time-consuming and probably quite tedious as well. Suffice it to mention, therefore, that among the hoary routines found in the text are the one in which the would-be philanderer flirts with a mysterious woman who is actually his wife, the one where the cozener of young ladies is himself cozened, and even the one in which a group of country bumpkins is taken in by a couple of city slickers.

Most of the deception in this first act revolves around four young men, friends of Leandro, named Lucrecio, Adrián, Roberto, and Claudio. The four are, in a way, antecedents of the *graciosos* of the later plays, because although they are *caballeros*, they act as foils to Leandro, and also serve the function, typical of *graciosos*, of both satirizing and exemplifying the ills of society. Lucrecio and company also appear in Acts II and III, where again they are associated with the motif of *inganno,* but as the play progresses, their role becomes much more limited.

Toward the end of the play, however, Lope does permit them one final prank. Learning that one of their acquaintances is being married, they decide to dress in costumes and crash the wedding feast. Once inside, they proceed to read satirical verses that mock the venality and inconstancy of women in general and of their own mistresses in particular. The guests, naturally, are very annoyed, and for their efforts attack them with blows and insults and throw them out into the street. This comeuppance, so fully deserved, coincides with the assassination of Patricio and presumably is meant to represent, as does the latter, the rewards of deceit and bad faith.

Comedies never dwell on the defeat of vice, for that would spoil their prevailing festive mood. The removal or discrediting of the blocking characters is a necessary first step in the creation of the new society for which comedy seems to clamor, but that accomplished, the play must move on quickly to the second step, celebration of the young lovers, who symbolize the hopes of the future. Thus, at the end of *Las ferias*, Patricio is no sooner killed than the body is whisked out of sight, and Leandro and friends no sooner ejected into the street than they are beaten off the opposite side of the stage. The scene is now left to Leandro and Violante alone. As is usual in these circumstances, boy proceeds to embrace girl, each pledges his respective hand, and both together advance to receive the applause of the audience.

Naturally, Lope has been careful to insure that the triumph of Leandro and Violante seem legitimate. On various occasions during the course of the play, each has given proof of the superiority of his values over those of the other characters. In the first act, for example, in the midst of the generalized familiarity of the fair, Violante steadfastly and all but uniquely maintains a decorous reserve. She also refuses to tease for gifts as do the other women. As for Leandro, he too stands out at the fair, both literally and figuratively. Shunning the other young men who gather on corners to gossip and plot practical jokes, he walks alone, "with a serious expression and a modest sadness, his bearing calm, and his glance sweet and gentle" (612a).

Such demonstrations of merit are clearly designed to convince us that Leandro and Violante deserve no one but each other. This is the only consideration that really matters. In other words, it is not particularly important that, in pursuit of their love, Leandro and Violante had to pass through a period of less than honorable activity. A sin is always a sin, but as Lope says in another play, "a transgression caused by love deserves to be pardoned."[33]

So one-sided are Lope's sympathies in this play, so exalted the treatment of the young lovers, that one is impelled to speculate on the circumstances behind its composition. If the Morley-Bruerton date for the play, 1585–1588, is correct, as it surely is, the play came into being either during or just after Lope's liaison with Elena Osorio.[34] That affair, as is well known, was one of the traumatic experiences of Lope's life, and it was still being remembered in works of diverse nature years after its termination.[35] It is thus only natural that a play that was written at roughly the time of the affair and that is, besides, of a marked romantic character, would show its impress in some way. Now clearly, *Las ferias de Madrid* is not a literal representation of the facts of the experience.

What it is, I suggest, is a transmutation into the realm of the ideal, a fantasized version in which—as Lope would have wished—the husband of Elena is disposed of, leaving Elena and Lope free to marry and live forever after in undisturbed happiness.

This interpretation can, of course, neither be proven nor disproven by reference to the text. But the play does appear to furnish evidence that Elena was indeed on Lope's mind at the time of its composition. The evidence is contained in the wedding scene, in those verses in which the four young men charge women with fickleness and an incurable desire for material security. The accusations are made in the form of miniature dramatic monologues, two of which, as Rinaldo Froldi has observed,[36] seem to allude to Francisco Perrenot de Granvela, Lope's rival for the affections of Elena. One of these monologues, that delivered by Claudio, is a lament addressed by a "shepherd" to his "lady" and reads as follows:

> Dejas un pobre muy rico
> y un rico muy pobre escoges;
> si te ofendo no te enojes.
>
> (620b)

You leave a poor man who is very rich and choose a rich man who is very poor; if I offend you, do not be angry.

The other, recited by Roberto, satirizes a rich gentleman recently arrived from the Indies who, according to Roberto, "overturned . . . years of service with divine and all-powerful gold." There are two speakers in this monologue, the *indiano* himself and "gold," and what they say is so opaque as to ruin the joke:

> No por mí, sino por vos,
> tierra donde yo nací,
> no por vos, sino por mí.
>
> (620a)

Not for me, but for you, land where I was born, not for you, but for me.

36

Clarity, however, if not humor, is served by the following gloss, supplied by the author of the verses:

> Habla el indio primero con la tierra
> diciendo que le quiere su señora
> por la tierra, donde hay tanta riqueza;
> y luego el oro responde a la tierra
> que no por ella fué querido el indio,
> sino por el que al fin lo vence todo.
>
> (620a)

The *indiano* speaks first with the land, saying that his lady loves him because of the land, where there is so much wealth; then gold replies to the land that it was not because of it that the *indiano* was loved, but because of that which in the end conquers everything.

If these two monologues do, in fact, allude to Granvela, then the fantasy seemingly acted out in the play was not of what might be but of what might have been. Once the attachment to Granvela had been established, Lope could apparently entertain little hope that he would ever again have the right to Elena's favors—at least not exclusively. Whatever the case —whether the play represents Lope's affair with Elena as he wished to have it, or whether it represents that affair as he would have wished to have had it, or whether, even, it has no particular connection with Elena at all—it is clear that *Las ferias de Madrid* springs from a source very close to Lope's heart. Like all comedies, it presents not the world as you know it, but the world "as you like it." The tendency to displace reality in the direction of the personally desirable is a characteristic of most of the first honor plays and, indeed, of the early plays in general. Here that tendency finds its logical culmination. The result is that we are given this time not simply a play that begins in seemingly serious vein and then ends comically, but one that breathes the pure spirit of comedy throughout.

3

Plays of the Middle Period: Vengeance Celebrated

THE generalizations about the early honor plays set forth in the preceding chapter apply to most of the honor plays written before 1600. There are, however, exceptions. *El toledano vengado* is possibly one such exception (Morley and Bruerton date the piece 1596–1604, but doubt the authenticity of the text). Another is a play, already briefly mentioned, that for many, myself included, is one of the most memorable works of Lope's theater: *Los comendadores de Córdoba* (1596).[1]

Los comendadores de Córdoba

Los comendadores is radically different from the three plays discussed at the end of the previous chapter. Here, there is no attempt to justify the actions of the offenders; neither is there any disinclination to allow them to suffer the full consequences of their transgression. In fact, the vengeance taken upon the offending parties in this piece is among the most brutal of those found in Lope. *Los comendadores,* in short, is a play that anticipates in most of its features the honor plays of the middle period. Indeed, it may be considered the first of Lope's mature honor plays. At least I know of no other in the manner of the middle period that unquestionably antedates it.

In considering *Los comendadores de Córdoba,* one feels acutely the lack of knowledge about the young Lope and about the plays of the early years. *Los comendadores* is obviously an anomaly: its structure is very unusual for the period; so is its ending. The latter, moreover, involves an act of vengeance on the order of those that Lope, in later years, claimed to find abhorrent. In view of these facts, several questions seem inevitable. How did Lope come to write *Los comendadores de Córdoba?* What were his feelings about the action of the play? Under what circumstances was it produced? Unfortunately, the questions must, for now at least, remain unanswered. The amount of information that we possess is simply not sufficient to permit us to deal with them. In any event, the really significant question is not what prompted Lope to write this play (I am assuming still that the play was the first of those fashioned in the style of the middle period, but the matter is basically irrelevant), but why, after a number of years, virtually all of the honor plays came to be struck from the mold that it furnished.[2] A simple answer would be that the public preferred plays like *Los comendadores* to those that characterize Lope's early period. But if that is true, why did the public prefer such plays? The answer to this question has to some extent been adumbrated in the Introduction, but a more complete answer requires a closer look both at *Los comendadores de Córdoba* and at the audiences for whom it was written.

Like many of Lope's honor plays, *Los comendadores* has a basis in fact. Specifically, it dramatizes a famous vengeance taken by Fernando Alfonso de Córdoba upon the discovery of the infidelity of his wife. The actuality of this event is attested by contemporary documents.[3] It is not from historical records that Lope derived the inspiration for his play, however, but rather from legend. In particular, he seems to have drawn on several poetic versions of the vengeance in the writing of *Los comendadores.* The first of these is the well-known anonymous *romancillo* that begins, "¡Los comendadores, / por mi mal os vi!" ("Knights-commander, to my sorrow have I seen you!"). Lope's tangible borrowings from this *romancillo*, which was evidently very popular in the sixteenth century,[4] seem to be few: at the beginning of Act III he glosses its initial lines; besides these lines and one or two motifs—that of horses and riding, for example, which runs throughout the play—there is very little that is taken directly from the song. One might assume from this that the contribution made by the *romancillo* to the play was not very significant. Such is not the case, however. Indeed, Lope was greatly indebted to the song, for, by virtue of its wide popularity, it furnished him with an audience already familiar at the beginning of the play with the main events of the story, and thus able to appreciate the dramatic irony that informs many of the important scenes and gives them their power.

A second probable source is a poem recently brought to light and published by Margit Frenk Alatorre.[5] The poem, which is both anonymous and untitled, is contained in a manuscript of the late sixteenth century that is now the property of the Palace Library of Madrid. It tells much the same story as the *romancillo,* but employs a more sophisticated metric scheme and incorporates a greater wealth of detail. It would thus seem to be of a later period than the *romancillo,* although as Mrs. Alatorre implies, it cannot be dated with any certainty. What does appear certain is that Lope had this poem—or another very similar to it—in mind during the composition of *Los comendadores,* for there are one or two complications in his plot that are found in this poem and in none of the other known versions of the story. These complications are relatively inconsequential in themselves, but important insofar as they demonstrate the unusual breadth of inspiration behind the play.

A final source, and the principal one for the construction of the plot of *Los comendadores,* is a ballad by Juan Rufo. This ballad, which also seems to owe something both to the *romancillo* and to the recently uncovered poem, exists in two considerably varying versions. The first appeared in print for the first time, so far as is known, in the miscellany entitled *Seiscientas apotegmas* that Rufo published in Toledo in 1596. The second also seems to have appeared initially in 1596; it constitutes the opening ballad of Luis de Medina's compilation of the *Flores del Parnaso, octava parte* (Toledo, 1596), from which collection it passed into the *Romancero general* (1600). The *Apotegmas* version of the ballad is undoubtedly the more authentic of the two, and it is plainly the version Lope used (although he may have seen the *Flores* version as well); where the two texts differ in a manner relevant to the play, at the end, for example, where the killings are enumerated, it is the *Apotegmas* reading that Lope follows.[6]

Though Rufo's ballad is long—indeed, one of the lengthiest in the language—it is long not because of any particular narrative complexity but because Rufo has chosen to weight his story with moralizing disquisitions. Basically, his account is quite simple. It tells how Fernán Alfonso, Señor de Belmonte and Veinticuatro de Córdoba, learns of the adultery of Da. Beatriz, his wife, and undertakes to kill her. The climax of the tale is chilling. Announcing to his wife that he will be gone for a few days on a hunting expedition (the irony is intentional), the Veinticuatro retires to a nearby wood, where he awaits nightfall. Then, under cover of darkness, he creeps back to the house, scales the outside wall, and enters. The scene he encounters inside is what he had anticipated: Beatriz and her confidante, Da. Ana, bound in the embrace of their respective lovers, D. Jorge and his brother, D. Fernando. Now comes the celebrated and frightful vengeance. Acting with perfect self-control, the Veinticuatro kills the two women and the two men—the "Comendadores de Córdoba"—and then, one by one, every other living occupant of the house: several servants, a number of dogs and cats, a monkey, a parrot, and an ape.

Although Lope shaped his story with close attention to Rufo's version, the spirit of *Los comendadores de Córdoba* is quite different from that of its source, as anyone who reads both pieces may easily discover. The difference has little to do with the fact that the one work is by a definition a drama, the other a ballad: drama and ballad have intermingled so extensively in Spain that their properties long ago ceased to be mutually exclusive—if indeed they ever were. It has to do, rather, with how each author has interpreted the lessons of the incident. Though Rufo, like Lope, was impressed by the heroism of Fernán Alfonso, the story of the Veinticuatro and

41

the *comendadores* was for him primarily a kind of cautionary tale that revealed not only the foolhardiness of those who transgress the laws of Heaven—

> Esta es la mísera suerte
> De los que, con mal instinto,
> A la amistad verdadera
> Prefieren sus apetitos.[7]

This is the miserable fate of those who, with base instinct, prefer [the satisfaction of] their appetites to true friendship.

but also—in the case of the Veinticuatro—the danger of trusting too much in one's destiny:

> Estando, pues, la Fortuna
> Cansada de haber subido
> Este insigne caballero
> Al punto de más peligro
> Determinó derriballe
> Desde la cumbre al abismo.[8]

Fortune being weary, then, of having raised this illustrious gentleman to the point of greatest danger, she decided to hurl him from the summit into the abyss.

For Lope, however, what is chiefly significant in the story is not that Da. Beatriz and the *comendadores* suffer just retribution for their sins, or that the Veinticuatro, like many great men, experiences an unforeseen fall as the result of a caprice of Fortune, but that the Veinticuatro, having been cast into adversity, exerts will and strength together not simply to recover his former position, but actually to climb above it. The process by which the "villains" of the piece condemn themselves was of interest to Lope, but chiefly in relation to the process by which the hero saves himself. The latter constitutes the real action of *Los comendadores*. Once having appreciated this fact, we are in a better position to understand the play itself.

Aristotle said that the action of a drama was revealed

through a set of simultaneous "imtiations," the imitations being those that inhere in the principal parts of the play: the plot, the characterization, the words, and so on. In the theater, of course, most of us do not attempt to perceive and assess independently the contributions of the different parts. Rather, we are likely to concentrate our attention on what seems to us to be the heart of the drama, the interplay between the major characters. In *Los comendadores de Córdoba,* Lope has deployed his main characters along three planes of morality. On the lowest is Da. Beatriz, a woman who is significantly different from the heroines of most of Lope's later honor plays. When first seen, she is engaged in a dispute with Da. Ana (who in Lope is not Beatriz's confidante but her niece through marriage) over which is the most attractive of the *galanes* who have recently passed in the street. The purpose of the incident is obvious: to provoke the audience to doubts about Beatriz's dedication to her husband. Those who catch the hint do not have to wait long for confirmation of their suspicions. For minutes after the conversation with Da. Ana, the *comendadores* are knocking at the door, and the first sight of D. Jorge—the *comendadores* are related by blood to both the Veinticuatro and his wife, but have been long absent from Córdoba—ignites in Beatriz a violent passion.

At this point in the play, some readers may be reminded of Phèdre, the prototype in modern literature of the wife who is prey to a love that is not merely adulterous but incestuous. There is little real resemblance between the two women, however, for Beatriz, unlike Phèdre, makes no effort to resist her passion. Indeed, her sole interest, from the moment she is conscious of its existence, is to see her love consummated. She is willing to make known her feelings during her first conversation with D. Jorge and thereafter to employ all manner of guile and artifice to achieve the sexual fulfillment they both desire. Though she could not help knowing that what is for her incomparable ecstasy is for her husband a grievous offense, she will not allow herself to articulate this thought until the moment of retribution. Then she speaks: "Conozco que os he ofendido" ("I recognize that I have offended you") (*Ac.*, XI, 297b). The choice of verb here is significant: not *sé*—"I know"—but *conozco*—"I am aware," "I admit," "I recognize." It is because Beatriz refuses to "recognize," until it is too late, what she has always known that she is, in the eyes of Lope and his public, so greatly censurable.

The case of the *comendadores* is rather different from that of Beatriz. Though they are no less guilty of the sin of adultery, they are aware at least of the immorality of their acts: thus, D. Jorge laments, as he feels himself succumbing to the fatal attractions of Beatriz, "Oh, sad misfortune, where are you leading me?" (267b). Such awareness should not be underestimated, for recognition of the truth is the necessary condition of corrective action. True, D. Jorge and D. Fernando never do abjure their sins and repent, but for them at least the possibility is open.

It is significant that, when first presented to the audience, D. Jorge and D. Fernando are depicted as models of both valor and circumspection. The beginning of the play finds them recently returned from the siege of Granada (like Rufo, Lope laid his story in the year 1492), and each has come back mantled in glory. Neither, however, has any particular desire to claim credit for his deeds. In fact, they seem somewhat surprised that their uncle, the Bishop of Córdoba, should manifest pride in them, and they profess to be unworthy of the compliments tendered them by their friend D. Luis.

This apparently natural modesty is further exemplified by the *comendadores'* refusal of D. Luis's offer to lend them two spirited stallions so that they can parade in eye-catching splendor through the streets of Córdoba. The offer is one that we may suppose most of Lope's *galanes* would find irresistible. D. Jorge and D. Fernando, nevertheless, decline, courteously but firmly: they feel no need to attract attention to themselves and know their equestrian ability to be limited.

D. Luis, however, is importunate, and the result is that D. Jorge and D. Fernando agree finally to ride the horses. Thus, the scene, which began by impressing us favorably with the qualities of the *comendadores,* ends by inducing in us a feeling of apprehension. This stems in part from the young men's fear of being thrown, a fear that is unarticulated but quite perceptible in the speeches of the later part of the scene: inevitably, this anxiety brings to mind the instances in other Lope plays, notably in *Peribáñez,* where a fall from horseback presages a disastrous plunge into unrestrained sexuality.[9] Our apprehension also depends in part on a discovery we have made about D. Jorge and D. Fernando: though basically modest and sensible, they will, under duress, check their better instincts and yield to the pressure applied.

It is this weakness that is eventually to prove the undoing of the *comendadores.* The concept of the fatal flaw has in recent years fallen out of favor with both Shakespearean and Classical scholars, but it necessarily retains its pertinence for students of the *Comedia,* a drama more unqualifiedly moralistic than Elizabethan or Greek tragedy.[10] The fatal flaw of Beatriz, is that she remains existentially unaware of what, intellectually, she knows; that of D. Jorge and D. Fernando is that, although perfectly aware, they are not strong enough to direct their actions as this awareness dictates.

The situation contains the germ of tragedy, but it is not allowed to grow. In *Las ferias de Madrid,* Lope is quite careful to elicit the audience's sympathy for the would-be seducer. In *Los comendadores de Córdoba,* he is equally careful to prevent that sympathy from developing. Because they are young and inexperienced, we would probably feel pity for D. Jorge and D. Fernando, were it not for the fact that they disregard several opportunities to end their heedless course—such as an enforced separation from their mistresses in Act II—and stubbornly ignore a whole series of portents of impending disaster. They must thus be regarded as not simply conscious but even obstinate transgressors.

Earlier I noted that the process by which the Veinticuatro punishes the malefactors of this play and realizes his vengeance is, for him, a process of earthly salvation. It is hardly surprising that the important steps in this process represent corrections of the errors that lead to the condemnation of Beatriz, D. Jorge, and D. Fernando. Beatriz loses her life because of her deficient awareness; D. Jorge and D. Fernando forfeit theirs because they cannot bring their will to bear on what they are aware of. To rescue himself from dishonor, the Veinticuatro must first become aware and then exert his will as this awareness dictates.

The stages in the Veinticuatro's salvation are marked by what might be called his three homecomings: first, his return early in the play from the siege of Granada (like the *comendadores,* the Veinticuatro had served his king there with great distinction); next, his return at the beginning of Act III from a visit to the court in Toledo; and finally, his return at the very end of the play—surreptitious this time—from the feigned hunting expedition.

The first homecoming constitutes the nadir of the course the Veinticuatro is to trace from honor, through dishonor, to honor regained, for by this time D. Jorge and Da. Beatriz have already succumbed to their "fierce love," and the Veinticuatro fails to detect it. Indeed, he places himself in a most ludicrous position by expatiating on the joys of marriage while the machinery set up to deceive him is already in motion:

> ¿Qué piensa quien no se casa?
> La libertad envejece.
> ¡Oh, alegre y dichoso estado!
> Si la cabeza me duele,
> tengo al fin quien me consuele,
> que es, mi mujer á mi lado.
> Siente, en efecto, mi mal,
> alégrase de mi bien,
> y, en efecto, tengo quien
> lo sienta con rostro igual.
> Si me ausento, me desea,
> si vengo, me da sus brazos,
> no con fingidos abrazos,
> como de otros bien se crea.
> Mira mi hacienda, y regala,
> es médico y es consuelo:
> si es buena, es prenda del cielo,
> y del infierno si es mala.

(272a)

What is that person thinking of who does not marry? Freedom causes one to grow old. Oh, happy and fortunate state! If I have a headache, there is someone at least to comfort me, my wife, standing by my side. She is pained by my misfortune; she rejoices in my good fortune; truly, I have someone who can feel all things as I do. When I am away, she desires me; when I return, she takes me in her arms, and not with feigned embraces, as might well be thought of others. She looks after my household, she indulges me, she is my physician and my consolation. [A wife,] if she is good, is a gift from heaven, and if she is bad, from hell.

At this point, the Veinticuatro is living in a state of dangerous unawareness. His situation moves the modern reader to sympathy, but for Lope, it is an occasion only for abrasive irony. Those who allow themselves to be deceived are not to be pitied.

Between his first homecoming and the second, the Veinticuatro fortunately acquires the needed awareness. It is a credit to Lope's dramatic sense that he makes the audience privy to the moment of perception and arranges matters so that this moment forms the climax of Act II. The King sees one day upon the hand of D. Jorge a ring that he, the King, had given to the Veinticuatro in gratitude for his many services. Encountering the Veinticuatro shortly afterward, he upbraids him severely, thinking that his gift had been valued lightly. The Veinticuatro can only reply that he had given the ring not to D. Jorge, but to his wife, a perfectly natural action. To this the King answers, "Si á tu mujer se la diste, / que tu mujer te la dé" ("If you gave it to your wife, let your wife give it back to you") (285a). The Veinticuatro is obsessed by this remark, and as he meditates on its meaning, he comes to realize the truth:

> ¿Qué es esto que en este punto
> ha pasado por mis ojos?
> De mis mortales enojos
> debe de ser el trasunto.
> Mas ya de mi honor difunto

la triste sombra se ve.
¿Cómo la dió? ¿Cómo fué?
Mas ¡oh buen Rey!, bien dijiste:
"Si á tu mujer se la diste,
que tu mujer te la dé."

.   .   .   .

¡Ay de mí! ¿Qué estoy pensando?
¿Cómo aquéste la trujera,
cuando ella no se la diera?
Luego ya fué cierto el cuándo.
Diósela, ¿qué estoy dudando?
¿Quién no dirá que así fué
porque no me guarda fe?
Rey, mucho en esto dijiste:
"Si á tu mujer se la diste,
que tu mujer te la dé."
¡Ea, que me vuelvo loco!
La honra ayudan las leyes:
las palabras de los reyes
siempre dicen mucho en poco.
¡Á qué furia me provoco!
Pero por la posta iré;
que más por la posta fué
honra que en mujer consiste:
"Si á tu mujer se la diste,
que tu mujer te la dé."

(285a–b)

What is this that in this moment has passed before my eyes? It must be a semblance of my mortal cares. Already the dismal shadow of my dead honor can be seen! How did she give it to him? How was that? Oh, good King, you said it well: "If you gave it to your wife, let your wife give it back to you." Woe unto me! What am I thinking? How could he be wearing it if she did not give it to him? But the "how" is now a certainty. She gave it to him, why am I doubting it? Who will not say that it was so because she is unfaithful to me? Sire, much was conveyed when you said: "If you gave it to your wife, let your wife give it back to you." Ay, I'm going mad! The cause of honor is supported by the law. The words of kings always say much with little. What a rage I am provoking myself into! I shall return by the post stage, for the honor of women is in itself something staged: "If you gave it to your wife, let your wife give it back to you."

Having thus "provoked himself into a rage," the Veinticuatro returns home a second time. Now the tables are turned, and it is the Veinticuatro who is aware and Beatriz and the *comendadores* who are deceived. The new situation is clearly pleasing to the Veinticuatro, and, with a zest that modern audiences would find unseemly, he plays with the ignorance of his enemies, deflecting onto the three of them the irony that was formerly directed at him. The enjoyment to be derived from such games is, however, momentary at best, and thus, having received from his faithful servant Rodrigo a full account of the many adulteries committed beneath his roof, the Veinticuatro moves quickly toward his real objective, the cleansing of house and reputation.

The Veinticuatro's third and final homecoming represents the application of will to awareness and is the obvious culmination of the action of the play. What little critical comment *Los comendadores de Córdoba* has received has been elicited, for the most part, by the extreme ferocity of the Veinticuatro's acts on this occasion. More interesting than the vengeance itself, however, is the long monologue spoken by the Veinticuatro immediately before. This monologue, which is obviously inspired by a similar speech in Rufo's ballad, is invaluable for the insight it gives into the psychology not only of the Veinticuatro but of Lope's heroes in general:

> Hoy, ¿en qué me diferencio
> de otro furioso Roldán?
> ¡Ah, honra, veisme aquí ya
> en vuestro teatro puesto,
> como todo hombre lo está;
> que nacimos para esto,
> desde que Dios sér nos da!
> Uno representa el Papa
> con su pontificia capa,
> otro el Rey con su corona,
> otro su misma persona,

que su puesto ocupa y tapa;
otro con él corresponde,
es Duque, y menos que él,
éste Marqués, y aquél Conde,
y otro le sirve y responde,
porque aquél se sirve de él;
tal es, y un hombre ciego,[11]
oficial y ciudadano,
tal pone el pueblo en sosiego,
con vara ó pluma en la mano,
y honor representa luego.
Y mirad lo que le plugo
al cielo en darme este yugo;
que entre las figuras todas,
la honra, autor de mis bodas,
me vino á dar el verdugo.
¡Ea, desnuda la espada,
no te mueva compasión!

(296a)

Today, in what way am I different from any other "Orlando furioso"? Ah, honor, now you see me placed here in your theater, as all men are [sooner or later], for we are born for this from the moment God gives us being. One man plays the part of the Pope with his pontifical cape, another the King with his crown, a third [the Crown-Prince, the Viceroy?], the person who is the same as the King, the one who occupies and fills his position. Another corresponds [in his sphere] to the man preceding; he is a Duke and of lesser stature. This man is a Marquis, that one a Count, and still another, the one who serves and attends to the Count, for the latter requires to be served by him. One man, besides being blind (?), is a tradesman and citizen; another keeps the town in peace, with pen or rod of authority in hand, and is the symbol there of honor. And look how Heaven was pleased to burden me: for honor, the author of my marriage, has decided to give me, out of all possible parts, that of executioner! Now then, unsheath your sword, do not be moved by compassion!

The first thing that strikes one in this speech is the curious discrepency between the tone of the first part—one of complacency and a kind of grim satisfaction in the face of the task ahead—and that of the end—one of self-pity and of sympathy for the future victims. We are not surprised by the latter; it seems normal for the Veinticuatro to feel at least some compassion for those he is about to kill, for he had affection for them once, and is bound to them still by ties of blood and family. What does surprise us somewhat, perhaps, is the feeling that shows through the first lines of the speech. How, we wonder, is it possible for the Veinticuatro to anticipate with seeming eagerness the bloody act that must now take place, especially in view of the humanity we have also observed? Obviously, there is a paradox here that some may be inclined to resolve by ascribing insincerity to one or the other of the apparently antithetical attitudes. Actually, the Veinticuatro *is* both sorry and content that the moment for vengeance has come. His contentment has nothing to do with any defect in his character. It has to do, rather, with his realization that he is about to undergo one of the critcial experiences of his existence: depending on how he meets the challenge of the next few minutes, the "life" of the Veinticuatro will either be triumphantly regained or lost forever.

As the Veinticuatro himself explains in his soliloquy, every man is assigned at birth a certain role to play on earth. Some are asked to be kings and princes, others, dukes and counts; the majority are cast as simple laborers.[12] Each role, however, no matter how humble, includes a certain number of episodes where one's very life as a man of honor is placed on the line. The Veinticuatro could not have foreseen the particular challenge to his honor presented by his wife and D. Jorge, but he could have foreseen, and obviously did foresee, that his manhood would eventually be tested in some fashion. It is because he is eager to prove himself, and because he knows full well that dishonor avenged is not simply honor restored but honor strengthened and augmented, that he faces his testing with fortitude and some degree of anticipation.

In the preceding pages, *Los comendadores* has several times been characterized as a story of worldly salvation. The Veinticuatro's monologue enables us to know the conditions of such salvation as they were understood by Lope's audiences. They are, first, constant consciousness of the responsibilities and obligations of the role into which one has been placed on earth; and second, the ability, deriving from courage and strength of will, to discharge faithfully those responsibilities and obligations.[13] These conditions, the first in particular, constitute the reason that the heroes of the *Comedia* are so extremely self-preoccupied. He who would avoid false steps must always remain mindful of who he is, which is to say, *what* he is—not simply Charles, but Charles V, King of Spain and Emperor of the Holy Roman Empire; not simply Rodrigo, but Rodrigo Téllez Girón, Grand Master of the Order of Calatrava, not simply Fernán Alfonso, but Fernán Alfonso, Señor de Belmonte and Veinticuatro de Córdoba.

"Soy quien soy," "I am who I am," says the Golden Age hero often in moments of crisis or decision. The phrase is susceptible to misinterpretation. What it expresses, as Leo Spitzer and, more recently, José Antonio Maravall have made clear, is not a determined individualism—such a feeling would be anachronistic—but a particular kind of awareness, an awareness like that manifested by the Veinticuatro at the end of *Los comendadores de Córdoba*.[14] It implies recognition not so much of one's psychological configuration as of one's social configuration, that is, of one's place in society and of the behavior expected of one as a certain member of the social hierarchy. It would not be an exaggeration to say that *Los comendadores de Córdoba* amounts, ultimately, to a celebration of this kind of awareness. Those who, like Beatriz, fail to attain it, are destined for certain disaster. Those who, like the *comendadores,* attain it but refuse or neglect to respect it are equally damned. But those who, like the Veinticuatro, pursue this awareness and direct their actions in accordance with its urgings possess the secret of heroism. For the vengeance of the Veinticuatro is, in this play, an indisputably heroic act. It is an act that rescues a nearly forfeit life, one that through destruction creates. Nothing could be more worthy of esteem. Lest anyone doubt or deny this, the King himself is made to appear in the last scene of the play, there to confirm and memorialize the greatness of the Veinticuatro's deed:

Hecho famoso y notable,
tan digno de eterna fama,
que de un Rey, noble te llama,
y de un Reino memorable.
Sois, don Fernando, tan dino
de premio por tal venganza,
que hasta un Rey parte le alcanza
del honor que á vos os vino.
Hónrase Córdoba más
que por Séneca y Lucano
de tener tal ciudadano.

(299a)

Great and notable deed, so worthy of eternal fame that a king proclaims you noble, and a kingdom, memorable. You are, Don Fernando, so deserving of reward for such a vengeance that even a king may share in the honor which has come to you. Córdoba is more honored by having such a citizen than by Seneca and Lucan.

These lines are highly reminiscent of the ending of the *Poema de Mio Cid.* Also reminiscent of the *Poema* is the Veinticuatro's reaction when the King informs him that, as a sign of monarchical approval of the vengeance, he is to be given as his bride one of the noblest ladies in the kingdom: "All that I have lost I have regained" (299b). Like the Cid, the Veinticuatro suffers a grave affront at the hands of his enemies; like the Cid, he is banished, because of this affront, from the company of the honored; and like the Cid, he is able eventually to rise out of the limbo of dishonor and to regain his original privileged state by strength of will and body alone ("Your bravery has put everything right," says one of the characters to the Veinticuatro at the end of the play [299b]). It is, I suggest, precisely because of this approximation to the trajectory of the Cid's life that the action of *Los comendadores de Córdoba* exercised such a strong hold on Spanish audiences of the Golden Age. As noted earlier, the greatest value for a Spaniard was "to be," the worst possible fate, to be known as a person "without being." *Los comendadores de Córdoba* depicts a man who, from an initial condition of fullest possible "being," lapses into one of total "nonbeing," only to restore himself at the end, dramatically and suddenly, to his former life. It is obvious that few tales could be better calculated to arouse the sympathetic and passionate interest of most Spaniards. The men and women who constituted the theatrical public of the late sixteenth and early seventeenth centuries, however, must necessarily have found the implications of a play like *Los comendadores de Córdoba* especially attractive. For these men and women were unique among those who lived in Spain in the roughly one hundred and fifty years that intervened between the accession of Isabella I to the crown of Castile and the death of her great-great-grandson, Philip III. Like their forebears, the Spaniards who crowded the theaters during the last decade of the sixteenth century and the first two of the next believed fervently that to "be" was the supreme value, possibly the only great value. Unlike the immediately preceding generations, however, they saw their "being" not simply challenged but severely menaced. Tracing how such a situation came to exist is, as well as being interesting in itself, important to an understanding of the honor plays, and I turn now to the development of this phenomenon.

An Excursion into History

The threat to their inner "being" experienced by Spaniards at the turn of the sixteenth century derived chiefly from an aggregate of crises, military-political, social, and economic, suffered by the Spanish nation at that time and in the years immediately preceding. Of these crises, those that Spain sustained in the military and diplomatic sphere have been, at least until recently, the ones that most engaged the attention of historians. The others, however, were quite as serious and equally or more consequential in determining the spirit of the age.

The sequence of military setbacks endured by the Spanish during the last years of the reign of Philip II and the first few years of that of Philip III is well known to all students of European history. The series began with England's defeat of the Great Armada in 1588—characterized by R. B. Merriman as Spain's "supreme disaster" under Philip II[15]—and continued with Essex's sack of Cadiz in 1596; the failure of the lesser armadas, also England-bound, in 1597 and 1601; the aborting of the Irish Expedition in 1602; and the neutralizing, in instance after instance, of the Spanish armies in France and the Netherlands. The record of these reversals is contained in the treaties signed by Spain with its traditional enemies as the one century ended and the other began: 1598, peace with France; 1604, peace with England; 1602, Twelve Years' Truce with the Dutch.

Whether or not Spain was seriously weakened by the succession of defeats and stalemates that it sustained during the twenty years that followed the terrible defeat of 1588 is a much debated historical question. There were many at the time who thought that it had been. The pessimism of Quevedo in this regard is well known. The prominent historian Mariana was of a similar opinion, warning in 1609 that unless Spaniards mended their ways and abjured vice and frivolity, "our losses [in the future] will be greater than those up until now, and there will be no end until we are flung from the peak where we were into great misfortune and servitude."[16] Our concern, however, is not so much with the state of Spain's physical defenses at the turn of the century as with that of its psychological ones. These, unquestionably, had been considerably undermined by the events of the preceding years. Accustomed to prevailing, and needing to prevail in order to "be," the Spaniards were now forced to the realization that they could be bested—decisively and repeatedly. This was surely a blow of the greatest magnitude to the imperative dimension of both nation and individual citizens, and if the shock of it was too great to be absorbed at once, still it must be held in large part responsible for that "sense of insecurity" which J. H. Elliott speaks of as settling over the country during the closing years of the sixteenth century and the opening ones of the following century.[17]

Contributing to that same sense of insecurity was the general economic collapse that Spain suffered at this time,[18] a collapse reflected in the several decrees of bankruptcy that Philip II was forced to issue during his reign. The reasons for the failure were various: spiraling inflation, induced in part by the huge imports of bullion from America; an unfavorable balance of trade, particularly with the colonies in the New World, which were gradually rising to self-sufficiency, a profoundly regressive system of taxation, which placed the greatest burden upon those least able to bear it, the artisans and laborers. Among the many things that may be held jointly responsible for the collapse, however, one stands out as being especially instrumental. That was the disastrous decline into which Spanish agriculture fell during the second half of the sixteenth century. The causes of this decline have been well documented; they relate principally to the steady rise in costs during this period and the disappearance of the American market. But of greater interest to us than the causes of the crisis are its effects. The most significant of these was a marked shift of the population, from rural areas into urban ones. Eventually, this shift was to place an unbearable strain on the resources of the towns and cities, and the result was the squalid conditions so vividly depicted in novels like *Guzmán de Alfarache*.

At the end of the sixteenth century, the ill health of the Spanish countryside was apparent to everyone. There was talk of drastic remedies, but before any of these could be applied, agricultural interests were staggered by a pair of unexpected and truly devastating blows. The first of these was a series of crop failures so severe that the price of grain more than doubled in the three years between 1595 and 1598. The second was a recurrence, beginning in the year 1595, of the bubonic plague. The exact number of victims claimed by the plague has never been determined; but it is estimated that as many as 500,000 may have succumbed.[19] A large percentage of those who died were from the country, because the malnourished peasants were particularly vulnerable to the epidemic. The loss of those men and women was a catastrophe for Spanish agriculture, as was the departure of the *moriscos*, who were expelled from the peninsula early in the next century. A state of grave weakness now threatened to degenerate into total collapse.

That, as was suggested above, Spaniards actually did react to the economic disorder of the turn of the century with an acute sense of anguish is attested by numerous documents of the time. Their concern was undoubtedly not primarily for their own well-being; personal poverty, as the *escudero* in *Lazarillo de Tormes* demonstrates, could be borne with fortitude and at least an air of indifference. It was more likely to be their family's welfare that preoccupied them, because to allow those for whom one is responsible to suffer reflected not only on one's humanity but also on one's capability as *paterfamilias*, and consequently on one's honor. That honor should be called into question was, of course, not to be permitted, which may be one reason why the Cortes of Castile protested loudly and frequently about the chaos prevailing at the end of the sixteenth century.[20] The great distress felt by the Cortes can best be appreciated by reading the record of their proceedings at length, but the following extract from a petition of the year 1594 (several years, be it noted, before the worst of the economic crisis) gives an accurate notion of the vehemence of their sentiment: "How can one engage in commerce when one is forced to pay three hundred ducats in taxes on a capital of a thousand ducats? . . . In the regions where 30,000 *arrobes* of worsted were formerly worked, scarcely 6,000 are now consumed. It results from this, as well as from the tax imposed on wool, that the number of flocks is also diminishing. Agriculture and the raising of cattle, industry and commerce are ruined; there is now not one region of the kingdom which does not lack inhabitants; any number of houses closed and uninhabited are to be seen; *in short, the kingdom is perishing.*"[21]

The third of these crises, what I earlier called social crisis, was that provoked by the anti–New Christian prejudice of the Old Christians. This prejudice was hardly unique to the age; its history extends back many years—ultimately, to the first outcroppings in the Middle Ages of hatred for the Jews. But the manifestations of the prejudice were probably most clearly marked in the years under discussion, and it is those manifestations that concern us here. As several recent studies have made clear,[22] to be acknowledged a New Christian during the height of the preoccupation with "purity of blood" was to be excluded from all the university colleges, all the military orders, from many of the religious orders, and from many of the better positions within the state bureaucracy. It was to be subjected to nearly complete ostracism and to the constant surveillance of one's neighbors. It was to be liable to denunciation to the Inquisition and to the dreadful consequences that Inquisitional investigation not infrequently entailed. Most terrible of all, to be marked a New Christian was to live completely without honor. It was assumed that there was no true nobility outside the caste of the Old Christians, and as the Golden Age wore on, this belief came to be held ever more strongly.

Perhaps the best indication of how unpleasant a fate it was to be regarded a New Christian is that people were willing to go to extravagant and what seem to us ludicrous lengths to avoid being so labeled. Ignorance was cultivated (because learning was held to be a characteristic of the Jews); gravity and tranquillity were carefully affected (the Jews were also said to be "a very restless people"); quantities of ham and bacon were ostentatiously consumed.[23] Recourse to such extreme measures was no guarantee that a person would automatically be accepted as an Old Christian. There were those who, in spite of their possession of the signs of the dominant caste, continued to be regarded with suspicion. For these, there was only one alternative: to confront the rumors and to try to prove them false. If the scandal was in fact unfounded, it could usually be laid to rest by bringing forth reliable character witnesses and appropriate and trustworthy documents. If there was truth in it, the problem was immeasurably greater. Considerable ingenuity and effort were then required for the construction of an elaborate lie, which might not, in any case, be believed: certificates had to be forged, witnesses bribed, a whole new genealogy fabricated.[24]

Thus did politico-military, economic, and social crises act in concert in the 1590s and 1600s to threaten the "being" of Spaniards and thereby to induce at every level of Spanish society an acute sense of vulnerability. This sense of vulnerability, so inimical to the values on which Spanish life was structured, was especially devastating when compared with the glory of the preceding decade, roughly 1575–1585, which had been distinguished by Philip II's greatest triumphs in the area of foreign relations. Naturally, this feeling of vulnerability inspired a variety of reactions. Some people—a very few—were impelled by their insecurity to question the very foundations of existence in Spain; others, the so-called *arbitristas,* accepted the traditional values but called for multiple reforms; still others—one thinks of the ascetics—avoided having either to accept or to reject by retreating into closed, personal worlds. It is very doubtful that the vast majority of Spaniards ever felt tempted to assume any of these postures. For most, the idea of giving up the world in which they lived was inconceivable. It was equally inconceivable that they would question the values that had sustained Spain for hundreds of years or that they could believe the nation needed radical reform. These people, the majority, remained committed to life in the world and fundamentally unshaken in their faith in Spain, in Spanish values, and in themselves. They were, nevertheless, unsettled by recent events and in need of reassurance—reassurance that the traditional Spanish values were still viable, that through the exercise of discretion, fortitude, and bravery, both they themselves and Spain could continue to "be." Such reassurance they were given by the *Comedia* in general and, with special effectiveness, by honor plays of the type of *Los comendadores de Córdoba.*[25]

Ritual, Myth, and Romance

Our recently enhanced understanding of seventeenth-century Spain permits us to grasp an important truth: the whole of the theater of the time was, like the primitive drama from which it ultimately descends, profoundly ritualistic in nature.[26] Not only the *autos sacramentales,* in other words, but the *comedias* as well existed, if not exclusively then in large part, for the purpose of gathering people together so that they could celebrate, in communion with each other and by means of a dramatic representation, those ideals and values that they held to be self-evident. Unlike the great English and French drama of the time, the Spanish seventeenth-century drama did not as a rule aspire to the communication of new perceptions.[27] Its interest was, rather, in affirming the worth of the traditional truths, and thus it asked the audience not to stand back and contemplate but to come forward and participate.

This essential feature of the *Comedia,* the tendency to promote ritualistic participation in the celebration of shared values, has been remarked in diverse fashion by a number of recent writers. Charles V. Aubrun, for example, has described the theater of the seventeenth century as a "temple in which a single fervor unites public, players, and author in a common task, the celebration of an active ideology (or mythology)."[28] José Hierro sees the *Comedia* in quite similar fashion, but expresses his understanding rather differently. "For the Spaniard of the Golden Age," he writes, "the *Comedia* was a framework of lyrical passages, of beautiful words which illuminate the heart. He did not see the work as a solid structure. He entered into it, allowing himself to be transported. He became the protagonist, forgetting that he was a spectator. The lyricism served him as a bridge with which to join into— humanly—the lives of those beings put in motion upon the stage."[29] What Hierro says finds perfect confirmation in an essay of Azorín that describes the performance of a seventeenth-century play in an old Spanish village.[30] The climax of the piece finds the hero in a difficult situation: menaced by grave danger, he must turn his mind from the threat in order to speak words of love to his lady. He rises to the challenge splendidly, and in watching him do so, one of the spectators, a dignified older gentleman, becomes visibly agitated; his eyes begin to glow with excitement, his hand moves up to his chin, and his fingers nervously stroke his grizzled beard.

Commenting on Azorín's anecdote, Ortega writes: "The good Castilian went to see the famous play not in order to contemplate some exemplary action, but to let himself be swept away, to get drunk on the stream of adventures and perils experienced by the characters."[31] To move every member of the audience to enter into the sufferings and triumphs of the stage heroes and thereby to affirm the values that sustained those heroes in their moments of crisis, was, then, the proper business of the *Comedia.* Its proper business and also, in a sense, its acknowledged business: again I quote the lines in the *Arte nuevo de hacer comedias en este tiempo* where Lope says that of all possible plots,

> Los casos de la honra son mejores
> porque *mueven con fuerza a toda gente*...[32]

Cases of honor are the best, because they move all people pro-foundly...

These two lines from Lope's "Poetics" have frequently been remarked upon, but their real importance has not always been appreciated.[33] They are, in fact, highly significant, for they suggest that Lope was intuitively aware both of the ritualistic function served by the theater of his time and of the burden which that function placed on the dramatist: the obligation to create for the audience viable "myths"—by which I mean simply the story acted out in ritual.[34] There may be some readers who find it difficut to believe that Lope could have been so aware. These should be reminded that several years before Lope established himself as a dramatist Cervantes had already sensed the need for the fabrication of myths. Such, in any case, is the conclusion that one draws from *La Numancia,* a play that gives every indication of having been conceived quite consciously as the instrument of ritualistic celebration of Spanish history and of Spanish values.

Indeed, the history of the *Comedia* in the last decade of the sixteenth century and the first two decades of the seventeenth may not inappropriately be summed up as a continuous search—carried on with varying degrees of awareness—for myth. What separates Lope from the Cervantes of *La Numancia,* from Juan de la Cueva, and from Guillén de Castro is not so much a different conception of the theater as a different degree of success in carrying out that conception. *La Numancia, El reto de Zamora,* and *Las mocedades del Cid* are, for reasons that cannot be examined here, incompletely realized myths (in the sense of that word given above). *Los comendadores de Córdoba* is, by contrast, superbly effective as myth, as is attested by the fact that within a very few years, the pattern of its action became standard for the honor plays. The reason for the particular effectiveness of *Los comenda-*

dores de Córdoba as myth has already been suggested. It is that, in a time when the feeling of personal and group vulnerability was general and consecrated Spanish values had begun to be questioned by some, the story of the Veinticuatro offered reassurance that a man could lose everything and then, relying only on himself and the values of his ancestors, recover it all again. The word "everything" is used here advisedly. As the Golden Age *comedias* make clear over and over again, no possible combination of misfortunes could be worse than the loss of honor. To be without honor was to be dead in all but actuality: "Dishonor for an honorable man is, ultimately, to cease to be," says a character in a play of this period.[35] In *Los comendadores de Córdoba,* then, audiences were celebrating something more than a hero's fall and restoration. They were celebrating what was for them the almost literal death and rebirth of a man. It was this that made their celebration a matter of such intense satisfaction.

If we, as modern readers, are able to believe in the reality of the Veinticuatro's rebirth, then we too, in all probability, will feel some sense of contentment at the ending of his story. For as Maud Bodkin has shown in her *Archetypal Patterns in Poetry,*[36] the pattern of death and resurrection in literature is one that has had at all times and in all places the power to compel assent and approval. Indeed, so responsive is this pattern to the most basic needs of the human psyche that it serves as the foundation of a good deal of the world's mythology and informs the traditions surrounding most great culture heroes. Only somewhat less outstanding has been its role as a structuring principle in more sophisticated, which is to say written, literature. Here, of course, its appearance is frequently masked, which means that whatever effect it makes upon the reader is necessarily commanded by a chain of subconscious or semiconscious associations. There is, however, one type of narrative, closely related to the wish-fulfillment dream, in which the archetypal pattern of death and rebirth appears regularly in a form both prominent and undisguised. That type we call romance, and it is as an analogy to narrative romance that honor plays like *Los comendadores de Córdoba* can best be understood and appreciated.

This idea may at first seem surprising. Consider, however, the characteristics of romance as they have been defined by Northrop Frye, the contemporary critic who, more than any other, has rehabilitated the notion of genres in literature.[37] The essential element of romance, Frye informs us, is "adventure." This element may take various forms; it may, for example, spin itself out in a seemingly endless series of more or less inconsequential and minimally differentiated incidents, or it may be embodied in a single major adventure. In the latter event, the story revolves around two main characters: a protagonist or hero, the exemplar of perfect manhood in his society, and an antagonist or enemy. It is the job of the protagonist to complete the adventure successfully; it is the job of the antagonist to oppose the completion of the adventure, and in fact, by his opposition to the hero, actually to constitute the adventure. Once joined, the conflict between protagonist and antagonist can have only one end: the triumph of the former over the latter. Before the victory can take place, however, the hero must prove his worthiness. This he does, first, by seeking out his enemy with steadfast purpose and, second, by entering into courageous and skillful combat with him. Thus, the adventure is divided into three phases: "the stage of the perilous journey and the preliminary minor adventures; the crucial struggle, usually some kind of battle in which either the hero or his foe, or both, must die; and the exaltation of the hero."[38] The three phases being analogous to the three recognizable movements of tragedy, Frye would have us call them by the names traditionally used to identify those movements, *agon* (conflict), *pathos* (death-struggle), and *anagnorisis* (discovery, or, in this instance, recognition of the hero).

This idea of adventure as central to romance admittedly has connotations of frivolousness that do not seem to accord well with a play like *Los comendadores de Córdoba*. But it is apparent that for Frye adventure means primarily *agon,* all-out struggle, conflict on a large scale. And clearly, the *Comedia* is, as a whole, informed by such conflict, and so is *Los comendadores* in particular. From the beginning of the play, the action directs itself with single-minded purpose toward the instant when the Veinticuatro—the model of Spanish manhood—engages those who have critically wounded his honor. This is the moment of *pathos,* and as always, what is being risked is life itself: the life of the Veinticuatro's honor is staked against the mortal lives of Beatriz, D. Jorge, and D. Fernando. As was observed earlier, the drama of the moment is heightened by the device of having the Veinticuatro do battle on two fronts. First, he is made to acquire domination over his own emotions, his natural feelings of sympathy for the intended victims. Then, having won the first contest— having succeeded in subjugating his instincts to the role imposed on him by society—the Veinticuatro takes on the external enemy. In this struggle there is, of course, no real danger that the Veinticuatro will lose, but then in romance there never is. The hero skirts death, he is even, on occasion, touched by it, but inevitably he comes back to life again. This is the whole point. Because romance is basically wish-fulfillment fantasy, the protagonist, after demonstrating his bravery and fortitude by battling the forces of darkness and death, must then emerge into the light with undiminshed powers— must be resurrected if need be—to receive the acclaim due him. This acclaim constitutes what Frye calls the *anagnorisis,* or discovery, and we observe it in *Los comendadores de Córdoba* when, at the end of the play, the Veinticuatro is summoned to receive the recognition of his King.

The analogy with romance, helpful to an understanding of *Los comendadores de Córdoba,* is even more important for the comprehension of certain of Lope's middle-period honor plays. I am thinking in particular of *Peribáñez* and *Fuenteovejuna.* Both of these plays show an approximation to romance that is greater than that of *Los comendadores de Córdoba,* and the approximation of *Fuenteovejuna* is noticeably greater than that of *Peribáñez.* This suggests that we have within this group of plays a kind of development, a development that though not consistent is nevertheless manifest, and that is comparable in its way to the larger evolution from early honor plays, to middle-period plays, to late plays. Not coincidently, the movement toward romance that characterizes the middle-period honor plays is accompanied by another development, the increasing use of elements of ritual. I say "not coincidentally" because both developments are the more or less inevitable consequences of Lope's acquiescence in the public's demand for ritualistic theater, drama that will "move all people."

That ritualistic drama will tend to assimilate itself to ritual is, doubtless, obvious. That it will also tend to assimilate itself to romance is less obvious but equally true. As Lord Raglan shows in *The Hero,* a prototypical form of romance was the original myth of ritual, and rituals—and ritual-like dramas—have been dependent on romance ever since.[39] What they have chiefly appropriated from the latter is an archetypal narrative uniquely suited for the expression, and celebration, of values. At the center of the narrative, always, is the hero, and in him are embodied the ideals of the celebrating people. The efficacy of these ideals is assumed, but it is made patent as a result of the hero's adventures and ordeals. Traditionally these lead to—or are even entirely supplanted by—a major, climactic adventure. Here, the hero meets a supreme challenge, one that often seems to bring an end to his life. But his demise is only temporary. Ultimately, he is reborn, and his rebirth occasions recognition and rejoicing that the values which sustain him, and the communing people, are superior to all alien forces, even death.[40]

In the rest of this chapter, I shall consider in detail two later middle-period plays, *Peribáñez* and *Fuenteovejuna.* Each of these marks a further step in the progression toward ritual, on the one hand, and toward romance, on the other. Together they constitute the summit of the art of Lope's middle-period honor plays.

Peribáñez y el Comendador de Ocaña

The story of *Peribáñez* (1605–1612, probably 1605–1608)[41] is familiar to most readers of Spanish literature and requires no synopsis here. Unlike *Los comendadores de Córdoba,* it does not have a known source in history, but this is not to say that it does not derive ultimately from some historical event. Quite possibly it does, since there seems to have existed in Lope's time a ballad dealing with the material of the play.[42] It

is generally supposed that this ballad was the immediate inspiration for the play and that it is quoted, either verbatim or
in part, in Llorente's song in Act II:[43]

(Ac., X, 132a)

con la vuesa guarnecida."
que no á vos, Comendador,
con su capa la pardilla,
"Más quiero yo á Peribáñez
desta suerte respondía:
mientras Pedro está en Toledo,
cuanto hermosa y cuanto linda;
La mujer es virtuosa
de amores la requería.
el Comendador de Ocaña
hermosa es á maravilla;
La mujer de Peribáñez

The wife of Peribáñez is wonderfully beautiful; the Comendador of Ocaña plied her with attentions. The wife is virtuous,
as virtuous as she is beautiful and comely. While Pedro was in
Toledo, this is how she responded [to the Comendador]: "I love
Peribáñez, with his humble brown cape, more than you, Comendador, with your embroidered one.

This song, similar in function to the famous *copla* in *El
caballero de Olmedo* and to the equally famous lyrical ballad
from Act II of *Fuenteovejuna*, crystallizes in a few short lines
the essence of the play: it evokes the principal characters and
suggests their basic natures; it formulates the dramatic conflict that shapes the action; and it implies the lesson of the
story.[44] That lesson we have already seen in *Los comendadores de Córdoba*. It is that the inherent worth of all true
believers is the same, that one is therefore under a strict
obligation to act out, cheerfully and conscientiously, the role
to which one has been assigned on earth, and that, because
of this obligation, self-awareness, in the sense given earlier, is
a quality to be esteemed and rewarded, while self-oblivious-
ness and self-deception are qualities to be despised and
punished.

One of the recurring features of the old Spanish *romances* —seen in such a ballad as the one sometimes entitled "Querellas entre Fernán González y el Rey de León"—is the sharp and prolonged contrasting of one world or sphere of life with another, a feature that serves to emphasize the basically dramatic nature of these poems. In his seminal article on *Peribáñez*, Edward M. Wilson pointed out how, in similar fashion, the worlds of Peribáñez and the Comendador are in this play carefully and consistently distinguished from beginning to end.[45] The world of Peribáñez is the world of the peasant. It is characterized, linguistically, by the use of language that is plain and unassuming and, emotionally, by an attachment to the simple things of life, to the objects and experiences of the country. The world of the Comendador is the world of the nobleman. Its linguistic peculiarity is constant striving for elevation of style, its emotional bias, toward life's refinements. The two worlds are brought into contact initially through the person of Casilda, and it is in expressing their common love for her that both Peribáñez and the Comendador most effectively characterize their respective spheres: "The husband [sees] in Casilda the fruits of the earth which he cultivates; the suitor calls her an angel, a diamond, a heavenly jewel."[46]

Despite the distinctions, both large and small, that Lope perceives between the two worlds, there can be little doubt that he feels that they should, and can, live in harmony.[47] That they do not here is due to the fact that both Peribáñez and the Comendador to some extent lose their self-awareness and repudiate the social rank to whose responsibilities and duties they must remain faithful. Of the two lapses, much the more serious is the Comendador's. Charged, like all feudal lords, with preserving the life and well-being of his vassals, he instead conspires against the chastity of one of them and against the honor of another. The sin is very grave, and cannot be considered less so because it is the only aberration in an otherwise upright and circumspect existence.[48] The Comendador himself knows this: at several points in the play he expresses fear for his future should he continue to follow what he calls his "mad idea."[49] Unfortunately, like the young men of *Los comendadores de Córdoba,* he lacks the moral strength to abandon a course once taken, even though it is clearly destructive. His ignominious end is thus what he had vaguely foreseen: death at the hands of a social inferior. As the Comendador himself acknowledges, it is a punisment well deserved: "I have been killed justifiably" (144a).

Compared to the Comendador's lapse, Peribáñez's loss of self-awareness does not seem very important. It consists only of accepting from the Comendador certain expensive gifts, in particular a set of wall hangings embroidered with the Comendador's escutcheon. A peasant is not a nobleman, however, and his walls are properly decorated not with coats-of-arms but with crosses of "grain and straw, a few poppies, camomile and broom" (133b). Peribáñez's acceptance of the hangings is thus an act of foolish presumption, the unwarranted appropriation of the attributes of a superior social rank. It is also an act fraught with danger, for it puts Peribáñez under obligation to the Comendador ("My wife and I, until now your vassals, are from this day on slaves of your house" [119b]), and has the effect of encouraging the Comendador in the pursuit of Casilda.

Fortunately, it is not long before Peribáñez learns of the Comendador's designs on his wife. His first act thereafter is to rid his house of the shameful hangings, for he perceives immediately the connection between the "false character" he has assumed and the Comendador's attack on his honor. Now Peribáñez is once again self-aware in the double sense of acknowledging who he is, which is to say what role he is playing, and of knowing what he must do in order to "be himself" properly. Equipped with that self-awareness, he can make plans for the vengeance that will restore him to a state of honor.

The course of Peribáñez's progress from honor, through dishonor, to honor restored is marked at each important stage by what might be termed scenes of ritualistic confirmation. Several of these scenes, which remind us of those instances in which Shakespeare uses ritual and ceremony to focus the feelings of the audience, involve the participation of a group of peasants who act as a kind of chorus within the work. The first of them is the opening scene of the play. Here, the peasants are called on to celebrate the just-consecrated marriage of Peribáñez and Casilda. They do so by performing a folk dance, the *folía,* to the accompaniment of a May song filled with warmth, love, and respect:

> Dente parabienes
> el Mayo garrido,
> los alegres campos,
> las fuentes y ríos.
> Alcen las cabezas
> los verdes alisos,
> y con frutos nuevos
> almendros floridos.
> Echen las mañanas,
> después del rocío,
> en espadas verdes
> guarnición de lirios.
> Suban los ganados
> por el monte mismo
> que cubrió la nieve,
> á pacer tomillos.
> 　　　　　*Folía.*
> Y á los nuevos desposados
> eche Dios su bendición;
> parabién les den los prados,
> pues hoy para en uno son.　　*Vuelven á danzar.*
> 　　　　　　　　　　　　　　(110b–111a)

Let greetings be given you by florid May, by the happy fields, the springs and rivers. Let the green alders raise their heads, and the flowering almonds, bearing their new fruit. Let the morning give forth—the dew having gone—an adornment of lilies, set among swords of green. Let the flocks go up the mountain, once covered with snow, to graze upon the thyme. (*Folía.*) God bless the newlyweds, and the fields extend their congratulations, for today the two are as one. (*They resume the dance.*)

With a few simple images—greening fields, flowering lilies, fructifying trees—the song evokes the smiling face that nature puts on in May. For Lope and his contemporaries, as for people of all eras, nature in spring signified harmony and concord, growth and abundance, vitality and hope. These are the things that their friends and neighbors wish for Peribáñez and Casilda, and they are the things that in time presumably do characterize their union.[50]

The marriage celebration signals the apogee of Peribáñez's life, to that point, as a man of honor. Unhappily, it is all too soon interrupted by the noisy entry of Bartolo, who announces that the Comendador has fallen from his horse, thus setting in motion the chain of events that will lead eventually to Peribáñez's disgrace. This, too, is confirmed by a song of the peasants, the one quoted earlier. Here, the words are sung by one man alone, the others, presumably, gathered around as a nonparticipating, though approving, audience. Though apparently simple, the song is actually quite complex and equivocal in intent. While it is on the one hand a celebration of the virtue of Casilda, it is on the other a proclamation of the dishonor of Peribáñez. In this proclamation there is, inevitably, an element of reproof, and one is reminded of the *vitos* of which Pitt-Rivers has written, mocking songs sung before the houses of social offenders in rural Andalusia to force them into acceptance of prevailing moral standards.[51]

Just as *Peribáñez* opens with a ritual celebrating Peribáñez in his state of unblemished honor, so does it close with a ritual celebrating him in his state of honor recovered. The scene is one that we have seen in *Los comendadores* and will see again in *Fuenteovejuna*: the King of Spain is sitting in state; before him is brought a man who has supposedly breached the laws of the kingdom; the King listens to the man's story, hears of honor lost and regained, and ends by declaring that the man is not only to be pardoned but, what is more, extolled as a paragon of virtue and a model of Spanish manhood. Like the Veinticuatro, Peribáñez emerges from the ritual with more honor than before, for the King confirms him in his rank, conferred originally by the Comendador, of captain, and gives him permanent "permission to bear arms, both defensive and offensive" (147b).

There is one other ritual in *Peribáñez* that deserves attention. It is the ceremony, occurring early in Act III, in which

le regalan

Peribáñez is knighted. Clearly, Lope conceived of the ceremony as significant, for he presents it in detail and with considerable dramatic emphasis. But its meaning within the context of the play is by no means unambiguously clear, and it has been subject to varying interpretations. One construction of the incident often advanced is that it is intended to furnish the basis for Peribáñez's concern with his honor. Another is that it serves to make justifiable Peribáñez's killing of the Comendador.[52] Though neither of these interpretations is convicing in the last analysis, each of them raises points of interest and importance, and they are, therefore worth examining in some detail.

The view that the purpose of the ceremony of investiture is to provide an explanation for Peribáñez's feelings of wounded honor rests on the belief, formerly widespread, that in the *Comedia* honor is a value that only the nobility can appreciate. This belief is supported by no less an authority than Ramón Menéndez Pidal, who years ago wrote that "it seems that in the theater honor is the exclusive patrimony of the noble class. If a peasant presumes to honor, it usually is just in passing, and even then it arouses special wonder; or it turns out—and this is the most frequent situation in the plays—that he is a peasant in appearance only, for in reality he is a nobleman, brought up among peasants as the result of some chance happening of his childhood."[53] More recent investigation, however, based on a broader knowledge of the texts than Menéndez Pidal commanded, has shown that his characterization is simply not true. In other words, there are in actuality a rather large number of plays in which peasants—true peasants and not noblemen in disguise—display a genuine and sustained concern for their honor. It was the particular contribution of Alexey Almasov, in a study that has not had the recognition it deserves,[54] to have pointed out and documented this fact. And it was the particular contribution of Noël Salomon, in his slightly later and monumental monograph, *Recherches sur le thème paysan dans la "comedia" au temps de Lope de Vega,*[55] to have called attention to the uniqueness of the fact—in the other European theaters of the time honor *is* the exclusive patrimony of the nobility—and to have provided in explanation of it a theory that is, although undeniably partial, thoughtful and illuminating.

Salomon's initial premise is shared by a number of other writers.[56] It is that the phenomenon of what has been called peasant honor is a function of the general celebration of rural Spanish life that came increasingly to characterize the *Comedia* after 1600. For Salomon, however, that celebration relates almost entirely to economic factors. Specifically, he sees it as stemming directly from the collapse of Spanish agriculture in the final decades of the sixteenth century and the ensuing depopulation of the countryside and rapid, unhealthy growth of the cities. One result of that collapse was the creation of a large body of physiocratic writings, works that by stressing the usefulness and dignity of farming aspired to bring about a revival of life in the country. Though I simplify his argument for the sake of concision, Salomon's thesis is that the Golden Age plays that exalt rural existence are in part a dramatic reflection of those physiocratic writings, in part a collective dream of evasion projected by an urban population increasingly depressed by the noise, filth, and misery of their cities.

If Salomon's explanation falls short, as I think it does, it is because it is too narrowly gauged. The idealized vision of the country and of country people in such plays as *Peribáñez, Fuenteovejuna, El alcalde de Zalamea,* and *La serrana de la Vera* indisputably was conditioned by the belief that agriculture must be revived and that life in the towns and cities was becoming ever more unpleasant. But it was conditioned as well by other, less transient, views. Chief among these is the conviction that it was in the countryside that the traditional values of Spanish society had best been preserved. Américo Castro has recently analyzed this conviction.[57] It made its appearance rather early in Spanish history and was greatly reinforced in the sixteenth century by the growing realization that it was the peasants who, more than any other social group, exemplified the imperative of "purity of blood." During the Middle Ages, the relatively easy contact between urban Christians and Jews resulted in considerable intermarriage between the two castes, especially at the higher levels of society. The Christian peasants, however, had little or no opportunity to marry outside their class and faith. Thus, as time went on, they could, and did, lay claim to a virtually unblemished ancestry. Because of their purity, the peasants were in possession of the first, and most important, requisite for honor. It was a requisite that many lacked, including quite a few who ranked higher in the social hierarchy. This fact is vitally important. More than any other, it explains both the increasing aggressiveness with which the peasants asserted their right to honor in the late sixteenth and early seventeenth centuries and the increasing willingness of the members of the upper classes, collectively if not individually, to consider seriously that claim.

Some of the aggressiveness with which the peasants asserted their purity, and hence their honor, may be observed in *Peribáñez* when Belardo refers contemptuously to the noblemen as "Jews" (138b), and when Costanza dismisses them as "hidalgos cansados" ("tired hidalgos") (138a),[58] "cansados" being here a punning reference to their belonging to the "old," that is, Jewish, faith.[59] Peribáñez himself is not so arrogant. He is, however, resolutely proud of his stock, as we see from his description of himself before the King in the final scene of the play:

> Yo soy un hombre,
> aunque de villana casta,
> limpio de sangre, y jamás
> de hebrea ó mora manchada.

> (147a)

Although of the peasant class, I am a man of clean blood, never tainted by that of Jews or Moors.

It would seem that a man who takes such pride in his lineage has no need to become a knight in order to feel honorable. And of course the evidence of the play demonstrates that this is so. Peribáñez's concern for his honor is apparent long before the ceremony of investiture and thus can have no logical connection with it. To be sure, Peribáñez himself implies that there *is* a connection, in a speech to the Comendador:

73

Vos me ceñisteis espada,
con que ya entiendo de honor;
que antes yo pienso, señor,
que entendiera poco ó nada.

(136b)

You girded me with the sword [of knighthood], so now I
understand about honor; before, Sire, I believe I understood
little or nothing.

Peribáñez's words, however, need not be taken at face value,
for their evident intention is less to state a fact than to com-
municate a warning. The Comendador has to this moment
consistently discounted the possibility that Peribáñez would
act to avenge an injury, believing, like many of his class, that
a peasant is incapable of caring for his honor. Peribáñez's remarks serve to advise him that if he continues to do so, it will
be at his peril.

It is, then, only with difficulty that we can suppose that
the ceremony of investiture is meant to "explain" Peribáñez's
feelings of wounded honor. Equally problematical is the interpretation that the ceremony is intended to justify, that is, ex-
culpate, Peribáñez's killing of the Comendador. There is,
admittedly, some question whether before his dubbing Peribáñez had the legal right to take up arms against the Comendador.[60] The difficulty is not that the Comendador is a
feudal lord, and Peribáñez his vassal. Under the laws of
feudalism, if the lord through some action seriously inimical
to the welfare of the vassal—such as seeking to reduce the
latter to servitude, plotting against his life, or committing
adultery with his wife—breaks the feudal contract, the vassal
is automatically released from further obligation and given
license to seek redress in all appropriate ways.[61] The difficulty
is rather that Peribáñez is a peasant, a member of a class
whose right to employ weapons was at all times and under all
conditions strictly limited. Some jurists of the time maintained
that in cases of self-defense—the definition of which presumably could be extended to include the defense of one's
honor—peasants *were* authorized to use arms. Others maintained that they were not. The matter was therefore moot,

and thus it can be argued, and has been argued, that the knighting of Peribáñez makes legal, and therefore proper, what might otherwise have been construed as an act of questionable legality.

The argument is on its own terms convincing. It fails, however, to contend with the fact that in the last scene of the play the King, the arbiter of right and wrong, condones the action of Peribáñez without ever being informed that he had been knighted. The King knows only that Peribáñez was dishonored, that he avenged his dishonor, and that he is willing to accept whatever consequences his revenge may entail. The King is rather surprised by Peribáñez's deed—"What a strange thing! That so humble a farmer should be so concerned with his honor!" (147b)—but far from finding it censorious and punishable, he finds it deserving of reward.

His judgment is based less on the rules of law than on those of fairness: "Justice is what this is called" (147b). Evidently, Lope wished the public to regard Peribáñez's deed not in terms of what is lawful and what is unlawful, but in terms of what is fitting and what is not. Lope's motive is, I believe, apparent: if he could impose this perspective, the cause of peasant honor would be considerably strengthened.

A modern audience would have little difficulty in accepting Lope's view. Those of Lope's own time would have found it more troublesome. Indeed, for many members of those audiences it might well have been impossible to assess the rightness of Peribáñez's conduct apart from the matter of legality. Knowing his public as well as he did, Lope was undoubtedly aware of this problem. The ceremony of investiture was, I think, his answer to it. By giving Peribáñez full legal right to carry arms, and thereby to defend his honor, the ceremony serves as a safeguard against the possibility that the play would be rejected through concern over the legality of Peribáñez's vengeance.

Naturally, there are other ways of looking at the investiture. Seen from the point of view of dramatic structure, for example, it is a stratagem in Peribáñez's desperate struggle to retain his honor. After all, it was Peribáñez himself who initiated the ritual with his request for knighthood. One probable motivation is that Peribáñez foresaw in his knighting an opportunity to warn the Comendador of his intentions should the latter refuse to quit stalking Casilda, and, of course, Peribáñez did in fact use the occasion for that purpose. It seems likely that Peribáñez perceived the ceremony also as a means of preventing misinterpretation of the assassination that he was determined to carry out if necessary. This killing, as Peribáñez appears to realize, might well be understood as an expression of the resentment of a social inferior. Such an interpretation would, however, degrade an act induced not by feelings of rancor and envy but by those of wounded honor. Thus, in his final words to the Comendador, Peribáñez emphasizes the "equality" that now prevails between the two at the same time that he hints darkly of his resolve not to be mocked:

> Y pues iguales los dos
> con este honor nos dejáis,
> mirad cómo le guardáis
> ó quejaréme de vos.
>
> (136b)

And since you have made the two of us equal with this honor, look to how you preserve it, or I shall have a quarrel to pick with you.

The ritual of investiture leads directly to the concluding, and climactic, section of the play. This is structured upon the three movements of romance. First comes the *agon*, or conflict, which here, as in *Los comendadores de Córdoba*, begins as a literal night journey. As spectators we do not witness this journey, but it nevertheless becomes for us almost as vivid as a represented experience through Peribáñez's highly emotional description:

> ¡Bien haya el que tiene bestia
> destas de huir y alcanzar,
> con que puede caminar
> sin pesadumbre y molestia!
> Alojé mi compañía

y con ligereza extraña
he dado la vuelta á Ocaña.

. . . .

No acabo de agradecerme
el haberte sustentado,
yegua, que con tal cuidado
supiste á Ocaña traerme.

. . . .

Otras veces me has traído;
pero fué pesando poco;
que la honra mucho alienta:
y que te agradezca es bien
que hayas corrido tan bien
con la carga de mi afrenta.

. . . .

¡Oh yegua! ¡En menos de un hora
tres leguas! Al viento igualas;
que si le pintan con alas,
tú tendrás desde agora.
Ésta es la casa de Antón . . .

(140b–141a)

Fortunate the man who has an animal of the sort that can flee and give chase, so that he may ride without worry and care! I quartered the company, and with remarkable speed have returned to Ocaña . . . I never cease thanking myself, mare, for having nourished you, you who knew to bring me back to Ocaña with such devotion . . . Other times you have brought me back, but then I weighed little, for honor uplifts. Thus, it is right that I should thank you for having run so well under the burden of my disgrace . . . Good old mare! Three leagues in less than an hour! You are the equal of the wind; and if the wind is painted with wings, then you will have them from now on. Here is Anton's house . . .

After the *agon* comes the *pathos*, or death struggle. The wager in this case is similar to that in *Los comendadores de Córdoba:* the resurrected honor of Peribáñez for the life of the Comendador. Not unsurprisingly, Peribáñez is, at the last minute, reluctant to strike down the man who is his overlord and supposed protector. He is soon reminded, however, that his greatest obligation is to honor itself, and he expresses the thought with words that Pedro Crespo would undoubtedly applaud:

> ¡Ay, honra! ¿Qué aguardo aquí?   (*Ap.*)
> Mas soy pobre labrador:
> bien será llegar y hablalle . . .
> Pero mejor es matalle.
> *Adelantándose con la espada desenvainada.*
> Perdonadad, Comendador;
> que la honra es encomienda
> de mayor autoridad.

(143b)

Oh, honor! What am I waiting for? (*Aside.*) But I am only a poor peasant: it would be well to go up and speak with him . . . But it is better to kill him. (*Advancing with his sword unsheathed.*) Forgive me, Comendador, but honor is a command of higher authority.

The life of Peribáñez's honor—and his own—is not, of course, fully resurrected until his deed of vengeance has been confirmed. Thus, we have the *anagnorisis* of the final scene of the play. The situation has already been described. Peribáñez presents himself before the King and Queen, pleads that he ought to be allowed to make a defense for his alleged crime, and, receiving permission, goes on to do so so successfully that the King is moved not simply to forgive him but to express "recognition" of the valor of his conduct. Out of this recognition comes Peribáñez's "rebirth," which takes place in two phases: first the King grants Peribáñez the corporeal life that had almost been extinguished; then he gives him a "new" life of greatly increased honor.

Modern formal criticism has taught us to see clearly that in the fully integrated work of literature the individual parts reflect and anticipate the whole. We are therefore not surprised to discover that the archetypal pattern of death and rebirth that underlies the action of *Peribáñez*, thus serving as the foundation of the entire piece, informs as well numerous separate details. It is present, for example, in the temporal setting of the play, for, as Alan Soons has reminded us,[62] *Peribáñez* takes place at the time of the Feast of the Assumption, dedicated to celebrating the death and subsequent ascension to heaven of the Virgin Mary. It inheres also in the secondary intrigue devoted to the statue of Saint Roch, where it is suggested both by the statue itself (which instead of being replaced is "restored" to new life) and by the life of Saint Roch, a fourteenth-century saint venerated chiefly because of his cures of plague victims and his own miraculous recovery from the disease.[63] Finally, and perhaps most interestingly, the pattern of death and rebirth infuses the significant images of the play.

These images, as Wilson was the first to note,[64] are predominantly natural in character, and they fall principally into two categories: those related to Peribáñez and those related to the Comendador. Even though the latter are fewer in number than the former, they stand out in the play because of their consistency: most evoke a wild and dangerous beast of some sort. The very first time the Comendador is mentioned, he is compared to a hawk. The last time he is spoken of, he is pictured as a preying wolf. And in between he is frequently and conspicuously identified with the bull that caused him to fall from his horse and whose disruption of the marriage feast foreshadows the Comendador's later attempted disruption of the marriage itself.[65]

These animal images are significant, for they tell us that in *Peribáñez* we have moved a step closer to archetypal romance. All romance, as we have seen, is characterized by a mortal struggle between the protagonist and his antagonist. In the purest form of romance, however, the antagonist is almost always a beast or monster: the dragon killed by St. George, or the Gorgon slain by Perseus, or the Leviathan that, according to the Old Testament, the Messiah is destined one day to overcome. What all these beasts and monsters have in common is affinities with death and sterility. Indeed, they are the source of death and sterility: because of them the once fertile land is laid barren and waste. One effect of the animal imagery of *Peribáñez* is thus to create the impression that the Comendador is more than a simple seducer of women. The

Comendador is made to seem a serious threat to established social order, a destructive foreign body whose removal both justifies and demands the most extreme measures.

In contrast to the Comendador, linked always with the world of animals, Peribáñez is associated chiefly with plants. Earlier, I quoted the charming May song sung by the townspeople to celebrate the marriage of Peribáñez and Casilda, a song laden with images of trees and flowers. The same images are Peribáñez's chosen vehicle for expressing his love and admiration of Casilda:

> El olivar más cargado
> de aceitunas me parece
> menos hermoso, y el prado
> que por el Mayo florece,
> sólo del alba pisado.
>
> (110a)

The olive grove most laden with fruit seems to me less beautiful, and the meadow that flowers in May, trodden only by dawn.

And Casilda herself, when describing to Inés and Costanza the happiness of being married to Peribáñez, recalls that joyous moment of the day when he returns from working the fields, grateful for the fruits of his labors and eager to enjoy them. The eventual result of such passages is that we identify Peribáñez with everything that the Comendador negates— with fertility, with creation, with growth, and with life.

At the beginning of the play, the life with which Peribáñez is associated is principally new life: flowering almonds, fields in May, the first sprigs of thyme. These images are faithful to Peribáñez's circumstances at that moment. Soon, however, Peribáñez's life becomes troubled, and as his situation changes, so does the imagery: the fresh meadows of spring are replaced by the harvest fields of early autumn. We are reminded constantly of these fields during the last two acts of *Peribáñez,* as the farm hands come and go and as they discuss the progress of the reaping. They seem at first merely to represent life cut down in its prime, and this is the symbolism that Peribáñez himself appears to draw from them:

¡Con qué diversa alegría,
oh campos, pensé miraros
cuando contento vivía!
Porque viniendo á sembraros,
otra esperanza tenía.
Con alegre corazón
pensé de vuestras espigas
henchir mis trojes, que son
agora eternas fatigas
de mi perdida opinión.

(131b)

Oh fields, with what different emotion did I think to look upon you, when I was living in contentment. Because at the time I came to sow you, I had other hopes. With happy heart I planned to fill my barns with your spikes, which now suggest the abiding anguish of my ruined reputation.

Later, however, as they suffer the effect of the historical allusions of the play—the repeated references to the life of Saint Roch and the Assumption of the Virgin—the harvest fields come to stand for something rather different: not, any more, life simply and irrevocably ended, but life that subsides temporarily so that it may burst forth again with increased vigor. The symbolic meaning of the fields of *Peribáñez* thus becomes fused, in the end, with the meaning of the grain of wheat of which Jesus speaks in *John* 12:24: "Verily, verily, I say unto you, except a grain of wheat fall into the earth and die, it abideth by itself alone; but if it die, it beareth much fruit." In reading the play, the passage from *John* comes inevitably to mind, and in its wake, the wealth of literary and cultural associations on which it depends for much of its poetic resonance. These associations have been perceptively analyzed by Maud Bodkin:

In the passage [from *John*] . . . there is a clear correspondence with a pattern of ancient poetic myth and ritual. The corn buried in the ground and rising to fruitfulness, used as a symbol of eternal life attained through death, recalls passages relating to pre-Christian mysteries . . .

81

As we dwell in thought upon these passages, the image of the buried wheat gathers the significance that belongs to it through the course of racial experience. Through the strange sacrament of the communication by words of long past thought and feeling, we become aware of remote dread and hope, lamentation and rejoicing, associated with the most primitive human needs. We are transported to a world whose less discriminating mode of thought has upon us the power of an inchoate or unconscious poetry. Within that world, the sequence of rain, flood, and springing corn constitutes a holy rebirth wherein man participates and finds an expression of his own nature. The wheat-image becomes dynamic, transfigured by its aura of suggestiveness, of inexhaustible significance for feeling.[66]

As we would expect, the images and symbols that attach themselves to Peribáñez are, like those that surround the Comendador, typical of romance in general. For in romance, as Frye tells us, the imagery tends to be both natural and polar: "the opposite poles of the cycles of nature are assimilated to the opposition of the hero and his enemy. The enemy is associated with winter, darkness, confusion, sterility, moribund life, and old age, and the hero with spring, dawn, order, fertility, vigor and youth."[67] Between the thematic associations of the prototypical hero of romance and those that distinguish the hero of *Peribáñez* there would seem to be one discrepancy: Peribáñez's link not just with spring but with autumn as well. That discrepancy is probably more apparent than real, however. For autumn in *Peribáñez*, as in the Bible and innumerable other texts, is a multivalent symbol: not the opposite of spring, but merely its logical conclusion—and also its necessary prelude. As envisioned in these various works, autumn is the one season that encompasses and recapitulates all the others. It is the maturation of growth and its subsidence, but it is also its recommencement. As such, it is perfectly suggestive of the process of life traced by the action of *Peribáñez*.

Fuenteovejuna

A play frequently spoken of in conjunction with *Peribáñez* is *Fuenteovejuna* (1611–1618, probably 1612–1614). The pairing is the inevitable result of the fact that the two plays share certain obvious features: both have as their antagonist or villain a Comendador of one of the great military orders of Spain; both (unlike, for example, *Los comendadores de Córdoba*) take place in the country; and both celebrate the exploits of peasants. These obvious similarities are mentioned repeatedly in the histories of Spanish literature and those studies that attempt to give an overview of the *Comedia*. There remain to be recognized, however, other points of contact between *Peribáñez* and *Fuenteovejuna* that, although less immediately apparent, are of no less importance. In the pages that follow, I shall examine some of those significant points of likeness, as well as two or three differences that dissociate the two works and that, to some extent at least, make *Fuenteovejuna* appear the more sophisticated play.

First among the differences is the fact that *Fuenteovejuna* relates a verified incident in history and is based on a written source, the *Chrónica de las tres órdenes y Cauallerías de Sanctiago, Calatrava y Alcántara* (1572) of Fray Francisco de Rades y Andrada.[68] The chronicle tells how "Fernán Gómez de Guzmán, Comendador Mayor of Calatrava, who resided in Fuenteovejuna, a town located in his commandery, afflicted the inhabitants of that town with so many and such grievous wrongs that, no longer being able to endure or overlook them, they decided with common accord and will to rise against him and to kill him."[69] In presenting this material, Lope for the most part follows Rades quite closely.[70] He does, however, depart from the chronicle in some significant respects. For one thing, much more than Rades, who was himself a member of the Order of Calatrava, he stresses the exact nature and degree of the Comendador's excesses. For another, and contrariwise, he makes little of the "great cruelties" that the villagers supposedly perpetrated upon the body of the Comendador at the same time that he strives, as will be noted later, to make the entire incident of the uprising seem both legal and proper. Finally, totally departing from Rades, Lope makes the Comendador the prime mover behind the Calatravan annexation of Ciudad Real that took place at the same time (1476) as the revolt of Fuenteovejuna, thus compounding the Comendador's villainy and joining to the main plot of his play an associated subplot.

This subplot, which involves the direct participation of the Catholic monarchs, has been the object of a great deal of critical scrutiny.[71] But to my knowledge, it has never been studied in specific relation to similar subplots in Lope's other middle-period honor plays.[72] Most do have a secondary action of some sort. In the two plays already discussed, for example, the story of the Veinticuatro's lost and recovered honor is enacted against the background of the conquest of Granada (1492), while Peribáñez's story is played counter an account of King Henry III's expedition (1406) against the rebellious Moors of Andalusia. In both of these works, the subplot (if that is the correct word) is linked to the main plot through the play's protagonist: at the beginning of *Los comendadores de Córdoba,* the Veinticuatro has recently laid aside the weapons of war; at the end of *Peribáñez,* Peribáñez is, presumably, about to take them up. The device seems to corroborate the interdependence of each play's two plots.

The function of these subplots is clearly to reaffirm the lesson of the principal action and to demonstrate its applicability to matters of national interest. Let us look at *Los comendadores de Córdoba.* The moral of the story of the Veinticuatro is that the "death" induced by dishonor need not be lasting, that by engaging one's enemies with courage and fortitude, one could belie the insulting implications of their acts and thereby restore one's honor. The action in the background of the play, the conquest of Granada, illustrates the same thesis. Here, the honor is that of Spain itself, the agents of dishonor the Moors—pagan foreigners who conquered and arrogated a substantial portion of a once integral land in the same way that D. Jorge conquers the body and affections of Da. Beatriz. The shame was great and endured for almost eight centuries. Finally, however, in 1492, the Spanish people under Ferdinand and Isabella succeeded in reducing Granada, the last bastion of Moorish strength, and in so doing recovered the right to be honored. The deed, as Ferdinand tells his assembled nobles, is worthy of long remembrance:

> Estoy, nobles caballeros,
> de vosotros bien servido,

pues vuestros blancos aceros
habéis en sangre teñido
de aquellos bárbaros fieros.
Y aunque es de Dios la victoria,
Él quiere que vuestra gloria
no se obscurezca de olvido,
pues habéis engrandecido
la fe con tan larga historia.

. . . .

Vúelvanse á sus casas todos,
pues volvieron de mil modos
por España y por su honra,
desde la infamia y deshonra
del primer rey de los godos.

(Ac., XI, 264a–265a)

I am, noble knights, well served by you, for you have tinged the white of your swords with the blood of those fierce barbarians. And although the victory belongs to God, He desires that your glory not be dimmed by oblivion, since you have magnified the faith with so grand a story...Let all now return home, having in a thousand ways defended Spain and her honor, following the infamy and shame of the first king of the Goths.

What the subplot of *Los comendadores de Córdoba* does, then—and the same is true of the subplot in *Peribáñez*—is to widen the scope of the play. Without its subplot, *Los comendadores* might conceivably be thought to be merely the story of a particular man faced with a particular challenge to his honor. With the addition of the subplot, the real subject of the play is necessarily seen to be not one man's injured honor but the problem of wounded honor in general, a problem that finds its solution in the exemplary vengeance of the Veinticuatro.[73] In a sense, therefore, the subplots in *Los comendadores de Córdoba* and *Peribáñez* respond to a universal imperative in literature: the need to transcend the limits of the singular and the specific and capture the common and the generic. That imperative has still more profoundly informed the conception of *Fuenteovejuna*. In this play, Lope has employed not just one subplot but two, both serving the same purpose as the subplots of *Los comendadores de Córdoba* and *Peribáñez*. In addition, he has substituted for the protagonist who simply suggests the common and the generic, one that actually is common and generic. For the first time in Lope, and for one of the first times in literature, we have in *Fuenteovejuna* a group hero.

Though some have professed to doubt it,[74] there cannot really be any question that honor is the dominant theme of *Fuenteovejuna*. All of the plots in the play deal with it. Let us call these plots: (1) Fuenteovejuna versus the Comendador, (2) Ciudad Real versus the Order of Calatrava, and (3) Spain (Ferdinand and Isabella) versus Portugal (Alfonso). In each there is an attack on the integrity of some unit of society by a hostile outside force, and in each the attack is met and, ultimately, avenged. Their common concern is emphasized by the fact that the arch-villain of the piece, the Comendador, participates, at least indirectly, in all three. The chief antagonist in the first plot, an important principal in the second, and a thoroughly committed accomplice of the opposition in the third, the Comendador lurks at the center of the play like a malevolent genius. The evil he radiates reaches out to befoul, eventually, the whole of the country: Fuenteovejuna, Ciudad Real, Spain; village, city, nation.

The plot most relevant here is that of Fuenteovejuna versus the Comendador. As in the main plot of *Peribáñez*, the antagonists in this plot are carefully distinguished. On the one side are the inhabitants of Fuenteovejuna, the villagers. They define themselves unmistakably (though, as we shall see, not always with perfect consistency) as peasants. Their speech is frequently quite rustic:

> Yo, Laurencia, he visto alguna
> tan brava, y pienso que más;
> y tenía el corazón
> brando como una manteca.
>
> (*Ac.*, X, 533a)[75]

I've seen other girls, Laurencia, just as spirited as you, and even more, I think; but they had hearts as soft as butter.

And their pleasures are the pleasures of the country:

¡Pardiez! más precio poner,
Pascuala, de madrugada,
un pedazo de lunada
al huego para comer,

· · · · · · · · · · ·

y más precio al mediodía
ver la vaca entre las coles,
haciendo mil caracoles
con espumosa armonía;

· · · · · · · · · · ·

y después un pasatarde,
mientras la cena se aliña,
de una cuerda de mi viña,
que Dios de pedrisco guarde;
y cenar un salpicón
con su aceite y su pimienta,
y irme á la cama contenta,
y al inducas tentación
rezalle mis devociones,
que cuantas raposerías
con su amor y sus porfías,
tienen estos bellacones . . .

(533b–534a)

By heaven, Pascuala, I give more for putting a slice of bacon on the fire at dawn for breakfast . . . and for watching the beef [in the pot] at noon, bobbing continuously among the cabbages in frothy harmony; . . . and later for passing the time, while the supper is cooking, with a bunch of grapes from my vineyard (may God preserve it from hail); and for supping on salmagundi, with its oil and pepper, and going off to bed happy to say my prayers until [I fall asleep at] "and lead us not into temptation"—[all these things I give more for] than all of the cunning tricks of those scoundrels, with their importunings and their declarations of love . . .

Finally, their social gestures are those of people who serve, and are served by, the land:

Fuente Ovejuna
y el regimiento que hoy habéis honrado,
que recibáis os ruega é importuna

87

un pequeño presente, que esos carros
traen, señor, no sin vergüenza alguna,
de voluntades y árboles bizarros,
más que de ricos dones. Lo primero,
traen dos cestas de polidos barros;
de gansos viene un ganadillo entero,
que sacan por las redes las cabezas
para cantar vueso valor guerrero.
Diez cebones en sal, ¡valientes piezas!
sin otras menudencias y cecinas,
y más que guantes de ámbar sus cortezas.
Cien pares de capones y gallinas,
que han dejado vïudos á sus gallos
en las aldeas que miráis vecinas.
Acá no tienen armas ni caballos,
no jaeces bordados de oro puro,
si no es oro el amor de los vasallos.

(537a–b)

Fuenteovejuna, and the council of the town, which you today have honored, ask and beg that you receive from us a small present, brought, Sire, in these carts which are, not without embarassment to us, more noteworthy for their rustic construction and their goodwill than for rich offerings. First, they bring two baskets of earthenware; then comes a whole flock of geese, which poke their heads out of their cages to sing your military valor; ten salted hogs—wonderful specimens!—whose hides are more [soft] than amber-scented gloves, and along with them sausages and jerked beef; finally, a hundred pairs of capons and hens, which have made widowers out of the roosters in the villages you see all around. Here there are neither arms nor horses, nor harnesses inlaid with pure gold—unless the gold is that of the love of your vassals.

On the other side is the Comendador, a professional soldier. In his speech figure none of the dialectalisms and homely comparisons of the townspeople. Rather, he has constant recourse to the imperative mood—"advertid," "id," "esperad," "sali[d]," "suelta," "llevalde," "azotalde," "no tengas miedo," "no se alborote"—and frequently uses, in contexts far removed from the field of battle, words with distinct military overtones,

such as *reducir, prender, defenderse, reñir, rendirse.* The fact
is that the Comendador's outlook has been wholly conditioned
by his military training, just as that of the people of Fuenteovejuna has been molded by the circumstances of their peasant life. For him all human relationships necessarily reflect
the military categories of stronger and weaker, victor and
vanquished, and his one existential concern, expressed in every thought and action, is to dominate others, particularly
women:

> Un hombre de amores loco
> huélgase que a su accidente
> se le rindan [las mujeres] fácilmente...
>
> (544a)

A man who is maddened by love is delighted that [women]
give in to his passion easily...

Since he has no existence apart from that of conqueror, his
identity is well—and devastatingly—captured by the villagers
in their song of welcome in Act I:

> Sea bien venido
> el Comendadore
> de rendir las tierras
> y matar los hombres.
>
> (537a)

Let the Comendador be welcomed back from taking lands and
killing men.

Like their counterparts in *Peribáñez,* the Comendador and
the townspeople of Fuenteovejuna derive from, and represent,
separate and distinct worlds. To those worlds I have given the
conventional labels "the military" and "the peasantry." The
people of the fifteenth century, however, following Don Juan
Manuel, defined them with earthier, more poetic names. They
spoke, that is, of *defensores* and *labradores,* joining those two
terms to that of *oradores* in order to analyze in a single,
rhyming phrase the social hierarchy of the day. In the fif-

teenth-century view, of course, there was no inherent cause for strife between the three principal ranks of society. To be sure, human beings being what they are, there would always be a certain amount of mutual incomprehension and envy (as Lope hints, even the peasants had something that the members of the other orders might have coveted: their indisputable *limpieza de sangre*). But these were properly held in check by the awareness that there was in the universe a divinely ordained scheme of things, and that within this scheme all ranks of society from the highest to the lowest, and within each rank all the individual members, had a function to perform that was both specific and indispensable. Serious discord could arise only if men refused to accept the existence of God's plan, or if they failed to understand it properly, misconstruing either their own role or someone else's. This, it would appear, is what happens in *Fuenteovejuna*.

It goes without saying that the principal cause of discord in this piece is the Comendador. From the beginning, Lope's presentation of him is notably calculated. Witness how he allows him the opening speech of the play, and how this speech, ostensibly a question, is made to seem an assertion: "Does the master know that I am here in town?" (531a). The impression created by the Comendador's first words is that of a man who is acutely aware of his own importance, and this impression is strongly reinforced by his next several speeches:

Comend.	Y ¿sabe también que soy
	Fernán Gómez de Guzmán?
Flores.	Es muchacho: no te asombre.
Comend.	Cuando no sepa mi nombre,
	¿no le sobre el que me dan
	de Comendador mayor?

Comendador. And does he also know that I am Fernán Gómez de Guzmán? *Flores.* He's just a boy; don't be so surprised. *Comendador.* Even if he doesn't know my own name, is it not enough for him that I am given that of Comendador Mayor?

The Comendador's obsessive self-assertion in the first few moments of the play prepares us for the scene that follows, which otherwise might seem improbable and unconvincing. After a momentary delay, whose effect on the waiting Comendador is disclosed in the lines just quoted, the Grand Master of the Order of Calatrava comes in to greet his guest. At once, the Comendador bursts out rancorously:

> Tenía
> muy justa queja de vos;
> que el amor y la crianza
> me daban más confianza,
> por ser, cual somos los dos,
> vos maestre en Calatrava,
> yo vuestro comendador
> y muy vuestro servidor.
>
> (532a)

I had just complaint of you, for the love I bear you and [my knowledge of] your upbringing gave me expectation [of a more courteous welcome], the two of us being who we are: you, the Master of Calatrava, and I, your Comendador and devoted servant.

Attempting to calm the Comendador, the Grand Master is reprimanded sharply—"It is your obligation to honor me, for I have risked my life for you in many struggles" (532a)—and then, the worst of the storm having passed, harangued at length about his duties and obligations.

All of this is slightly astonishing. The Grand Master is doubly the Comendador's superior, his social superior by virtue of his distinguished lineage and his political superior through the authority vested in him as head of the Order of Calatrava. But the Comendador treats him with a lack of respect that borders on insolence and a lack of deference that smacks of scorn. What are we to make of this? Chiefly, it would seem, that the Comendador is a man so convinced of his own worth that he accepts few, if any, limitations on his relations with those above him, a surmise borne out by the leading role he assumes in the short-lived insurrection of the Order of Calatrava against Ferdinand and Isabella.

But if the Comendador does not feel constrained in his behavior toward those above him, neither does he feel con-

91

DISCORD.
audience can see in his behaviour.

strained in his behavior toward those below him. And this is infinitely worse, for license in one's dealings with one's superiors is mere presumption, a perversion of God's scheme that is more or less easily corrected, but license in one's dealings with one's inferiors is tyranny, and its rectification requires extraordinary measures. The record of the Comendador's malefactions in Fuenteovejuna is apparently limitless: he has insulted the town elders, mocked the authorities, mistreated the men and boys, seduced and raped the women and girls. In speaking of these acts, the words that come most frequently to the lips of the townspeople are the more or less synonymous terms *excesos* and *demasías*. They may seem strangely pallid to a modern reader, but in actuality, as Carlos Serrano points out, they are both expressive and appropriate.[76] For the Comendador is a man who continually goes beyond what is proper and legal, who continually exceeds the established limits of the authority that has been granted to him. And he does so not because he is unaware of those limits,[77] but because he prefers to ignore them as too confining.

In this way, the Comendador comes to redefine the feudal relationship. Traditionally, the feudal lord protected the life and property of his vassals. If he performed his duties satisfactorily, the vassals were obliged to render various services to him. They were not, however, bound to him like chattel. The Comendador chooses to regard the people of Fuenteovejuna as if they were, converting them, in effect, into personal possessions: "Are you not mine?" (537b) he asks Pascuala and Laurencia one day. As a result of this perverse notion, the townspeople become equated in the Comendador's mind with the creatures that roam his forests and the animals that inhabit his stables. Thus, he judges a stubborn old man to be deserving of the same punishment one would inflict on a disobedient horse:

Comend.	¡Hola! La vara quitalde.
Esteban.	Tomad, señor, norabuena.
Comend.	Pues con ella quiero dalle,
	como á caballo brioso.

(550b)

Comendador. You there! Wrest the staff from him. *Esteban.* Take it, Sire, with my blessings. *Comendador.* Now I shall beat him with it, as I would an unruly horse.

Thus, also, he envisions a young woman he stumbles across while hunting as the deer he has been stalking:

> No es malo venir siguiendo
> un corcillo temeroso,
> y topar tan bella gama.

(540a)

It's not a bad thing to be following a frightened little buck, and to come across such a beautiful doe.

Although the Comendador's words here are bantering, they couch an obvious truth: he *does* prey upon the girls of the village as if they were wild animals.[78] Moreover, as the following exchange makes clear, he feels absolutely no sense of shame in doing so:

Esteban.	¿Vió Vusiñoría el galgo?
Comend.	Alcalde, espantados vienen esos criados de ver tan notable ligereza.
Esteban.	Es una extremada pieza. ¡Pardiez, que puede correr á un lado de un delincuente ó de un cobarde en quistión!
Comend.	Quisiera en esta ocasión que le hiciérades pariente[79] á una liebre, que por pies por momentos se me va.
Esteban.	Sí haré, ¡par Dios! ¿Dónde está?
Comend.	Allá, vuestra hija es.

(542a)

Esteban. Did Your Lordship see the greyhound yet? *Comendador.* Mayor, those servants are amazed to have seen such remarkable speed. *Esteban.* It's a marvelous animal. By Jove, it can keep pace with any criminal [on the run] or any coward

[confessing] under torture! *Comendador.* On this occasion
I should like you to match him with a hare which is always get-
ting away from me. *Esteban.* I'll do it, by God! Where is the
hare? *Comendador.* There, it's your daughter.

The Comendador's remarks are outrageous. Not only does he
savage Esteban's honor and sensibility by comparing his own
pursuit of Esteban's daughter to that of a greyhound coursing
its quarry, he compounds the injury by equating the girl with
a hare, in medieval iconography a common symbol for the
female sex organ.[80]

By reducing the villagers to the level of animals, as is his
wont, the Comendador is, of course, himself transformed into
a beast. Being obtuse, he cannot appreciate this. But the irony
is not hidden from the peasants: just as he sees them as
"does" and "horses," "hares" and "dogs," so do they envision
him as a "wild beast," a "lynx," a "wolf," a "tiger," and finally, a "devil." These creatures have the same qualities found
in the images that attach themselves to the Comendador in
Peribáñez: untamed fury, awesome strength, the instinct for
blood. Like his counterpart in *Peribáñez,* then, the Comendador of Fuenteovejuna is established as an analogue to the
monster-antagonists of the "pure" forms of romance. The role
that he enacts is that of the sower of discord and disharmony,
the rebel against Nature, the enemy of society.

Of course, the Comendador does not simply enact the role
of the enemy of society, he *is* the enemy of society. The distinction is important, for it shows that in *Fuenteovejuna* we
have moved one step beyond *Peribáñez* and another step
closer—a significant one—to archetypal romance. There is
nothing latent or potential about the danger presented by the
Comendador, nothing merely symbolic about his actions:
Fernán Gómez is a clear and real threat to the town of Fuenteovejuna. Indeed, it would not be too much to say that, like
his prototypes in earlier romances, the Comendador stands
poised in menacing attitude above his domain, ready to drain
it of its strength and eager to exact tribute in the form of
desirable maidens. At the beginning of the play, the fate of
Fuenteovejuna thus would seem to be that which so often

befalls the imaginary lands that serve as the setting of romance, the fate of being reduced to waste and ruins.

It is interesting to note that, just as Fernán Gómez de Guzmán is characterized in such a way as to remind us of his analogues in more pure, less displaced forms of romance, so is the town of Fuenteovejuna evoked in a way that is reminiscent of *its* analogues, those mythical lands of which I have just spoken. Many readers, undoubtedly, have noted that Fuenteovejuna has no particular, concrete reality. Unlike the town of Ocaña in *Peribáñez,* for example, it exists only as a kind of *locus amoenus.* We know that it has trees, fields, and a stream—according to Ernst Curtius the three indispensable ingredients of a "pleasance"[81]—but we know very little else about it. We never see the places where the people work, we never see the homes where they live, we never really see the streets where they meet and socialize.

The Fuenteovejuna of the play, in other words, is not the real, historical Fuenteovejuna but a literary invention, a pastoral paradise such as might be suggested by its very name: Sheep Well. It is therefore to be expected that the inhabitants of the town would comport themselves not like real human beings but like the characters of pastoral narrative, characters whose existence they recall, in many cases, with their own— quite literally—flowery names. And so, of course they do.[82] The Fuenteovejunans, one might say, are always peasants; they are not always, however, the peasants of ordinary life. Sometimes, for example, they address each other with elaborate forms of courtesy: thus, in Act I Frondoso hails Laurencia and Pascuala with a gallant "God preserve you, beautiful ladies." (534b). They are also capable of erudite debate on intellectual topics, as in the much-discussed dispute in Act I, where the claims of Platonic love are supported by Barrildo and others while Mengo upholds those of "natural love," and in the similar dispute in Act II, where Leonelo and Barrildo argue the value of books. And finally, they are given to expressing even prosaic thoughts in the most highly rhetorical manner, as may be noted in the following dialogue—brimming with learned words, parallel phrases, and *esdrújulos*— between Esteban and one of the councilmen of the town:

Esteban.	Así tenga salud, como parece,
	que no se saque más agora el pósito.
	El año apunta mal y el tiempo crece,
	y es mejor que el sustento esté en depósito,
	aunque lo contradicen más de trece.
Regidor.	Yo siempre he sido, al fin, deste propósito,
	en gobernar en paz esta república.
Esteban.	Hagamos dello á Fernán Gómez súplica.

(540a)

Esteban. So the town may enjoy health, it seems to me that no more grain should be taken from the public granary. The harvest augurs poorly, the year is coming to an end, and it is best that the provisions remain in deposit, even if thirteen or more gainsay it. *Councilman.* I have always been of the same mind, in order that our community may be governed in peace. *Esteban.* Let us then plead the case with Fernán Gómez.

Leo Spitzer in his important article on the play has conveyed much of the unreal, almost mythic atmosphere of Fuenteovejuna of which I have been speaking. The village, he says, "is an idyllic island of Primitivism," "an island of metaphysical peace, the realization of the Golden Age in the midst of our age of iron."[83] This is excellent as far as it goes. What Spitzer fails to note, however, is the irony present in Lope's evocation of "idyllic Fuenteovejuna." Sometimes this element of irony is self-generated, as in the conversation just quoted between Esteban and the *regidor;* sometimes it is focused by one character on another, as when Laurencia responds to Frondoso's courtly greeting with an abrupt, "Do you call us *ladies,* Frondoso?" or when Pascuala expresses her impatience with the rather pompous debate on love with the remark that the topic "tries the wits of the learned in their academies and schools" (536a). However produced, irony is more or less omnipresent throughout the early scenes of the play. At first this may seem somewhat puzzling. Lope is clearly attached to the people of Fuenteovejuna; why, then, does he make them seem slightly ridiculous?

The answer I would hazard is that Lope regards the townspeople as being implicated in some degree in the fate that befalls them. Fuenteovejuna, as Spitzer says, is "an island of metaphysical peace" where the ordinary preoccupations do not seem to matter very much, while questions of philosophy and ontology loom very large indeed. This "realization of the Golden Age" is, however, as Spitzer also points out, surrounded by an "age of iron," an age that is all too familiar with inequity, violence, and barbarism. There is, thus, a tremendous disparity between Fuenteovejuna and the "outside world." Lope never attempts to account for this disparity; it is not of interest to him to do so. But the fact that it exists must surely be assumed to bear some of the responsibility for the troubles that beset Fuenteovejuna. The people of Fuenteovejuna are unworldly to a very large extent: as Alan Soons says, they have been living "outside history," "protected from the influences of time and human villainy."[84] They are thus unprepared at the beginning of the play to meet the challenge presented to them by the Comendador. How is this challenge to be answered? Not, obviously, with learned disputations, bookish conversation, and courtly courtesies. It is to be met with concerted public action, and once the townspeople have appreciated this fact, they are well on the way to realizing their true, as distinct from their apparent, destiny.[85]

Among the recent developments in criticism of *Fuenteovejuna* has been a "Platonic" reading of the play, which finds its initial justification in the famous debate on love in Act I.[86] In this debate, it will be remembered, Barrildo declares that, as a "certain Plato" taught, love is harmony, specifically, a harmony of souls that arises from an appreciation of virtue. Mengo, his opponent, is skeptical of this notion. Love exists, he admits, but it is basically *amor natural,* the desire for fulfillment and preservation, self-love.

In the text, the debate on love ends inconclusively. To Barrildo's query, "Who wins?" Pascuala, one of the listeners and would-be judges, replies that neither she nor Laurencia is competent to decide and that the question ought to be referred to the sacristan. We might assume from this that Lope feels that neither Barrildo nor Mengo has spoken the full truth. The Platonist critics make no such assumption. They assert, or imply, that Barrildo's view of love is the one to which Lope subscribes and that he has conceived the action of the play as an illustration of the dynamics of Platonic love.

I fail to see that this is so. To be sure, the movement of the work is from (a hypothesized) harmony, to disharmony, to harmony restored. This movement is characteristic of the honor plays as a group, however, and even, as Arnold G. Reichenberger has pointed out, of the *Comedia* in general.[87] Thus, if the evolution toward harmony in this play is to serve as a guide to the reading of the work, then it must manifest particularities that distinguish it from similar movements in other works. The most important of these, probably, is the manner in which harmony is finally reestablished. That manner, I think it is evident, has little to do with Platonic love. But it has a great deal to do with *amor natural,* a concept that as defined by Mengo reminds us not of Plato but of Aristotle:

> Amor hay, y el que entre sí
> gobierna todas las cosas,
> correspondencias forzosas
> de cuanto se mira aquí;
> y yo jamás he negado
> que cada cual tiene amor
> correspondiente a su humor
> que le conserva en su estado.
> Mi mano, al golpe que viene
> mi cara defenderá;
> mi pie, huyendo, estorbará
> el daño que el cuerpo tiene.
> Cerraránse mis pestañas
> si al ojo le viene mal,
> porque es amor natural.
>
> (535b)

There is love [of a kind], one which in itself governs everything, the necessary interrelations of all that is seen hereabout; and I have never denied that each person feels love, corresponding to his nature, which preserves him in his state. My hand will defend my face from the on-coming blow; my feet, taking flight, will block the harm the body is receiving; my eyelashes will close if something bad is headed toward my eye—because it is natural love.

According to Mengo, then, "natural love" is unashamedly ego-centric. It cannot, however, be reduced simplistically to physical fulfillment alone. One "naturally" loves anything that gives one satisfaction. The immediate objects of natural love are, therefore, or may be, various. A person may derive gratification from being chaste; he or she will then, as does Laurencia, love chastity. That same person may also find contentment in knowing that his friends are happy. Insofar as this is the case, he will work to secure the well-being of those friends and thus, like many in *Fuenteovejuna*, be led by self-centered love to perform acts of altruism.[88] Of course, whatever else one loves, one must first and foremost love one's own life. Without life there can be no love at all, and thus the ultimate concern must always be simply to exist.

This is the truth that Mengo preaches. It would be wrong to imply that it is, for Lope, the whole truth. But it is a very important truth, and it is one that at the beginning of the play has little meaning for the townspeople of Fuenteovejuna. Having known only their pastoral paradise, their "idyllic island of Primitivism," they lack the instincts of normal "political beings" (the phrase is Soons's) and thus allow themselves to be the prey of one who would not just brutalize their bodies but who would also destroy their honor—without which they have no real existence. In the face of the Comendador's aggressions, they act for a time like the meek animals—the *gamas* and the *liebres*—with which he identifies them. Laurencia's severe denunciation of the men of the town early in Act III is, in other words, although out of touch with events and purposely exaggerated, not without its element of truth. That the men themselves recognize this is attested by the swiftness with which they react to her impassioned harangue:

> ¿Vosotros sois hombres nobles?
> ¿Vosotros padres y deudos?
> ¿Vosotros, que no se os rompen
> las entrañas de dolor,
> de verme en tantos dolores?
> Ovejas sois, bien lo dice
> de Fuente Ovejuna el nombre.

Dadme unas armas á mí,
pues sois piedras, pues sois bronces,
pues sois jaspes, pues sois tigres...
Tigres no, porque feroces
siguen quien roba sus hijos,
matando los cazadores
antes que entren por el mar
y por sus ondas se arrojen.
Liebres cobardes nacistes;
bárbaros sois, no españoles.

(552a)

Are you men of noble character? Are you fathers and kin? You, whose insides do not burst with grief on seeing me in such sorrow? You are sheep, the name Fuenteovejuna says it well. Give *me* some weapons, for you are stones, you are bronze, you are jasper, you are tigers...; no, not tigers, because they follow fiercely after those who steal their offspring, killing the hunters before they can reach the sea and hurl themselves into the surf. You were born cowardly rabbits; you are barbarians, not Spaniards.

In the purer forms of romance, the imperiled land is normally saved by a mysterious knight who rides in from a distant place to slay the tyrant-monster. The people of Fuenteovejuna can hope for no such delivery. If they are going to be saved, they must save themselves, and this they can do only by ceasing to be sheep and hares and by becoming instead what Laurencia, in a slip of the tongue, calls them in her diatribe: tigers. The Fuenteovejunans, in other words, must learn to behave like political beings who, when faced by a threat to life or possessions, react with the defensiveness that results from natural love. Once again, it is a matter of awareness. Only by forsaking the limited point of view of the pastoral world for precise recognition of what it means to be a member of fifteenth-century Spanish society can the peasants forestall the disaster that seems to menace Fuenteovejuna—"The harvest augurs poorly, and the year is coming to an end" (541a)—and preserve the town, not as a *locus amoenus* (that is now out of the question), but as a *locus habitabilis,* a place where life and honor are possible.

The requisite awareness—that which leads to justifiable self-defense—comes to Fuenteovejuna little by little. At the beginning, it manifests itself only in isolated acts of defiance. The first of these occurs at the end of Act I. Frondoso is talking with Laurencia in the meadow outside Fuenteovejuna when suddenly Fernán Gómez appears. The Comendador has been stalking a young buck, but the sight of Laurencia quickly convinces him that she would make a far more desirable prey. Before he can subdue her, however, Frondoso intervenes. Picking up the crossbow that the Comendador has laid aside—in order, as he says, not to frighten the "quarry"— Frondoso orders his overlord to be on his way, and then justifies his retention of the weapon on the grounds of self-preservation:

> ... pues me es
> guardar la vida forzoso,
> con la ballesta me voy.
>
> (540b)

Since I am forced to protect my life, I shall take the crossbow with me.

Frondoso's defiance of the Comendador is emulated in Act II by Mengo. The motive is, once more, essentially altruistic: Mengo asserts himself in defense of Jacinta, whom Flores and Ortuño, the Comendador's servants, are attempting to deliver to their insatiable master. If anything, Mengo's intervention is even more heroic than that of Frondoso, for the latter had for a weapon the Comendador's crossbow, while Mengo's only arms are his own:

Jacinta.   ¿Tienes armas?
Mengo.   Las primeras
              del mundo.

                                    (545a)

Jacinta. Do you have arms? *Mengo.* The first ones in the world.

Mengo's gesture is, however, basically unsatisfactory: it does not prevent the abduction of Jacinta, it merely delays it. In its ultimate vanity the act is no different from any other act effected singly; that is precisely the point. Lope wants us to understand that the unbounded barbarism of the Comendador cannot be checked by individual feats of heroism. What is needed is a mass effort, a popular uprising in the name of and justified defense of all the townspeople.

If nothing else, however, Mengo's act of defiance does point clearly to the one condition necessary for successful self-assertion: recognition of that irreducible and inalienable "being" that lies within oneself:

Pascuala.	Jacinta, yo no soy hombre
	que te puedo defender.
	Vase.
Mengo.	Yo sí lo tengo de ser,
	porque tengo el sér y el nombre...

(545a)

Pascuala. Jacinta, I am not a man and cannot be your defender. (*Exit.*) Mengo. Then I have to be it, for [of man] I have both the being and the name ...

As the words of Esteban and the *regidor* make clear, many of the men of Fuenteovejuna are already at the beginning of Act III quite aware of that "being." They need a spark to be moved into action, however. That spark is provided by Laurencia's speech. All doubts about the proper course of conduct removed, the Fuenteovejunans deliver themselves over to natural love—"love has moved them," remarks Frondoso to the Comendador, by way of explanation of the villagers' rebellion (553b)—and at once begin to put an end to oppression and dishonor.

The revolt of the villagers has been seen in two quite dissimilar ways. For Menéndez y Pelayo it is the act of a furious and uncontrolled mob.[89] For a more recent commentator, Antonio Gómez-Moriana, it is, on the contrary, an act that is not simply carefully pondered but executed with a surprising amount of discipline.[90] The truth probably lies somewhere

between these opposing views. The rebellion of Fuenteovejuna in the play is not the semicrazed riot it appears to be in
Rades (whose account quite possibly influenced the impression of Menéndez y Pelayo), but neither is it devoid of passion
or ferocity. The ferocity is not emphasized. But we know from
Flores's account of the uprising to the King that the body of
the Comendador was disfigured and that his house was sacked.
One may wonder, of course, why these details unflattering
to the townspeople have been included in the work at all.
Presumably, Lope felt that they gave the revolt a greater ring
of truth. After all, such actions have historically seldom been
exercises in patience and forbearance.

Besides, Lope knew that the audience's sympathy for the
rebellion was not likely to be undermined by a show of anger
on the part of the villagers. For, as depicted in the play, the
revolt is not just warranted but carried out substantially in
accord with both tradition and highly respected legal thought.
For one thing, the decision to rebel is not arrived at lightly.
On the contrary, it is taken so slowly and painfully as to
seem, when final, long overdue. Moreover, it is made with
the participation of all the townspeople and on the basis of a
clear and articulated grievance: the Comendador behaves like
a beast; his excesses have harmed everyone; continued tolera-
tion would threaten the very life of the town.

As Gómez-Moriana has pointed out, the public consideration of consequences and alternatives that precedes the revolt
of Fuenteovejuna fulfills the first condition of a legitimate
rebellion, as defined by St. Thomas Aquinas and the scholastic philosophers.[91] According to St. Thomas, a rebellion
against properly constituted authority could be condoned only
if there were no other recourse available and open discussion
had revealed that revolt had the clear support of a majority
of the people. But all the discussion in the world would not
suffice to legitimate a revolt if there were not in the first place
justifiable cause. As to what constitutes justifiable cause, St.
Thomas is quite explicit: it is tyranny.

For St. Thomas, as for Aristotle, the manifestations of tyranny are many: the lack of respect for the persons of the
people governed and for their property; the tendency to sub-

vert harmonious relations among the people and to destroy their mutual confidence, "for as long as one has confidence in the other, no plot will be set up against the tyrant's dominion";[92] the proclivity for corrupting public morality, since high moral standards are likewise a defense against oppression. Ultimately, as St. Thomas recognizes, all these manifestations of tyranny amount to the same thing. And thus it is that in the scholastic tradition the tyrant is defined quite simply as a man who recognizes no limits to his power and who acts as if his authority had been granted him for his own benefit instead of that of the people.

This definition enables us to see much of the intention behind Lope's characterization of the Comendador and the brilliance of that characterization. If the Comendador is from the literary and mythical point of view a monster, and from the religious point of view a devil, he is from the juridical point of view a tyrant. Significantly, however, the villagers do not apply that term to him until the last act of the play. Then, after they have acquired political awareness, they use the words *tirano* and *tiranía* with such insistence that not even the most insensitive reader or spectator can fail to be aware that a point is being made:

> Tiranos son; á la venganza vamos.
>
> (551b)

They are tyrants; let us take vengeance.

> ¡Mueran tiranos traidores!
> ¡Traidores tiranos mueran!
>
> (552b)

Death to the traitor-tyrants! To the tyrant-traitors, death!

> Ya el tirano y los cómplices miramos.
> ¡Fuente Ovejuna, los tiranos mueran!
>
> (554a)

Now we see the tyrant and his accomplices. Fuenteovejuna, let the tyrants die!

¡Vivan Castilla y León,
y las barras de Aragón,
y muera la tiranía!

(556b)[93]

Long live Castile and Leon and the stripes of Aragon, and death to tyranny!

Thus do the villagers prepare a legal defense later to be presented to the King and Queen.

Analyzed with reference to the structure of romance, the decision to rise up and kill the Comendador constitutes the beginning of the *agon* of *Fuenteovejuna*. This *agon* is much like that of the other middle-period honor plays, except that here the protagonist is a collectivity. In the rebellion and vengeance of the villagers, there is no individual, only group, responsibility. "Fuentevejuna did it" is the unvarying response of the people when asked by the examining magistrate who has killed the Comendador, and the reply serves not only as protection against individual punishments but as statement of fact. The uprising was planned by the massed people of the town, executed by them, and defended by them against reprisal.

The townspeople's defense of their action on the rack is an important element in their glorification. It is an incident so completely appropriate that had not history supplied it, literature would have seen fit to. Without the villagers' stoical endurance of physical torment, the killing of the Comendador might fail to impress us as a deed worthy of celebration: the defenders of the Comendador, after all, are a mere handful compared to the masses of rebels. By demonstrating their fortitude under torture, however, the townspeople prove unmistakably that there is no element of cowardice in the group vengeance. There is, in fact, a large measure of courage in Fuenteovejuna, and it is, moreover, the kind of rare courage that can laugh at pain:

Juez.   Al palo aplica
        la espalda.[94]
Mengo.   Quedo, que yo
      lo diré.

Juez.   ¿Quién lo mató?
Mengo.   Señor, Fuente Ovejunica.

(559a)

Judge. Apply your shoulder to the lever. *Mengo.* Wait, I'll tell. *Judge.* Who killed him? *Mengo.* Sire, little old Fuenteovejuna!

death struggle This torturing of the villagers makes up the second half of a phase of *pathos* of which the first half is the assassination of the Comendador. It may be said, therefore, that the people of Fuenteovejuna suffer a double "passion." As Esteban points out to them, they first experience a figurative death when their honor is destroyed by the Comendador:

> Un hombre cuyas canas baña el llanto,
> labradores honrados, os pregunta
> qué obsequias debe hacer toda esta gente
> á su patria sin honra, ya perdida.
> Y si se llaman honras justamente,
> ¿cómo se harán, si no hay entre nosotros
> hombre á quien este bárbaro no afrente?
> Respondedme: ¿hay alguno de vosotros
> que no esté lastimado en honra y vida?
> ¿No os lamentáis los unos de los otros?
> Pues si ya la tenéis todos perdida,
> ¿á qué aguardáis? ¿Qué desventura es ésta?

(551a)

A man whose gray beard is bathed in tears asks you, worthy farmers, what funeral honors should this people offer to its land, which is now dishonored, now lost. And if they are to be justly called honors, how are they to be done, if there is among us no man whom this barbarian has not affronted? Answer me: is there any one of you not wounded in honor and being? Do you not grieve one for the other? Well, then, since all of you have lost [both honor and life], what are you waiting for? What misfortune is this?

Then, lying on the rack, the villagers sustain another symbolic death, one that expiates whatever element of criminality

106

might attach to their killing of the Comandador and concurrently attests the valor that romance demands of all its protagonists.

Their courage thus "discovered," the people of Fuenteovejuna are ready to receive the traditional "recognition." To that end, Lope has them travel en masse to the court of Ferdinand and Isabella, where they are at once summoned before the monarchs. First, however, the examining magistrate is asked to tell what he has learned about the uprising. His account, far from being the condemnation that the Catholic monarchs would naturally expect, is actually an encomium of the villagers' bravery:

> Á Fuente Ovejuna fuí
> de la suerte que has mandado,
> y con especial cuidado
> y diligencia asistí
> haciendo averiguación
> del cometido delito.
> Una hoja no se ha escrito
> que sea en comprobación ;
> porque conformes á una,
> con un valeroso pecho,
> en pidiendo quién lo ha hecho,
> responden: "Fuente Ovejuna."
> Trescientos he atormentado
> con no pequeño rigor,
> y te prometo, señor,
> que más que esto no he sacado.
> Hasta niños de diez años
> al potro arrimé, y no ha sido
> posible haberlo inquirido
> ni por halagos ni engaños.

(561a)

I went to Fuenteovejuna in the manner you ordered and performed my duty with particular care and diligence, making inquiry into the crime committed. Not one page has been written that can stand as evidence; because, with single accord and brave hearts, when asked who did it, the people reply: "Fuenteovejuna." Three hundred have I tortured with no little severity, and I assure you, Sire, that I have extracted nothing more than this. I even put ten-year-old children on the rack, and it was not possible to find out anything, either through cajolery or through tricks.

After the magistrate has finished his report, the townspeople enter. They are awed by the sight of the monarchs—"Are those the King and Queen?" (561a)—but not so abashed that they cannot deliver a ringing defense of their actions. The defense stresses two points. First, the revolt was provoked by the Comendador, whose behavior toward them amounted to tyranny:

> La sobrada tiranía
> y el insufrible rigor
> del muerto Comendador,
> que mil insultos hacía,
> fué el autor de tanto daño.
>
> (561a–b)

The extreme tyranny and the insufferable harshness of the dead Comendador, who committed a thousand outrages, was the cause of all the harm.

Second, the revolt is in no way subversive, because the Fuenteovejunans remain firm in their allegiance to the crown and to the state:

> Señor, tuyos ser queremos.
> Rey nuestro eres natural,
> y con título de tal
> ya tus armas puesto habemos.
>
> (561b)

Sire, we wish to be your vassals. You are our natural sovereign, and it is with that justification that we have already put up your coat of arms.

In the face of such a spirited and convincing exculpation, Ferdinand has little choice but to approve the vengeance. It is true that he speaks of it as a "serious crime" and gives as reason for his pardon the fact that no written evidence could be gathered. His speech, however, seems perfunctory and formulaic, an effect that derives in part, as Gómez-Moriana has pointed out,[95] from its similarity to the words of the examining magistrate in the previous scene. One is thus led to the conclusion that it contains more than a little irony, a conclusion reinforced by the fact that Ferdinand ends by declaring his intention of temporarily assuming direct responsibility for Fuenteovejuna. The gesture is an implicit acknowledgment of the King's respect for the villagers and an explicit call for public recognition. The villagers thus leave court with their honor notably reaffirmed.

Like Peribáñez, then (and like the Veinticuatro de Córdoba also), the inhabitants of Fuenteovejuna travel a course from honor, to honor lost, to honor regained and augmented. Like Peribáñez, too, they see their progress along the course marked at each important stage by a ritualistic observance. The first of these ceremonies is the one that welcomes the Comendador back to Fuenteovejuna in Act I: the villagers sing ("Let the Comendador be welcomed back," and so on), present him with gifts, and pay him fine compliments; he, in turn, flatters them. The words are on both sides heavy with innuendo—the villagers have already become alarmed by the Comendador's unreasonable conduct—but the intent of the ritual is nevertheless unequivocal: to celebrate the state of harmony that supposedly prevails between overlord and vassals and the honor that each concedes to the other.

In Act II, there is a similar ceremony, prompted this time by the marriage of Frondoso and Laurencia. On this occasion, however, the songs honoring the wedding couple give way, suddenly and without explanation, to one telling not of harmony and honor but of disharmony and dishonor, the famous ballad "Al val de Fuenteovejuna":

> Al val de Fuente Ovejuna
> la niña en cabellos baja;
> el caballero la sigue
> de la cruz de Calatrava.
> Entre las ramas se esconde,
> de vergonzosa y turbada;

fingiendo que no le ha visto,
pone delante las ramas.
'¿Para qué te escondes,
niña gallarda?
Que mis linces deseos
paredes pasan.'
Acercóse el caballero,
y ella, confusa y turbada,
hacer quiso celosías
de las intrincadas ramas;
mas como quien tiene amor
los mares y las montañas
atraviesa fácilmente,
la dice tales palabras:
'¿Para qué te escondes,
niña gallarda?
Que mis linces deseos
paredes pasan.'

(549b)

Down to the valley of Fuenteovejuna comes the bare-headed
girl; she is followed by the knight with the cross of Calatrava.
She hides among the branches, because she feels ashamed and
disturbed. Pretending that she has not seen him, she pulls the
branches in front of her. "What good does it do to hide, charming maid? For my lynx-eyed desires pass through walls." The
knight came closer, and she, confused and disturbed, tried to
fashion a blind with the interlocking boughs; but because the one
who is in love crosses easily over seas and mountains, he speaks to
her these words: "What good does it do to hide, charming maid?
For my lynx-eyed desires pass through walls."

The introduction into the wedding celebration of this ballad,
which condenses into one symbolic encounter all of the
aggression to which Fuenteovejuna has been subjected, strikes
a puzzling and ominous note: a marriage seems to be no place
to insist on the town's dishonor.[96] The song proves to be all
too appropriate, however, for even as it is being performed,
the Comendador bursts through the assembled guests (just as
in the song his lust bursts through the protecting branches),
seizes Frondoso and Laurencia, and carries them off. His

barbaric act turns joy into mourning, music into silence, honor into disgrace.

With the justified murder of the Comendador in Act III, however, the order of the nouns is permanently reversed. Now the villagers can once again exhibit pride in their honor, and they proceed almost at once to do so. Gathering in the town square, they shout, dance, and take turns improvising *coplas*. These are unusually interesting. Their principal purpose is to celebrate the villagers' rebirth into a life of honor, and thus we might expect to find in them vivid and repeated recollections of the town's victory over the Comendador. What they offer instead are insistent affirmations of the Fuenteovejunans' feelings of allegiance to the King and Queen. Thus, each *copla* ends with the same hortatory refrain:

> ¡Muchos años vivan
> Isabel y Fernando,
> y mueran los tiranos!
>
> (556a)

Long live Isabella and Ferdinand, and death to the tyrants!

Clearly, an idea is being driven home. A revolt against a local tyrant is not necessarily a revolt against the state. The elimination of injustice is to be construed not as the unleashing of discord but as the reestablishment of concord. Out of disharmony oftentimes comes harmony.

In illuminating the evolution of their protagonists from honor, to dishonor, to honor once more, the rituals of *Fuenteovejuna* and *Peribáñez* are akin to the scenes of pageantry in *Hamlet,* whose function, in the words of Francis Fergusson, is "to show forth the main action or underlying theme, at various stages in its development."[97] But because honor plays like *Fuenteovejuna* and *Peribáñez* are themselves rituals of a sort, the rituals that they contain assume an additional significance not found in those of the more ironic *Hamlet*. They are the open doors through which the audience—an audience eager for celebrative participation—may enter into the play.

In general, the rituals operate by breaking down the barrier that normally prevails between private and public life, by appropriating unto the community what is otherwise the business of a single individual. We observe this clearly in *Peribáñez.* The honor with which the play deals is, basically, the concern of one person, Peribáñez. Through the various rituals examined earlier, however, the people of Ocaña assume a share in that concern. When Peribáñez celebrates the good health of his honor, they celebrate with him; when he suffers its loss, they also suffer; and when he is able to rejoice in its recovery, they partake of his joy. The townspeople thus come to participate intimately in the psychic life of Peribáñez, and because they do, the audience also finds it possible to do so.

In *Fuenteovejuna,* naturally, the intercalated rituals function somewhat differently. Here, there is no need to breach the barrier separating private from public life because there is no such barrier: protagonist and community are one and the same. There is, however, as in *Peribáñez* and the other middle-period honor plays, a need to elicit and structure the sympathetic participation of the audience. The feelings of the spectators must, as in the previous plays, be aroused and channeled, and this is done in the three rituals examined above in the usual fashion—through singing, dancing, and ceremony.

I have been speaking of *Fuenteovejuna's* three rituals, but there is, of course, a fourth as well. And it is perhaps the most important of all. For it is only with this ceremony, the audience before the Catholic monarchs, that the story—the romance—of Fuenteovejuna may be considered definitively concluded. The villagers have lost their honor and their "lives" and have regained them both. They now stand before Ferdinand and Isabella to have their restoration confirmed. The confirmation is given, and the play comes to its proper and joyful end. Joaquín Casalduero has described the moment well: it is, he says, "the happy dénouement of Christian tragedy, the joy of the 'third day' which follows after Death and which is its necessary complement."[98]

4

Late Plays: The Turn toward Tragedy

Tragedy and the Comedia

IN the introduction to his translation of the *Oresteia* of Aeschylus, Richmond Lattimore says of *The Libation Bearers* that "this is not a simple revenge play," for "here the emotions of Orestes and Electra are, like those of Clytaemestra, half-commited to the side against which they act; and Clytaemestra, in turn, loves the son whom she fears, who kills her, and whom she would kill if she could." He continues: "It is the *philos-aphilos* still, or love-in-hate, the murder committed not against an external enemy but against a part of the self ... So *Hamlet* is transformed from the vigorous revenge-intrigue drama it might have been into the tragedy it is, because Hamlet is emotionally involved with the queen and Ophelia, who are on the side of the enemy."[1] Here, I think, is the reason that there is no feeling of tragedy in the revenge murders that climax the three honor plays discussed in the last chapter. Those murders are all acts of positive value, committed with a notably clear conscience. Although there is a certain amount of sympathy for the slain, especially in the case of Da. Beatriz and the other victims of the Veinticuatro de Córdoba, that sympathy is held to a minimum and not allowed to mitigate the affirmation of the endings of the plays. The Veinticuatro, Peribáñez, and the people of Fuenteovejuna are very little "emotionally involved"—at least at the moment of the assassination—with those they murder. They can remain uninvolved because the killings are, in their minds, fully justified: each of the victims is, to appropriate a

113

characterization of A. C. Bradley, "a criminal who merely 'gets what he deserves.' "[2]

The phrase quoted occurs in Bradley's celebrated discussion of "Hegel's Theory of Tragedy." The paper makes the point, among others, that criminals of the sort described are unknown to both art and religion. Now we must, I think, acknowledge a good deal of exaggeration in this, unless we are prepared to write off a large chunk of Spanish literature, not to mention significant works in practically every other language. But if men and women who "merely get what they deserve" are not foreign to all art, they are, assuredly, foreign to that type with which Bradley is expressly concerned, tragedy. This, doubtless, is the explanation of the frequently remarked upon lack of tragedy in the Spanish Golden Age theater. For the *Comedia,* as many have sensed, and as A. A. Parker has convincingly demonstrated in a series of papers,[3] operates on the principle of distributive, or, as Parker calls it, poetic justice. With few exceptions, wrongdoers in these plays are punished, and punished quickly, while the righteous and the good are rewarded. This does not mean that the punishment invariably is commensurate with the crime or that the recompense is inevitably in proportion to the amount of goodness displayed. It does mean that justice is nearly always present to the extent that there is no moral guilt without suffering of some kind, and no virtue without some sort of recognition. It also means that in these plays it is normal that *only* the guilty suffer (and, of course, that only the virtuous receive rewards). Generally, then, as Parker says, "Spanish dramatists present no victims of destiny or mischance, but only of wrongdoing—their own, or someone else's."[4]

Changes of fortune in the *Comedia* are, thus, morally determined for the most part and morally explicable. Tragedy, however, as Northrop Frye remarks, "seems to elude the antithesis of moral responsibility and arbitrary fate, just as it eludes the antithesis of good and evil."[5] The fall into misfortune of the tragic hero is the result neither of capricious destiny nor, usually, of a violation of moral law (although a violation of some sort is always involved). Aristotle said that it was the product of *hamartia,* which word, according to one

114

of the most recent and illuminating commentators on the *Poetics,* has "no strong implication of moral fault or short-coming," but rather means, quite simply, an "error of judgment."[6] Perhaps this concept of *hamartia* has more relevance to ancient than to modern tragedy (that of Shakespeare, for example, or that of Racine), where it might seem that "error of judgment" is a rather euphemistic way of describing that action of the hero that brings on catastrophe. Whether innocent miscalculation, however, or something that seems to us, the spectators, more logically censurable, the errors of tragedy are rarely identifiable with mere sin or wrongdoing. Thus, speaking of Shakespeare, Frye describes the tragic process as "natural in the sense that it simply happens."[7] The hero moves somehow into a position of conflict with a power superior to himself and thereby invites disaster. Fate, which formerly had remained indifferent to him, now becomes external and hostile. The Wheel of Fortune turns, and as it does, the tragic hero slips and falls.

It is commonly held that of all possible views of life, the tragic is the most profound and true. I. A. Richards, for example, has written that tragedy "is still the form under which the mind may most clearly and freely contemplate the human situation, its issues unclouded, its possibilities revealed."[8] There are, nevertheless, perfectly comprehensible reasons why Spanish drama rejected, by and large, the tragic view of life. Even in tragedy catastrophe is never totally accidental. It results, ultimately, from a mistake of some kind, a breach of the established order: the hero is placed in circumstances where he must choose between alternative courses of action, and he chooses wrongly. The Spanish dramatists, however, and the public for which they wrote, could see no justification for choosing wrongly. For to make a mistake of this sort, a person must either be ignorant of the correct choice or, knowing which choice he must make, consciously, through weakness, make the wrong one. In the Golden Age view of things, however, man had been granted the higher faculties of Memory and Understanding specifically so that he might always be aware of the proper course of action, and that of Will specifically so that he would elect the alternative revealed as proper. The result, as Erich Auerbach has remarked, is that although "everything is a dream . . . nothing is a riddle demanding to be solved."[9] This does not mean that life was regarded as unexacting. On the contrary, it was recognized that in every existence Memory—which had the particular meaning in the seventeenth century of Memory of Death, the knowledge that earthly life is basically vain—Will, and Understanding had to contend with their mortal enemies, the World, the Flesh, and the Devil. Each, however, was sufficiently strong that all men and women could, within reasonable limits and by the grace of God, avoid error and effect their own salvation.[10]

Calderón's *La vida es sueño,* perhaps the most famous work of the entire *Comedia,* furnishes striking exposition of this doctrine. The play is a kind of antitragedy.[11] Whereas the typical tragic hero begins his dramatic life in a position of high estate, subsequently to drop to a very low one (thus effecting what Aristotle calls a "change from prosperity to adversity"),[12] Segismundo, the protagonist of this play, commences his trajectory at its nadir and then ascends along it to great heights: the Fall of Princes, we might say, has here been inverted to become the Rise of a Prince. What is significant about the rise is that it is realized against seemingly great odds. For Segismundo's long imprisonment has, it would appear, blocked the development of each of his three faculties: at the beginning of the play, Memory, Will, and Understanding (including that special kind of "awareness" discussed at length previously) all lie ineffective within him. Gradually, however, with the unfolding of the action, the three faculties are brought into service, and as each begins to make its proper contribution, Segismundo moves one step closer to the salvation that is ultimately his. The first of the faculties of which Segismundo acquires effective use is Memory. We perceive its workings in the magnificent monologue that closes Act II:

> ¿Qué es la vida? Un frenesí.
> ¿Qué es la vida? Una ilusión,
> una sombra, una ficción,
> y el mayor bien es pequeño;

> que toda la vida es sueño,
> y los sueños sueños son.
>
> $(2182-2187)$[13]

What is life? A frenzy. What is life? An illusion, a shadow, a fiction; and its greatest good is small, for all of life is a dream, and the dreams themselves are dreams.

Next in order of acquisition comes Will. Its triumph appears in Segismundo's decision to resist the impulse to possess Rosaura forcibly, and, rather than further to rob her of honor, to restore the honor she had lost previously:

> Rosaura está sin honor;
> más a un príncipe le toca
> el dar honor que quitarle.
> ¡Vive Dios! que de su honra
> he de ser conquistador
> antes de mi corona.
> Huyamos de la ocasión,
> que es muy fuerte.
>
> $(2986-2993)$

Rosaura is without honor; it is more fitting for a prince to give honor than to take it away. As sure as God lives, before I win my crown I shall win back her honor! Let us flee from this temptation, which is very strong.

Finally, Understanding too is acquired. It is not so easy as with Memory and Will to pinpoint the moment when it asserts itself. Segismundo's final monologue, however, his long address to the assembled nobles and soldiers of Poland, is informed in its totality by this faculty. Segismundo shows here that at the end of his long journey from cave to court, he can look back upon his life and find in it the essential pattern, the common humanity that links his existence to that of all men.

The implication of *La vida es sueño* is that if Segismundo, who must labor under the double burden of a seemingly hostile fate and a totally distorted view of reality, can overcome his fallen state in order, as he says, "to do what is right," then, surely, all men can. It is this attitude that explains the lack of commiseration in the Golden Age theater for those who commit serious mistakes. But, it would be wrong to imply that malefactors in the *Comedia* are never given compassion. There are exceptions. For example, Clifford Leech is undoubtedly correct in stating that in *El burlador de Sevilla* Tirso elicits for Don Juan our "reluctant sympathy."[14] Sympathy is also evoked from time to time on behalf of wrongdoers in Lope's plays, for example, *Las ferias de Madrid*. We find it also in the honor plays of the final period. There are, significantly, but two of these: *Porfiar hasta morir* (1624–1628) and *El castigo sin venganza* (1631). In each of them, Lope remained committed to the catastrophic ending that had proved so successful in the honor plays of the preceding period. Joined to this ending, however, is a marked feeling of pity for the victims of the vengeance. The effect is obvious: for the first time in the honor plays, tragedy is rendered possible.

La victoria de la honra *and* Porfiar hasta morir

Ernest H. Templin has remarked that "the lover [in the *Comedia*] is a sort of adolescent delinquent who has not reached the 'age of discretion.' "[15] Now clearly Templin's characterization is not equally valid for all those men and women who fall in love in the Spanish Golden Age theater. It is, however, a very apt description of the lovers who appear in Lope's early honor plays. It also points to the conception of love that obtains in those plays: that of a temptation of the flesh, appealing mainly to the young, and capable, if not resisted, of subverting both judgment and will. Love in the early honor plays—as in the *comedias de capa y espada*—is a force that those under twenty in particular have a very hard time withstanding and that, in a sense, takes unfair advantage of their inexperience. It is for this reason, in part, that youthful lovers are treated indulgently in those plays. Wrong is wrong, and is never really justified. Still, Lope seems to say, to be led astray by love is a natural part of the process of growing up, and since people are seldom hurt seriously by the mistakes of love, they may easily be forgiven: does not the old ballad teach that "yerros por amores / dignos son de perdonar" ("mistakes made in the name of love are worthy of being forgiven")?

The symapthy shown the victims of the vengeances wrought in *Porfiar hasta morir* and *El castigo sin venganza* is also justified at least in part by the fact of their sins' being "yerrors por amores." But the concept of love that governs in these works is, like that which we find in such a similarly late play as *El caballero de Olmedo* (1615–1626, probably 1620–1625), very different from the concept of love that informs the early honor plays. No longer is love a mere temptation of the flesh, the yearning, normal in the young at least, for physical fulfillment. It has become in these late honor plays a ferocious passion, a force so powerful that the will is not simply inclined under its weight but totally subjugated. It is an emotion that arises spontaneously, grows with astonishing rapidity, and ends by taking control of the entire being. Once in command, it has but one desire: to perpetuate itself. To this desire, everything is sacrificed—convention, scruples, shame. Even life itself is sacrificed, for nothing matters to the person in love except the extension and exaltation of his passion.

Clearly, this kind of love is a disease, a disease whose symptoms the patient may not repress and whose advance he is only partially capable of checking. It is natural, given this conception, that those who suffer from love should be pitied —even if the sinful consequences of their love must be punished. And this is indeed the attitude toward lovers in the very late honor plays, an attitude for which a work like *Fuenteovejuna* is apt to leave us unprepared. The step from the hostility of *Fuenteovejuna* to the compassion of the late plays was not taken all at once, however. For there is one middle-period play, at least, in which the satisfaction taken by the protagonist in his vengeance is attenuated by a real feeling of commiseration toward those he must kill. That play, which we may consider a kind of bridge between middle and late plays, is *La victoria de la honra* (1609–1615, probably 1609–1612).

The story related in *La victoria de la honra,* a work of uncertain source,[16] is that of Captain Valdivia, an *indiano* of mature years who has returned to Spain to settle down in Seville and enjoy his marriage to his young wife, Doña Leonor. The marriage promises to be long and happy until Fortune intervenes and sends into the lives of Valdivia and Leonor the impetuous Don Antonio. The latter, a young man of excellent family and apparently good character, has a chance encounter with Leonor one day, and immediately falls passionately in love. The unhappy consequence of Antonio's ardent love is that Leonor too becomes inflamed, and in the end, both are hopelessly compromised. At this point Valdivia, who has all along been aware of the catastrophe that threatened to overwhelm the three of them and who has worked conscientiously to avert it, can disregard the harm to his reputation no longer. With the help of his loyal slave, Hernando, he enters his house secretly and there takes the expected vengeance on the offenders of his honor.

The striking thing about the characterizations of Antonio and Leonor in this play is the amount of sympathy with which they are infused. Clearly, Lope wanted to make both lovers attractive and appealing. Thus, throughout the first act and a half, Leonor is a loving and obedient wife. She is completely aware of her duty to her husband and is determined to fulfill it:

> ¿Qué he hecho a aqueste mozuelo
> que contra la ley del cielo
> me sirve y me quiere agora?
> Yo soy casada, y soy noble;
> será dar pasos atrás,
> que mientras me siga más
> pienso resistirme al doble.
>
> (*Ac. N., X*, 425a–b)

What have I done to that young fellow who, against the laws of heaven, now loves me and serves me? I am a married woman and I am nobility. He will get nowhere, for the more he pursues me, doubly hard do I intend to resist.

Don Antonio, too, is endowed with many good qualities. He is strong and courageous. He is also, apparently, gallant and

generous toward everyone except Captain Valdivia. Like
Leonor, however, Antonio is unable to withstand the attack
mounted by Love—here envisioned, in anticipation of the
late honor plays, as an alien, destructive, and very nearly
irresistible force. Cupid, the *dios machín,* robs him of his
sense of honor, his self-esteem, and ultimately, of his respect
for his own life and soul:

Lope.	. . . dar la vida por un gusto loco
	no es para cuerdos, si de amor vencidos.
Antonio.	La vida, y aun el alma, tengo en poco.
Lope.	¿Estás en ti? ¿Qué dices?
Antonio.	Que me pierdo
	cuando en las cosas de aquel ángel toco.

(442b)

Lope. To give up life for a mad whim is not something that
sane people do, even if they have been conquered by love.
Antonio. I care little for my life or even my soul. *Lope.* Have
you taken leave of your senses? What are you saying? *Antonio.*
That I lose myself totally when I touch upon all things pertaining
to that angel.

If it is true, however, that Lope is in sympathy with the
young lovers of *La victoria de la honra,* it is also true that
he is greatly in sympathy with Valdivia. Sober, sincere, compassionate, Captain Vildivia is, we are led to believe, thoroughly undeserving of the misfortune that befalls him. Unlike the husbands of the early honor plays, and some of the
later ones as well, he has done nothing himself to bring that
misfortune about. Even so, he is completely understanding
and quite reluctant at first to exact the usual vengeance. In
the end, of course, he does act, but only after twice warning
Antonio's father of the disastrous course on which the boy has
set himself and after making it absolutely clear to his wife
that his honor is not to be trifled with. Indeed, so fair is
Valdivia in his actions throughout the play that when the
vengeance is finally taken, even Don Pedro, the father of
Antonio, is forced to admit its essential rightness.[17]

In view of the fact that Lope in this play empathizes both

with the plight of the protagonist and with that of the antagonist, it may well be questioned whether the ending of the play is not truly tragic. The answer has to be "no," because the ambivalence of feeling that is sustained throughout the play is resolved in the last lines strongly in favor of Captain Valdivia. As in the other middle-period honor plays, the closing scene of *La victoria de la honra* constitutes a celebration of the protagonist and his actions. Valdivia is constrained to explain his vengeance, does so satisfactorily, and is granted both pardon and approbation. The latter is insisted upon by the perhaps overgenerous Don Pedro. Proclaiming himself "envious" of the "glory" of Captain Valdivia, Don Pedro then goes on to match, as he says, "deeds to words," by giving to Valdivia in marriage the hand of his daughter, Doña Ana. The play thus comes to a close with the betrothal of the protagonist to the sister of the rival and victim, and whatever feelings of tragedy may have accrued to this moment are definitively and summarily dispersed.[18]

The rather peculiar course traced by the action of *La victoria de la honra,* a course that seems to be heading toward tragedy only, at the end, suddenly to veer away, is traced again in the late honor play *Porfiar hasta morir.* This play, as is well known, constitutes Lope's re-creation of the celebrated tale of Macías, the Galician troubadour who quite literally died for love. Since little is known about the historical Macías, each author who has related his story has been free to supply whatever biographical details seemed to him appropriate. According to Menéndez y Pelayo, those that appear in Lope's account are drawn chiefly from the *Nobleza de Andalucía* of Argote de Molina.[19] As given there, the essential facts of Macías's life are that he was a squire of the Grand Master of Calatrava (Lope makes it Santiago); that he loved a married lady, the wife of a nobleman also in the service of the Grand Master; that he was asked to forswear his love for the lady, but was unwilling to do so; and that he was finally killed by the dishonored husband, who dispatched him by hurling a lance through the window of the prison where he was being held, for his own safety, by the Grand Master.

In *Spain and the Western Tradition,* Otis H. Green suggests that in Lope's play Macías is a typical courtly lover, and he reproduces a number of passages substantiating this view.[20] He does not, however, quote one song that seems to me to recapture perfectly the spirit of courtly poetry and that occupies in *Porfiar hasta morir* a position similar to those occupied by the song of the harvester Llorente in *Peribáñez* and by the wedding song in *Fuenteovejuna*. This lyric gathers up the play's various thematic and formal patterns, condenses them, and then refracts them in a peculiarly illuminating way. It is the lyric that causes the death of Macías, the one composed by him in prison and then sung by a group of musicians before the Grand Master and his retinue:

> Dulce pensamiento mío,
> si en una obscura prisión
> el hierro es mi dulce gloria,
> la tiniebla es claro sol,
> decidla á mi bella ingrata
> cómo en la imaginación
> tan presente la contemplo
> cuando ausente della estoy.
>
> (*Ac.*, X, 103b)

Sweet thought of mine, if in a gloomy prison the iron bars are my sweet glory, and the darkness is a bright sun, tell my beautiful, ungrateful one how it is possible that, being absent from her, I see her in my imagination as if she were present.

In his song, Macías dramatizes his particular role of the moment, that of a man suffering a literal imprisonment that separates him from the lady he loves. He also evokes himself, however (whether knowingly or not, it is impossible to say) in the larger role he has chosen to play more or less from the beginning of the work, the role of the traditional courtly lover. In realizing this part, Macías has allowed himself to become another kind of prisoner, the proverbial "prisoner of love." What this signifies may be briefly stated. It means, first of all, that he has relinquished his own will in order to make himself the servant of his lady's. It means, second, that, since he is no longer his own master, he is dependent on his lady (who happens to have the appropriate name of Doña Clara, alluded to in the song) for whatever illumination and inspiration he may receive. It means, third, that being in service to his lady, he cannot aspire to be her equal in any way, and that she may consequently treat him however she sees fit. And it means, last, that, because he cannot possibly hope to attain his love, his absence from her is a natural thing and one that can be turned to his advantage.

All of these attributes of the courtly lover are present, at least by implication, in Macías's song. But the point now is not so much the ideas that Macías expresses as the way he expresses them: in courtly poetry, which here, in characteristic fashion, relies heavily on certain rhetorical devices. In particular, Macías makes use of the figure of verbal paradox. He says, for example, that, because he loves as a true courtly lover, his shackles have become his glory, and also that, for the same reason, darkness has for him been transformed into brilliant sun, absence metamorphosed into presence.

Verbal paradoxes of this kind derive their effect from the denial of the seeming contradiction between two counterposed antitheses. Their essential characteristic is the close juxtaposition of opposing concepts or images. Now it is precisely this juxtaposition of opposites that typifies Macías's manner of speaking throughout *Porfiar hasta morir*. One may open the text at random; virtually every speech of Macías will have at least one instance of this stylistic peculiarity. Two examples here must suffice. The first occurs early in Act I, immediately after Macías meets the beautiful Doña Clara. Asked by Doña Clara whether he would, perchance, know anything about certain relatives of hers living in Barco de Ávila, Macías replies:

> Señor de Valdecorneja
> al Toledo heroico llaman,
> y el Barco entre sus lugares
> no merece humilde fama.
> Pero nunca estuve en él,
> puesto que yo imaginaba
> que no la *tierra,* que el *cielo*
> es de los ángeles patria.

Mas siendo del Barco vos,
habrá para el *cielo* barca,
como la hay para pasar
á los *abismos* las almas,
como dicen los poetas;
de suerte que á vuestra *gracia*
pasarán los *venturosos*
que merecieron hallarla,
y á vuestras *penas* aquellos
que mate vuestra *desgracia.*[21]

(79a–b)

Heroic Toledo is called the Lord of Valdecorneja, and among the towns of that region, Barco is worthy of no little fame. But I was never there, for I supposed that not earth but heaven is the land of the angels. Nevertheless, since you are from Barco, there must be a bark that sails to heaven, just as there is, according to the poets, one to carry souls to hell. Thus, those fortunate ones who deserved to find it will receive your favor, and those struck down by your disfavor, your castigation.

The second example comes from the middle of Act II. At this point, Macías has just learned that Doña Clara is also loved —and courted—by the Grand Master's friend and vassal, Tello de Mendoza. He expresses his consternation as follows:

¡Ay de mí! Clara perdida,
vida, ¿para qué sois *buena?*
Que de tantos *males* llena,
más seréis *muerte* que *vida.*
. . . .
Tello de Mendoza ¡ay cielos!
¿ha de gozar de mi bien?
¿Cómo puede ser que estén
juntos mi amor y mis celos?
Mal pueden *fuegos* y *hielos*
tener en paz mi cuidado;
mas si *helado* y *abrasado*
no puede ser que me vea,
hará que posible sea
la *dicha* de un *desdichado.*

(87b)

125

Oh, woe! With Clara lost, of what good are you, life? For, filled with so many evils, you will be more death than life... Oh, God, is Tello de Mendoza to enjoy my treasure? How can my love and my jealousy exist together? Fire and ice in conjunction can give my soul no peace. But if I cannot live both frozen and burning, it may be possible for me to experience the happiness of the unhappy.

Though the constant oppositions and antitheses of Macías's speech become tiresome before the play is over, they are an important element in Lope's characterization of him. On one level, of course, they are merely conventional: troubadours in their songs express themselves with, among other things, paradoxes, oxymora, and antitheses; Macías is a troubadour; therefore, he has recourse to the same devices. Looking beyond the conventionality of Macías's speech, however, something that its very exaggerations almost force us to do, we sense the intention—as in the words that Lope gives to Peribáñez, Don Fadrique, Fernán Gómez, and others—to suggest a certain complex of values, a particular way of perceiving and experiencing the world. That particular way consists in a perspective that is essentially dualistic, in a vision in which all things exist in striking contrast to some opposing substance or idea. This manner of perceiving the world is not, of course, peculiar to Macías. It is characteristic of all courtly poets and even, as J. Huizinga points out, of medieval people in general.[22] Within *Profiar hasta morir,* however, Macías's "style" and the particular vision that that style implies are unusual and serve to separate him from the other characters. They also serve to explain, indeed tend to make inevitable, the way Macías's life comes to an end.

This relationship may be illuminated by a quotation from Huizinga's *Waning of the Middle Ages.* Discussing the typical dualistic view of medieval people, Huizinga says that "all things presenting themselves to the mind in violent contrasts and impressive forms, lent a tone of excitement and of passion to everyday life and tended to produce that perpetual oscillation between despair and distracted joy, between cruelty and pious tenderness which characterize life in the Middle Ages."[23] What Huizinga postulates here is an intimate connection between the way people see the world and the way they behave, specifically, that reality visualized as a series of sharp antitheses had in the fourteenth and fifteenth centuries the effect on the beholder of profoundly unsettling the emotions, of causing them to flow first in one direction and then in another. This is precisely the experience undergone by Macías. For like the troubadors of whom he is in this play the exemplar, Macías vacillates continually in his emotions: first between happiness and misery, then between optimism and despair, then between affirmation and denial.

Macías himself is not unaware of his erratic behavior, or so it would seem on the basis of his remarks to Doña Clara:

> Pues en mí todo se halla:
> cólera para ser luego,
> flema para edad tan larga,
> que, siendo el alma inmortal,
> tendré la vida del alma.
>
> (79b)

In me, everything is found: choler, for quickness of being, phlegm for a lengthy existence—something that, the soul being immortal, I shall enjoy through the life of the soul.

He makes no effort, however, to minimize the effects of his violent oscillations, the reasons being, evidently, that he enjoys them: "But I, who always found greatest pleasure in variety . . ." (86a). There is, of course, a certain morbidity in this, a morbidity that reveals itself more and more as the play wears on. Specifically, Macías comes to be increasingly obsessed with the opposition life-death, and to feel, apparently, in ever greater measure the attraction of the latter. Many passages demonstrate this, but a few examples will suffice to make the point. The first of these is from the long speech in Act II, Scene 2, in which Macías asks the King for the hand of Doña Clara:

> Y así, en hacerme este bien
> mostrarás, señor, quien eres;
> que en tenerla está mi *vida*,
> y en perderla está mi *muerte*.
>
> (87a)

And thus, in doing me this benefit, you will demonstrate, Sire, who you are: for in having her lies my life, and in losing her, my death.

Another example occurs in the confrontation between Macías and Doña Clara somewhat further on in the same act; at this point Macías knows definitely that Clara is not to be his:

> No sé cómo hable contigo,
> porque fué necedad siempre
> hablarles en cosas tristes
> á los que viven alegres.
> Casarte tú y morir yo
> son cosas tan diferentes,
> que no puede concertallas
> ni quien *vive* ni quien *muere.*
>
> (89b–90a)

I do not know how I can speak to you, since it has always been folly to speak of sad things with those who live happily. For you to marry and for me to die are such contrary things that they cannot be reconciled, either by the one who lives or by the one who is dying.

Still another instance appears in the closing lines of Act II, Scene 9, the scene in which Nuño, the *gracioso*, attempts to convince Macías to renounce his hopeless love:

> ¡Por Dios, Nuño, que me dejes;
> que á quien le cansa la *vida*
> será partido la *muerte!*
>
> (91a)

Leave me, Nuño, for God's sake; for one who is tired of life, death will be a boon!

The final example I take from Scene 9 of Act III; although he is unaware of the fact, Macías is here speaking for the last time with Doña Clara:

> Hermosa Clara, ocasión
> de mis versos y mis penas,

vuelve esas luces serenas
á mi obscura confusión.
No pido más galardón
de amor tan desatinado,
que saber que mi cuidado
halló lástima en tu pecho,
para *morir* satisfecho
de que fué bien empleado.

(100b)

Beautiful Clara, cause of my verses and my sorrow, turn once more upon my dark confusion those serene lights. I ask no other reward of such an ill-advised love than to know that my concern found pity in your breast, thus being able to die with the satisfaction that it was well directed.

In this last conversation with Clara, Macías speaks only of dying, suppressing entirely the first member of that antithesis which appears so insistently in his speeches almost from the beginning of the play. In the scene following, he tells Nuño not to expect, "for as long as you see me alive, anything except mad acts of love" (101a). It is shortly after this that he is taken off to prison, there to be murdered a little while later.

What, then, are we to make of the death of Macías? That it is, as some of the evidence seems to indicate, the very fulfillment of his wishes, a kind of suicide by proxy? Such a conclusion cannot, of course, be definitely proven. The most that can be said with certainty is that, in the words of Nuño, Macías "has allowed himself to die" (101b). Were Macías's death in fact a suicide for love, however, there would be little reason for surprise, for that is precisely the end yearned for, either consciously or subconsciously, by the most sincere and dedicated courtly lovers. What they seek in their love, as Denis de Rougemont informs us in *Love in the Western World,* is not satisfaction or contentment but passion, passion in the sense of suffering. This desire, seemingly so abnormal, has its roots in certain Orphic doctrines, in particular, the notion that man "reaches self-awareness and tests himself only by risking his life—in suffering and on the verge of death." Thus it is that the true courtly lover longs to be "branded," longs "to grow *aware* of what is on fire inside of him."[24] This awareness he finds in what many late Romantic writers, remote but direct descendants of the courtly lovers, called the Real Life, the life not of day but of night, the life of death.

Whether or not Macías is a true courtly lover in this sense is a question that necessarily remains open; it seems at least conceivable that he is. What can be affirmed categorically is that the thought of death is not at all dismaying to him. This being the case, it is difficult, if not impossible, to regard his end as really tragic. The very least common denominator of all tragedies is catastrophe; if, then, we have a play in which the hero views death not as catastrophe but as a release or even a kind of apotheosis, that piece, surely, belongs to a different order of literature. Most critics who have dealt with *Porfiar hasta morir* appear to have accepted this fact. Thus, despite the propensity of many writers to pin the label "tragic" on as many Golden Age plays as possible, the term has seldom been applied to this drama. Even Menéndez y Pelayo, among those most inclined to claim for tragedy every possible work, was in this particular case more circumspect. *Porfiar hasta morir,* he remarks in his discussion of the piece, is "a beautiful play, or rather, a moving dramatic elegy."[25]

A moving dramatic elegy: the description seems apt. For there is indeed something elegiac about the mood of this play. On the one hand, there is a profound sense of loss, a feeling that stems from our apprehension of the human worth of Macías. On the other hand, balancing that sense of loss, is an element of consolation: as we have seen, Macías is not only not afraid to die, he finds in death a secret fascination, and is drawn toward it by a kind of fatal attraction. Both the awareness of loss and the strain of consolation are important to that type of literature we call elegy, and when placed in conjunction, they give rise to the feeling that seems most to characterize it, the feeling of melancholy. Somewhat surprisingly, this feeling is not found very frequently in Lope's theater. I say "somewhat surprisingly" because, as will be noted later, melancholy was a mood to which Lope in his own life was far from a stranger.

El castigo sin venganza

Although all works of literature deserve to be judged by their own standards, without regard to any intention that their author might have had for them but evidently did not, it is perhaps inevitable that we should see *La victoria de la honra* and *Porfiar hasta morir* as plays that contain the seeds of tragedy, but seeds not allowed to come to fruition. Viewed this way, they assume a historical importance they might not otherwise have. They come to seem, that is, the necessary preparation for the single play in which Lope has projected a tragic vision comparable to that of Sophocles, Euripides, or Shakespeare. That play, one of the last and by universal acknowledgment one of the greatest that Lope ever wrote, is *El castigo sin venganza.*

The work that served as the principal source of *El castigo sin venganza* was identified some time ago. It is a Spanish translation of one of the *Histoires tragiques* of François de Belleforest, themselves adaptations of various of the *Novelle* of Bandello.[26] Superficially, Lope's play and Belleforest's story are quite similar: Lope has taken from his source the basic incidents of his plot, certain of the motivations of his characters, and even a few bits of dialogue. As is almost always the case with Lope, however, those things that are of primary interest in *El castigo sin venganza* are entirely his own invention. In particular, the tragic outlook of the play is totally absent from the story. Whereas Lope, as we shall see, finds the history of the Duke of Ferrara to be full of ambiguity and disturbing questions, Belleforest cannot conceive it as anything more than a simple cautionary tale. He makes no effort therefore to render any of the characters sympathetic. The Duke in his account is completely without redeeming qualities, an irresponsible libertine and nothing more. The Duke's wife is scarcely better: once aware of the grave insult done her by her husband, she determines, as she says, to pay him back in kind, and then, having decided on the instrument of her vengeance, proceeds coolly to seduce her step-son with both words and what the Spanish translator calls "dishonest ca-

131

resses."[27] As for the son, whatever he may have been in earlier years—Belleforest says that as a boy he had given "signs of virtue and valor"[28]—he turns out in the end to be passive and weak. Presented with such unattractive characters, we cannot but feel that the catastrophe that overtakes them is an act of poetic justice. This, of course, is precisely what Belleforest wants us to feel. Having told us previously that the scandal caused by the Duchess (in Belleforest she is actually a Marquise, just as the Duke is a Marquis) and her step-son was God's way of punishing the Duke for his licentious life, Belleforest concludes his story by moralizing explicitly on the deaths of the two lovers:

Thus ended the lives of those poor wretches, whose happiness was slight in comparison to the punishment they suffered, since from their pleasure they gained nothing except a [shameful] kind of death and the burial of their bones in the same tomb. What one may conclude from this is that one should consider well what one is beginning, and the consequences that may follow from it, before putting it into effect. For anyone can understand that if sin takes hold, it throws its roots so deep that they are difficult to pull out. This example is an excellent one for those who live without taking into account the power of the flesh and the devil, having relations with their relatives, heedless of the fact that many held to be wise erred in this respect, doing things disgusting to imagine that were punished with the death and disgrace of the malefactors.[29]

It is perhaps superfluous to say that the tone of this passage is quite foreign to *El castigo sin venganza,* which is informed not by the spirit of divine retribution, but by the true spirit of tragedy. We feel the presence of that spirit in the very first scene of the work, a scene that, like the opening scene of *Hamlet,* is dominated by obscurity and confusion. Thus, as the play begins, it is night, and we find ourselves in a street of Ferrara. The Duke is speaking with Febo and Ricardo, his two henchmen:

Ricardo.   ¡Linda burla!
Febo.   Por extremo.

Pero ¿quién imaginara
que era el Duque de Ferrara?

Duque.   Que no me conozcan temo.

(*Ac.,* XV, 237a)

   Ricardo. A pretty hoax! *Febo.* In the extreme! Who would imagine that it was the Duke of Ferrara? *Duke.* I am afraid that I will be recognized.

   The audience is never told the nature of the trick that has been played. These opening lines are, nevertheless, far from gratuitous, for they establish the motif of deception that runs throughout the first scene. Ferrara, as we soon discover, is a place where all men deceive. Some delude for a living: these are the actors who, in the practice of their art, mix the feigned with the real, or the poets who, according to the Duke, are like "those prestidigitators, all sleight of hand and little art, who produce out of their mouths ribbons of various colors" (237b–238a). Others delude for the sheer pleasure of it. The Duke himself is in this category, as is that "certain crafty husband" mentioned by Ricardo who appears to sell his wife's favors only to withhold delivery of the goods. Still others delude simply because it is prudent to do so: Cintia, for example, who, because she does not wish to admit the Duke to her house, pretends in this first scene not to recognize him and then, under cover of her pretense, goes on to excoriate him in a manner reminiscent of Casilda's speech to the Comendador in Act II of *Peribáñez.* No one, we are thus led to believe, is free from dissembling, and what is worse, even nature puts on masks. The shadow, for example, that seems to cover the evening sky is not shadow at all but rather "an embroidered cape with which heaven disguises itself" (237a).

   The dramatic ideas presented in this opening scene are, as we would expect, reiterated and developed in the course of the play. E. M. Wilson in his sensitive and sensible article on this work has traced the pattern made by the motif of deception.[30] I should like to draw attention to another motif, that of darkness.[31] As in so many tragedies—*Hamlet,* for instance, or *Macbeth,* or *Phèdre*—the atmosphere in *El castigo sin venganza* is prevailingly opaque and obscure. This gloom de-

rives to a large extent from scenic effects: not just the first scene of the play but the greater part of the last act too takes place at night. But verbal suggestion also plays an important part in creating the atmosphere of tenebrosity. For among the words repeated to a noticeable extent throughout the play are *noche* (used figuratively), *negro, sombra, oscuro, oscurecer.* The word *noche,* especially, occurs with great frequency and in a variety of contexts, ranging from Casandra's metaphorical description of her highway mishap and subsequent rescue—

> ...fué mi error la noche,
> mar el río, nave el coche,
> yo el piloto, y vos mi estrella.
>
> (243b)

...my blunder was the night; the river, the sea; the coach, a ship; I, the pilot; and you, my guiding star.

—to Federico's anguished expression of his profound depression—

> ...ruego á la muerte en vano
> que no aguarde á que la cera
> llegue al último desmayo,
> sino que con breve soplo
> cubra de noche mis años.
>
> (253b)

...in vain, I call upon death not to wait until the taper [of my life] gives its final flicker, but with one short puff to shroud my years in night.

—to the Duke's speech of gratitude to Aurora:

> Dame tus brazos, Aurora,
> que en mi sospecha y recelo,
> eres la misma del cielo,
> que mi noche ilustra y dora.
>
> (246a)

Give me your arms, Aurora; for in my suspicion and misgiving, you are the very Aurora of Heaven, which illuminates and brightens my night.

134

Maynard Mack has said that all great plays "present us with something that can be called a world, a microcosm—a world like our own in being made of people, actions, situations, thoughts, feelings, and much more, but unlike our own in being perfectly, or almost perfectly, significant and coherent."[32] Clearly, *El castigo sin venganza* belongs in the company of those exalted works of the theater that create microcosms of extraordinary inner coherence. If we were asked to characterize briefly the world of this play, we would say, I think, that it is one in which deceit is universal, in which mere appearance cannot easily be distinguished from reality, and in which even the simply apparent is obscured by a seemingly omnipresent darkness. Such a world will inevitably produce its own states of mind and its own modes of behavior. Thus, it is not surprising that Aurora should speak of "el confuso laberinto ciego / de mis fortunas tristes" ("the confused blind labyrinth of my unhappy fortunes") (245b–246a), or that Federico should assert that "bien dicen que nuestra vida / es sueño, y que toda es sueño" ("rightly do they say that our life is a dream and wholly a dream") (248a), or that the words *confusión, confundir, turbar,* and so on, should appear with great regularity in the speeches of the major characters. Neither is it surprising that these characters should be preoccupied with the idea of error (the words *yerro, error,* and *errar* constitute another verbal motif of the play) or that in spite of their efforts, sincere in greater or lesser degree, to avoid mistakes, they should eventually stumble and fall. The world of *El castigo sin venganza* is a world in which tragedy seems not simply natural but virtually unavoidable.

Until quite recently, it had always been assumed that the tragedy of *El castigo sin venganza* centered on the two lovers, Casandra and Federico. This assumption was not entirely illogical. In the first place, the tragic experience must, whatever else it may include, involve catastrophe, and the most striking catastrophe in this play is the one that befalls Federico and Casandra. In the second place, we quite naturally expect that the focus of emotion in tragedy will be on those persons who dominate the action, and read in a certain way, *El castigo sin venganza* does indeed seem to be dominated by the two

lovers. A more probing examination of the text reveals, however, that not only do Casandra and Federico not occupy the
leading position, but that, if one is discriminating in the use
of literary terms, their end is not really a tragic one. We are,
of course, moved by the deaths of Casandra and Federico. We
are not, however moved "tragically," by which I mean that
we are not impelled to experience that "paradoxical combination of a fearful sense of rightness (the hero must fall) and a
pitying sense of wrongness (it is too bad that he falls)" that
Frye, paraphrasing Aristotle, has declared to be the essence of
tragic feeling.[33]

The fact is that these two sentiments are basically irrelevant to the story of Federico and Casandra. With regard to
the matter of "wrongness," we do not, at the end of the play,
feel that it is too bad that Federico and Casandra have fallen
(we do not, in any case, feel that it is entirely too bad). The
reason has nothing to do with any lack of sympathy for the
young lovers: Amado Alonso, among others, has demonstrated
how Lope gains a good deal of initial sympathy for Casandra
and Federico and how, after they have fallen in love, he en-
deavors to maintain our compassionate interest by showing
them agonizing over their love and struggling to resist it.[34] It
has to do, rather, with the way in which the lovers themselves regard their fall. Casandra and Federico cannot, of
course, consider their deaths as accomplished fact, as can we.
They can, however, and do, envision catastrophe as the probable end of their affair, and they are not greatly disturbed by
the prospect.

Even the casual reader of this play must notice that death
is an iterated motif in the conversations of Casandra and
Federico. In another context, this preoccupation might point
to fear. What it suggests here is not fear but fascination. Like
Macías, perhaps, and like the courtly lovers characterized by
de Rougemont, Casandra and Federico are resigned to death
to the point where it seems to them less a necessary evil than
a positive good. Naturally, this attitude does not find expression all at once, but rather builds gradually during the course
of several scenes. Thus, when Federico first speaks of dying, it
is still with a fairly strong sense of attachment to life:

>   . . . quiero
> ser en todo desdichado;
> que mi desesperación
> ha llegado á ser de suerte,
> que sólo para la muerte
> me permite apelación.
> Y si muriera, quisiera
> poder volver á vivir
> mil veces, para morir
> cuantas á vivir volviera.
> Tal estoy, que no me atrevo
> ni á vivir ni á morir ya,
> por ver que el vivir será
> volver á morir de nuevo.
> Y si no soy mi homicida,
> es por ser mi mal tan fuerte,
> que porque es menos la muerte,
> me dejo estar con la vida.
>
> (251a)

. . . I wish to be unhappy in everything; for my despair has become such that the only appeal from it can be to death. And if I die, I should like to be able to return to life a thousand times, in order to be able to die as many times as I have come to life. In such a state am I that I do not dare either to live or to die, seeing that to live would be to begin to die once again. And if I am not my own murderer, it is because my misfortune is so severe that, death being less so, I permit myself to live.

That sense of attachment is considerably attenuated when, in a speech already quoted in part, the subject of death next appears:

>   Yo me muero sin remedio,
> mi vida se va acabando,
> como vela, poco á poco;
> y ruego á la muerte en vano
> que no aguarde á que la cera
> llegue al último desmayo,
> sino que con breve soplo
> cubra de noche mis años.
>
> (253b)

I am hopelessly dying. My life is coming to an end, like a candle, little by little. In vain, I call upon death not to wait until the taper gives its final flicker, but with one short puff to shroud my years in night.

By the end of the second act, life no longer matters at all:[35]

Casandra.	Yo he de perderme:
	ten, honor; fama, resiste.
Federico.	Apenas á andar acierto.
Casandra.	Alma y sentidos perdí.
Federico.	¡Oh, qué extraño desconcierto!
Casandra.	Yo voy muriendo por ti.
Federico.	Yo no, porque ya voy muerto.
Casandra.	Conde, tú serás mi muerte.
Federico.	Y yo, aunque muerto, estoy tal,[36]
	que me alegro, con perderte,
	que sea el alma inmortal,
	por no dejar de quererte.

(260a)

Casandra. I shall surely be ruined. Honor, hold fast; reputation, resist. *Federico.* I can scarcely move. *Casandra.* I have lost both reason and senses. *Federico.* Oh, what strange confusion! *Casandra.* Because of you, I am dying. *Federico.* I am not, for I am already dead. *Casandra.* Count, you will be my death. *Federico.* And I, although already dead, am in such frame of mind that I rejoice, even as I bring about your ruination, for the soul is immortal, and thus I shall never cease loving you.

Federico's remarks here are categorical: death is to be welcomed as the salvation of a love that life and time can only destroy. Having heard Federico speak thus at the end of Act II, we cannot easily feel pity for his death at the end of Act III. For if death is a salvation, how may it be regretted?[37] One can, of course, assume that Federico does not mean what he says, that he has, in a sense, become entrapped in his own courtly rhetoric, and there is indeed indication in Act III that the somewhat vacillating Federico is not fully committed to his choice of death over life. At a critical moment, however, the more determined Casandra strengthens his resolution, and together they decide to keep faith with their love, knowing only too well what the consequences will be.

We do not, then, experience much of a "pitying sense of wrongness" upon the death of Federico and Casandra. Neither do we experience much of a "fearful sense of rightness." For the latter, as defined by Frye, results from our feeling that the tragic character *must* fall—that he has, in other words, acted in such a way that it is right that he should fall—and in *El castigo sin venganza* we are not at all convinced of the appropriateness of the lovers' fall. (That they themselves appear to acquiesce in this disaster is for the moment irrelevant.) The problem is that we are not sure that Federico and Casandra are responsible for their actions. To be responsible in this way, one must be capable of acting in a manner different from the way one has acted or, what amounts to the same thing, capable of reversing a course of action already begun. Asking ourselves whether Federico and Casandra possess this capability, we would have to answer that the evidence seems to indicate otherwise.

From the beginning, there is something fateful about the relationship of Federico and Casandra. Riding to meet his future step-mother, Federico leaves the road to admire a river view that has caught his attention. Suddenly, he hears voices below and, against the advice of his servant not to go looking for trouble, hurries to investigate. The person in distress turns out to be Casandra herself, who, leaving her escort, the Marqués de Gonzaga, on the road above, had driven her coach to the river's edge and there overturned it. Just in time, Federico reaches the coach and rescues her.

In the opinion of the Marqués de Gonzaga, this first meeting of Federico and Casandra shows clearly the hand of God. Speaking with Federico after the incident, he says:

> El cielo, señor, ordena
> estos sucesos que veis,
> para que Casandra os deba
> un beneficio tan grande,
> que desde este punto pueda
> confirmar las voluntades,
> y en toda Italia se vea

amarse tales contrarios,
y que en un sujeto quepan.

(244b)

> Heaven, my lord, has ordained these events that you have wit-
> nessed in order that Casandra would owe you a debt so great that
> it might, from this moment on, join your wills in harmony, and
> that in all Italy there be seen the mutual love of such [formerly]
> contrary spirits, and how they can exist as one.

No doubt by the end of the play the Marqués would wish to
retract these words. We cannot help feeling, however, that he
is at least partially right, that there has been some supernatural power at work here, causing Federico and Casandra
to meet in circumstances of such emotional intensity that it is
all but unavoidable that they should fall in love. What this
supernatural power is we are not sure, but we inevitably
identify it with that force which brought Tristan and Isolde
together and bound them so inescapably to each other. In
making this association, we are no doubt influenced by certain
analogies between the story of Federico and Casandra and
that of Tristan and Isolde: the obvious resemblance between
the triangle Duke of Ferrara–Federico–Casandra and that of
King Mark–Tristan–Isolde, the similarity between the mission
that Federico undertakes at the beginning of the play and that
which Tristan undertakes on behalf of King Mark, and so on.

For a time, as we have seen, Federico and Casandra struggle
hard to resist the love that springs up with such portentous
suddenness between them (as early as the end of their first
encounter, both Federico and Casandra confess to confidants
that they have been touched by feelings of more than familial
affection for each other). Eventually, however, the flames of
passion burn too hot and chastity is overcome. Federico suc-
ceeds in bestowing an ardent kiss on Casandra's hand. From
that moment, there is seemingly no turning back: the poison,
as Casandra says, has risen from the hand to the heart, and
the will is paralyzed. Here, precisely, lies the difficulty for anyone who might otherwise feel a "sense of rightness" in the
fall of Federico and Casandra. For the actions of a coerced
will, as courts of law everywhere recognize, are not subject

to the usual judgments. Under these circumstances, normal ideas of guilt and innocence simply do not apply, and thus, however heinous the crime, however regrettable, it stands exempt from the customary atonement or retribution.

If, then, the tragic feeling that pervades this play cannot be said to be centered on the characters of Federico and Casandra, we must look for its focal point elsewhere. There is really only one other possibility, and that is the Duke. That the Duke does, in fact, stand at the heart of the tragedy of *El castigo sin venganza* is an idea now generally accepted by students of the play.[38] It was not always so. Earlier critics could not admit the notion of the Duke as tragic hero, arguing that the part he played in the drama was limited and that his character and acts were incompatible with tragedy. But these arguments are not well-grounded. The invalidity of the first of them was demonstrated by A. A. Parker, who pointed out, with the necessary supporting evidence, that the "Duke not only opens and closes the stage action but is the agent who determines the whole course of the plot."[39] The second argument, I suggest, is equally fallacious. For the character of the Duke not only is not incompatible with tragedy, it is of that precise type which is most characteristic of tragic literature.

Turn once again to Aristotle. The tragic hero, we are informed by the *Poetics,* should be "neither eminently virtuous or just, nor yet involved in misfortune by deliberate vice or villainy, but by some error of human frailty [*hamartia*]; and this person should also be someone of high fame and flourishing prosperity."[40] Here, as elsewhere in the *Poetics,* the tone is seemingly prescriptive. Aristotle's intention, however, was not so much to prescribe like a legislator as to describe like a philosopher or scientist. In particular, his purpose appears to have been to note down and analyze the best and most effective tragic practice of his time. It was this practice that became the model on which most later tragedians constructed their plays, and thus the phrases of the *Poetics* serve by extension as a brief characterization of tragic heroes in general: men who are, in Herbert J. Muller's restatement, "essentially but not pre-eminently good, whose misfortune is brought about by some 'error or frailty.' "[41]

141

That the Duke of Ferrara is possessed of human frailty is obvious to all, including himself; there will be occasion to examine the exact nature of this frailty shortly. For the moment, I want to stress the fact, sometimes overlooked, that he is also, to use Muller's expression, "essentially good." We are given a few examples of the Duke's "goodness" in the play: his concern for the happiness of his niece, Aurora; his quick response to the call of the church; his receptiveness (as shown in Act III) to the petitions of his subjects, and so on. For the most part, however, we do not so much see the goodness of the Duke in action as perceive its reflection in the feelings that the other characters of the play have for him. Despite his well-known excesses, the Duke is held in widespread esteem and affection. Federico, Aurora, Febo, the Marqués de Gonzaga, Ricardo—all these express during the course of the play some kind of love or fondness for the Duke. Against these, only two characters manifest active hostility toward him: Casandra, who has, of course, good reason to feel wronged, and Batín, the *gracioso*.

The hostility of Batín deserves some comment because it appears to be at least partially responsible for a recent and, to my way of thinking, quite mistaken interpretation of the Duke by T. E. May.[42] For May, the Duke is totally abhorrent: he is a "calculating tyrant," a "mere figure of greed and power," a being inhabited by a "monster of cruelty and pride." Worse yet, as May sees him, the Duke is a hypocrite who encourages his subjects to idolize him, even though he is himself fully aware of the vileness of his behavior. Thus, the third-act conversion, so important to any reading of the play, is in May's view a deliberate fake, a piece of trickery through which the Duke may enhance his reputation while going about his usual lascivious way. May does not feel compelled to spell out his reasons for doubting the authenticity of the Duke's conversion. It would seem, however, that his mistrust derives in large measure from the suspicions of Batín, who, upon being informed of the Duke's new way of life, remarks that "a cat will be a cat, and a dog will be a dog, in *saecula saeculorum*" (264b). Batín, then, is a disbeliever. His disbelief, however, need not necessarily command our own, for

142

he is, like so many *graciosos* of the *Comedia,* a resolute cynic. Bravery means nothing to him, as we see on the occasion of the first meeting of Federico and Casandra; neither does loyalty, as the last act proves; neither, apparently, does honor:

Batín.	¿Cómo te llamas?
Lucrecia.	Lucrecia.
Batín.	¿La de Roma?
Lucrecia.	Más acá.
Batín.	¡Gracias á Dios que con ella topé! que desde su historia traigo llena la cabeza de castidades forzadas y de diligencias necias.

(242b–243a)

Batín. What is your name? *Lucrecia.* Lucrecia. *Batín.* You're not the one from Rome? *Lucrecia.* Not so far away. *Batín.* Thank the Lord I've met her, for ever since I heard her story my head has been full of thoughts about violated chastity and useless remedies!

Batín, moreover, has cause to feel personal rancor toward the Duke, because the Duke's marriage to Casandra has, in everyone's mind, deprived Federico of a dukedom. For Batín, this means the end of his hopes, once so sure of fulfillment, for great rewards in the future, and he is certain to have resented such a reversal of his fortunes.

For anyone, then, not predisposed to suspect the motives of the Duke, there is no very good reason to doubt the sincerity of his conversion. We have seen that Batín's skepticism is not to be trusted (it might be added that Ricardo, a servant who knows the Duke rather better than Batín, explicitly rejects the latter's mistrust, and none is expressed by any other member of the Duke's retinue). And as for the objection, raised by some, that the change is unnaturally sudden, it should be remembered that we are dealing here not with real people but with literary characters, for whom standards of "naturalness," if applicable at all, are certainly very different. There is, however, a very compelling reason for

143

accepting the conversion at face value, and that is that the ending of the play gains immeasurably in tragic force thereby. For if the Duke's conversion is real, if he is in fact "a new man," then upon returning from the Vatican's war, he stands in a position much different from any he occupied before. It is that spot traditionally reserved for the heroes of tragedy, the top of the Wheel of Fortune. Now, for the first time, the Duke has real cause to think well of his life: he has come back from the war mantled in glory, having once again demonstrated his accustomed bravery, but more than this, he has come back chastened and purified, cleansed of the sins of the flesh that formerly tainted his existence. In this moment, it is understandable that the Duke should feel a little proud of himself: "Let my vassals know that I am a different man" (265a). Such feelings ought to be repressed, however, for they are laden with danger. Pride—*hubris*—may mean nothing in the life of an inconsequential man, but in that of a great man, it is a sure harbinger of disaster. And thus it is. Within moments of the inappropriate expression of his self-esteem, the Duke is made aware that his world has collapsed around him.

Were the Duke a reflective person, he might not have invited disaster by speaking as he did. But the point is precisely that he is *not* reflective. From the beginning of the play the Duke is governed by his feelings, his instincts, and his impulses, and this, I think, is the cause of his tragedy. It is not that the Duke's instincts and impulses are all, or even for the most part, bad; frequently they are not, as when he decides abruptly to marry Aurora to Federico, hoping thus to secure the happiness of both, or when in the first act he determines, rather abortively as it turns out, to reform his life. The problem is that the Duke is given over almost completely to his emotions, so much so that he deliberately avoids being provoked to thought and meditation, especially when they may center on himself. We see this clearly in the first scene of the play, of which I have already spoken at some length. At the end of this scene, the Duke is granted two different opportunities to increase his knowledge of himself and of his people, and he scorns both. The first opportunity is that presented by Cintia's denunciation of her ruler's scandalous behavior; in this case, instead of seizing the occasion, as Febo seems to be recommending, to come to some general conclusions about his reputation among the people, the Duke dismisses the supposedly overheard remarks out of hand:

> . . . el vulgo no es censor
> de la verdad, y es error
> de entendimientos groseros
> fiar la buena opinión
> de quien, inconstante y vario,
> todo lo juzga al contrario
> de la ley de la razón.

(239b)

The common people are not the arbiters of truth, and it is a mistake of the unsophisticated mind to trust one's reputation to those who, fickle and inconstant, judge everything contrary to the laws of reason.

The second incident is even more revealing. This time the Duke finds himself with the chance to witness the rehearsal of a play that is apparently being prepared for his wedding feast. He refuses flatly to take advantage of the occasion, however, saying that he is afraid of what he may hear. When pressed for further explanation, he reasons as follows:

> ¿Ahora sabes, Ricardo,
> que es la comedia un espejo,
> en que el necio, el sabio, el viejo,
> el mozo, el fuerte, el gallardo,
> el rey, el gobernador,
> la doncella, la casada,
> siendo al ejemplo escuchada
> de la vida y del honor,
> retrata nuestras costumbres,
> ó livianas ó severas,
> mezclando burlas y veras,
> donaires y pesadumbres?
> Basta, que oí del papel
> de aquella primera dama

145

el estado de mi fama:
bien claro me hablaba en él.
¿Que escuche me persüades
la segunda? *Pues no ignores
que no quieren los señores
oir tan claras verdades.*[43]

(240a–b)

Surely you know, Ricardo, that the theater is a mirror in which—as we listen to the examples they present of life and of honor—the fool, the sage, the old man, the youth, the strong man, the gallant, the king, the governor, the maiden, and the wife paint a picture of our customs, both the insignificant and the important, mixing jests and truths, pleasantries and sorrows. No more; for I heard in the speech of that first lady [Cintia] about the state of my reputation; in it, she spoke all too clearly to me. And now you persuade me to listen to another? You must realize that great lords have no desire to hear such clear truths.

The Duke that we see in *El castigo sin venganza* is, then, an incomplete person. He is a human being who rejects, or attempts to reject, what is most human in him, namely, his capacity for analysis, both of himself and of his circumstances. The result of this rejection is deficient awareness: as E. M. Wilson has shown, the Duke is frequently unaware of the true nature of things. In this respect he is similar to a number of the characters examined in the last chapter. More to the point, however, would be a comparison with such heroes of tragedy as Oedipus, Macbeth, and Lear. These, too, are unaware, but unlike, for example, Beatriz in *Los comendadores de Córdoba* or the knights-commander of *Peribáñez* and *Fuenteovejuna*, they are led by their unawareness to an end that is not merely pathetic or spectacular but truly tragic, the same kind of end as befalls the Duke of Ferrara.

Unawareness is not, of course, in itself the agent of tragedy, but rather the state of mind that produces that agent. The latter, as we have seen, is a blunder or error of some sort, a breach of what the Greeks called *Diké,* the established order of things. It is not easy to say with certainty what the Duke's tragic blunder is. He makes a number of mistakes in the course

146

of the play, several of them very serious. Clearly, he was wrong not to accept Federico's offer to accompany him into battle; much grief might have been avoided had he done so. Just as clearly, he was wrong to treat Casandra after their wedding with indifference and disrespect. For some, then, either of these two errors might appear to be the one fraught with tragic consequences. There is, however, a prior mistake whose nonoccurrence would have precluded the other errors and their effects, and it is this mistake that seems to me decisive. It is the Duke's decision to marry.

It is quite possible to specify why the decision to marry is blameworthy: the Duke is not really prepared to marry; the marriage is strictly one of convenience; with the marriage, Federico, the person whom the Duke loves most in all the world, is deprived of his obvious right of succession; and so on. All such reasons are ultimately irrelevant, however, for in tragedy we are not asked to justify why a particular mistake leads to catastrophe, but simply to accept the fact that it does. What is important is the inevitability of the process, an inevitability that has been well explained by Frye, who says that in his error, the tragic hero exchanges "a fortune of unlimited freedom for the fate involved in the consequences of the act of exchange, just as, for a man who deliberately jumps off a precipice, the law of gravitation acts as fate for the remainder of his life."[44] Thus it is in *El castigo sin venganza*. For with his decision to marry, the Duke sets in inalterable motion a chain of events that will not be broken until both his wife and his son are dead and he has experienced the complete ruination of his own existence.

Logically, perhaps, we ought strongly to condemn the Duke for the mistake that leads to so much tragedy. And yet, although disapproval is obviously a part of our reaction to the Duke, our feeling is not so vehement as might be expected. Why is this? The reason may have to do in part with our conviction that in the world of *El castigo sin venganza*, a world enveloped in darkness, confusion, and deceit, errors are all too easy to make. Significant, also, is the fact that we are inclined to empathize with the Duke's decision. For despite its faultiness, the decision was made on grounds that were

147

essentially humanitarian. What those grounds were the Duke explains to Aurora early in the play:

> . . . fué casarme traición
> que hago á mi propio gusto;
> que mis vasallos han sido
> quien me han forzado y vencido
> á darle [a Federico] tanto disgusto;
> si bien dicen que esperaban
> a tenerle por su señor,
> ó por conocer mi amor,
> ó porque también le amaban;
> mas que los deudos que tienen
> derecho á mi sucesión
> pondrán pleito con razón;
> ó que si á las armas vienen,
> no pudiendo concertallos,
> abrasarán estas tierras,
> porque siempre son las guerras
> á costa de los vasallos.
> Con esto determiné
> casarme: no pude más.
>
> (245b)

To marry was an act of treason committed against my own heart. But my vassals have been the ones who forced and compelled me to give him [Federico] so much grief. To be sure, they say that they had hoped to have him for their lord, perhaps because they are aware of my love, perhaps because they too love him. But they also say that the kinsmen who are entitled to succeed me will [if Federico becomes Duke] bring justifiable suit; and that if they rise in arms, efforts to reach accord having failed, they will devastate these lands, for wars are always waged at the cost of the vassals. Hearing this, I made the decision to marry; I could make no other.

It was, then, in order to spare his people the horrors of civil war that the Duke married. And who can say that such a war would not, in fact, have taken place, had the Duke not married, as he would have preferred, and allowed Federico to succeed him on the throne? The decisions of tragedy, as Hegel pointed out,[45] are never easy to make, and the alternative discarded may well involve consequences almost as terrible as those of the alternative chosen.[46] Such, we feel, is the case when Antigone is forced to choose between her duty to her brother and her duty to her king, and such might also be the case when the Duke makes his decision to marry. This being so, we can only regard the Duke's "wrong" decision with a certain amount of compassion, even though it was made, as Federico seems to imply in his first conversation with Batín, without the Duke's being fully aware of what he was doing.

Ultimately, perhaps, what induces us to look upon the Duke with sympathy, is our realization that, as with many great and powerful men, his faults are merely the reverse side of the coin of which his merits are the obverse. In him, defects and virtues are not merely allied, but quite inseparable. It is true that the Duke is heedless, impulsive, and unaware, but he is at the same time bold, generous, and brave. Could he be the latter without also being the former? Undoubtedly not. The Duke, then, is not a complete person, but he is in a sense an integrated one. The failing that leads eventually to his defeat should thus be seen, to borrow some words of William Troy, not as "a unit of [his] moral composition . . . but an aspect of his form as a whole. It is not a flaw in an otherwise beautifully shaped vessel (to take Goethe's metaphor for *Hamlet*) but an inner principle of dissolution within the vessel itself."[47]

The sympathy we cannot help feeling for the Duke is inevitably increased, and greatly, by the ending of the play. For now the Duke is faced by the truly awful problem of how to deal with the terrible consequences of his own blunder. There are, it would seem, three courses of action open to him: he can excuse the crime and pardon the offenders; or he can, in the manner of other dishonored husbands, exact a suitable vengeance; or he can, recognizing the transgression but refraining from personal vengeance, act in his capacity as chief magistrate of the dukedom to see that the malefactors receive the punishment they deserve. From the point of view of the seventeenth century, the Duke could with least justification choose the first of these alternatives. As the anointed head of a state, he has the obligation to insure that justice is done therein, and to pardon the offenders in this situation would not be, according to the thinking of the time, an act of justice but the compounding of transgression with further transgression; for the crime of Federico and Casandra is no ordinary one, but rather, as we are reminded by the numerous historical and mythological allusions of the play, a crime of the most appalling sort the human imagination can conceive. That leaves the other two possibilities. And it is, indeed, between these two possibilities that the Duke vacillates—agonizingly, dramatically—in the final scenes of the work.

Upon learning of the adultery of his wife and the treachery of his son, the Duke's first reaction is, not unexpectedly, to take the most frightful possible vengeance, especially on Federico:

> ¡Oh traidor hijo! ¿Si ha sido
> verdad? Porque yo no creo
> que emprenda caso tan feo
> hombre de otro hombre nacido.
> Pero si me has ofendido
> ¡oh si el cielo me otorgara
> que después que te matara
> de nuevo á hacerte volviera,
> pues tantas muertes te diera,
> cuantas veces te engendrara!
>
> (265b–266a)

Oh, treacherous son! But can it be true? Because I do not believe that any man born of another would commit so vile a crime. But if you *have* wronged me, heaven grant me the power, after I have killed you, to bring you back to life, for I would then give you as many deaths as I give you new lives.

These are, however, words spoken under the stress of the initial shock. Later, his fury somewhat calmed, the Duke decides that he will not, that he must not, exact a personal vengeance. The decision seems motivated by two factors. The first is the Duke's dim awareness that he himself, like the biblical David, whom he sees as a kind of analogue, bears a large part of the responsibility for the catastrophe that has befallen his family:

150

El vicioso proceder
de las mocedades mías
trujo el castigo y los días
de mi tormento, aunque fué
sin gozar á Betsabé
ni quitar la vida á Urías.

(265b)

The licentious conduct of my youth has brought about the punishment and the days of my torment, although I have neither slept
with Bathsheeba nor taken the life of Uriah.

The second, and seemingly more important, cause is the
Duke's stated belief that personal vengeance would in this
case be an offense to Heaven, particularly that part of it
directed against his own son:

Cielos,
hoy se ha de ver en mi casa
no más de vuestro castigo.
Alzad la divina vara.
No es venganza de mi agravio;
que yo no quiero tomarla
en vuestra ofensa, y de un hijo
ya fuera bárbara hazaña.

(269b)

Heaven above, that which is to be seen in my house today is
your punishment and nothing more. Raise the divine rod. This is
not a vengeance of my affront, for I have no desire to offend you
by taking revenge, and to do so upon one's son would be an act
of barbarity.

Thus does the Duke convince himself that revenge is inappropriate and even barbarous, and that although he cannot
avoid moving against Casandra and Federico, he will take
that action strictly as the representative of God's justice on
earth. Perhaps it would be better to say that the Duke tries to
convince himself, because it is not certain that he ever suc-
ceeds completely in doing so. The remainder of the monologue
just quoted reveals a strange mingling of thoughts about

151

divine judgment and thoughts about honor and personal insult:

> Éste ha de ser un castigo
> vuestro [i.e., de los cielos] no más,
>   porque valga
> para que perdone el cielo
> el rigor por la templanza.[48]
> Seré padre y no marido,
> dando la justicia santa
> a un pecado sin vergüenza
> un castigo sin venganza.
> Esto disponen las leyes
> del honor, y que no haya
> publicidad en mi afrenta
> con que se doble mi infamia.
> Quien en público castiga
> dos veces su honor infama,
> pues después que le ha perdido,
> por el mundo le dilata.

(269b)

[Heaven], this is to be your punishment and nothing more, for then its [seeming] severity may earn divine forgiveness, [the severity] being in reality moderation. I shall act as a father, not as a husband, administering, in the form of holy justice, punishment without revenge to a sin without shame. The laws of honor ordain this, as well as that there be no publicity of my affront, because that would double my infamy. He who punishes in public twice defames his honor, for after having lost it, he spreads [the loss] throughout the world.

The same mingling is found in the words of the Duke as he watches Federico carry out the punishment he has devised for Casandra:

> Aquí lo veré; ya llega;
> ya con la punta la pasa.
> Ejecute mi justicia
> quien ejecutó mi infamia.[49]

(271a)

Here I shall observe him. Now he is approaching her; now with the tip [of the sword] he runs her through. Let my justice be executed by the one who executed my disgrace.

These speeches, and others of a somewhat similar nature toward the end of the play, seem to suggest that the Duke never does entirely rise above his initial desire for vengeance. I do not wish to state this categorically; the speeches are sufficiently equivocal that they admit of different interpretations. But I would find it difficult to disagree with E. M. Wilson's contention that there is an ambiguity of motivation in the chastisement administered by the Duke.[50] At the same time it is important to point out that the Duke himself does not recognize this ambiguity. For him—as for the Marqués de Gonzaga and, yes, even Batín—the execution of Casandra and Federico is a genuine "punishment without revenge."

Does this mean, as May has submitted, that the Duke is an unmitigated hypocrite? No; only that he is at the end as he was before, which is to say, imperceptive, lacking in self-knowledge, and rather egotistical. We should not be surprised that he remains so. The Duke has changed his habits, but he has not changed—presumably because he cannot change—his basic nature. He is a sincere convert, but a convert who in many ways continues true to his former self.

One important part of that former self is the Duke's devotion to Federico. That, too, like David's devotion to Absalom, endures.[51] And thus, despite his knowledge that not to punish Federico would in itself be a kind of transgression, despite even the apparently not totally suppressed desire to be avenged upon him, the Duke finds that actually to plan the death of his son is almost unbearably painful:

> Sólo de pensarlo ¡ay triste!
> tiembla el cuerpo, expira el alma,
> lloran los ojos, la sangre
> muere en las venas heladas,[52]
> el pecho se desalienta,
> el entendimiento falta,
> la memoria está corrida,
> y la voluntad turbada.
>
> (296b–270a)

Merely in thinking of it, oh, unhappy man! my body begins to tremble, my soul expires, my eyes weep, my blood dies in my frozen veins, my breath catches in my chest, my understanding fails, my memory becomes confused and my will feeble.

The sentiments expressed here stand in marked contrast to those aroused earlier by the thought of the imminent execution of Casandra. She is an adulteress, moreover a quasi-incestuous one, and custom decrees that she should die. The Duke can accept this. But how, he asks himself, can a father accept the killing of his own son? Only by silencing the voice of his paternal love, and by reflecting on the possible consequences of not killing him:

> ¿Qué quieres, amor? ¿No ves
> que Dios á los hijos manda
> honrar los padres, y el Conde
> su mandamiento quebranta?
> Déjame, amor, que castigue
> á quien las leyes sagradas
> contra su padre desprecia,
> pues tengo por cosa clara
> que si hoy me quita la honra,
> la vida podrá mañana.
>
> (270a)

Love, what is it that you want? Do you not understand that God commands that sons honor their fathers, and that the Count is breaking His commandment? Love, allow me to punish him who scorns, to his father's harm, the divine laws, for I hold it as evident that if today he takes my honor, tomorrow he may take my life.

Albert S. Gérard has pointed out that the feelings of the Duke in this, his most anguished moment, are similar to those of Othello just before he strangles Desdemona.[53] The resemblance is well observed and pertinent to our understanding of *El castigo sin venganza*. We should not fail to note, however, that there are also significant differences between the endings of the two plays. Desdemona, for example, is in reality innocent of the sin of which she is accused; to kill her, therefore, as Othello does, is not an act of justice but pure assassination, a terrible blunder for which Othello must pay with his own life. Casandra and Federico, however, are guilty. The Duke's blunder does not lie in putting them to death, but in having, long before, created the circumstances that would make their downfall virtually certain. What these differences amount to, in effect, is that what is the "crime" of the protagonist in *Othello* is the "punishment" of the protagonist in *El castigo sin venganza*. Federico, as the Duke has said, is the one being in all the world whom he has most cherished; indeed, he is the only person whom the Duke has ever loved deeply. In acting against him, therefore, the Duke is, like Orestes at the end of *The Libation Bearers,* acting against a significant part of himself. Justice is done, but it is justice that holds little satisfaction for the judge. Retribution is made, but it is retribution in which the offended shares equally with the offender.

Having said that justice is done, I must acknowledge that there are those who deny that this is so.[54] They argue not that Federico and Casandra do not deserve to be chastised (that much is necessarily admitted), but that the Duke lacks the legal and moral authority to administer the chastisement. The first part of this argument is clearly specious. As the sovereign head of state, the Duke is not simply empowered but obligated to act within Ferrara as the supreme arbiter of both human and divine law. There is thus no need for him to set "himself up as the secular representative of God's justice," as C. B. Morris has written,[55] because he *is* that representative. What is more, he is the representative of God's justice regardless of his own faults and sins. This is not to say that he is not himself held accountable. For him there is also a reckoning, and he is not totally unaware of this. Or so we gather from the speech, quoted above, in which the Duke connects the collapse of his family and his honor to his own earlier transgressions.

Still, it is difficult for us not to wish that the Duke were more fully cognizant of the instrumental role he has played in the tragedy that has gathered about him. It is normal for tragic heroes to fail, and to fail greatly, but we are inclined to feel that the most satisfying tragic stories end with the protagonist recognizing wholly both the nature and the extent of his failure, and learning from his experience. Thus, perhaps, the special attraction exercised by such diverse works as *Prometheus Bound, Oedipus Rex, King Lear, Samson Agonistes,* and *Murder in the Cathedral.* In all of these, the protagonist emerges from his suffering with a changed perspective, a clarified vision that illuminates the meaning of past events and suggests a new direction to be followed—by others, if not by the hero—in the future. It is because of the new perceptions to which catastrophe gives rise in these and similar tragedies than one modern critic has spoken of the fall of the tragic hero as being, parodoxically, a "fortunate" one.[56] Of course, not all tragedies conclude with a phase of significant illumination, in some cases because the protagonist is simply incapable of being appreciably enlightened. It would seem, as there has already been occasion to observe, that the Duke is just such a protagonist.

Does the Duke's lack of real perceptiveness about the tragic situation in which he is caught up afford a means of understanding the executions he devises for Casandra and Federico? Certainly, the contemporary reader or spectator cannot help finding those executions puzzling. The problem is not, as some seem to think, that they are not performed openly, after a public trial.[57] That is indeed the way the offenders are punished in the stories of Bandello and Belleforest, but it is clear that in this particular Lope had necessarily to depart from his sources. For, as Amado Alonso has pointed out, that any man would publicizé to the world that he had been cuckolded, and by his own son, would have struck Spanish seventeenth-century audiences as scandalous, and that a head of state—in whom resides symbolically all the honor of the people—would do so would have seemed to them totally incredible.[58] No; the difficulty is not that the executions are performed secretly and without benefit of trial, but that they are performed with such deviousness. Why, we ask ourselves, does Federico have to be tricked into being the murderer of Casandra? And why does he then have to be denounced as a homicidally jealous step-son?

Can it be that, with the same shallow thinking that has characterized him throughout the work, the Duke has concluded that the subterfuges he has devised will work ultimately not only to his benefit but that of Casandra and Federico as well?[59] This is a possibility, if we assume that at the end of the play Casandra leaves this world with her reputation intact outside the palace and Federico leaves it branded as a murderer but not—which might be worse—as the cuckolder of his father and lover of his step-mother. The explanation is less than completely convincing, however, and I am forced to admit that, like so many others, I find the enigma of the manipulated executions both tantalizing and frustrating.

But it is important not to allow our puzzlement over this aspect of the play to make us insensitive to the very real tragic effect of the ending of the play. As noted earlier, this effect does not proceed directly from the deaths of Federico and Casandra, because the story of those two characters lies outside the normal range of tragic emotion. It derives, rather, from the circumstances in which the Duke of Ferrara here finds himself. The Duke whom we regard at the conclusion of *El castigo sin venganza* is different from any other character examined in this study and, indeed, from any other in the whole of Lope's theater. He is a man who, within the briefest possible span of time, has plunged from the height of human happiness to the depth of human misery. At one moment he was, as Northrop Frye has said of Milton's Adam, "on top of the wheel of fortune, with the destiny of the gods almost within his reach";[60] in the next, almost literally, he found himself deprived, and by his own doing, of virtually everything that he has valued in this world. By his own doing—here, as always, lies the ultimate source of the play's tragic feeling. The Duke, like all tragic heroes, is an autonomous being. He is free, free to choose, and he chooses wrongly. He must, then, accept a measure of responsibility for what has happened to him, and this he does, if with less than full awareness; the result is that we react to his fall with what was earlier termed a "fearful sense of rightness." At the same time, the Duke conceives the retribution to be incommensurate with the crime, and so, I think, do we, or at least we conceive it to be incommensurate with his actions considered as a whole. We also, then, experience a "pitying sense of wrongness." These feelings are not resolved when the play ends, nor should they be. For it is precisely in combination that they are able to suggest to us that double and paradoxical vision characteristic of tragedy: man is a being capable of the most appalling mistakes, but he is also a being imbued with a talent for greatness.

5

Conclusion

IN the market of literary reputations, the stock of individual authors rises and falls in accordance with fluctuations in the taste of readers and critics. Right now, Alemán, Góngora, Galdós, and Miró, to name just a few, are more highly regarded than they were a few generations back; while Herrera, Pereda, Campoamor, and Benavente have lost esteem. In contrast to that of many others, the perceived worth of Lope de Vega has remained fairly constant over the years. Nevertheless, our impression of him as a writer has changed considerably in recent times. Traditionally, people have thought of Lope as a man of great but facile talent, a dramatist who was content to develop a few formulas and then to repeat them unvaryingly, albeit entertainingly, until the end of his days. The view is now understood to be fallacious. Literary creation did come easily to Lope, but he was a careful and often meticulous writer, as well as a quick one. By the same token, his dramatic production, far from being so much mere self-repetition, is actually marked by a process of continuous modification and growth.

This process is best observed by isolating from the body of Lope's plays one particular kind of play and then examining in more or less chronological order its various manifestations. In this study, I have traced the evolution of Lope's honor plays, grouping them into three separate periods: early, middle, and late. The honor plays of the early period are undoubtedly the least well known, both to the specialist and the general reader. They are characterized by their aversion to vengeance, especially the extreme forms of vengeance with which the later plays typically end. In *Carlos el perseguido* (dated manuscript: November 2, 1590), an unfaithful wife is banished rather than executed; in *El castigo del discreto* (September 1598–January 1601), a good thrashing is considered sufficient punishment; and in *Las ferias de Madrid* (1585–1588), *Los embustes de Fabia* (before 1596, and probably 1588–1595), *La bella malmaridada* (dated manuscript: December 17, 1596), and *El desposorio encubierto* (1597–1603), there is no punishment at all. The existence of these plays as a distinct subgroup within the corpus of Lope's honor plays must not be overlooked, for as a collectivity they give the lie to two ideas sometimes encountered in writings on Lope's theater. The first of these is that cases of vengeance withheld or thwarted are exceedingly rare in Lope; Américo Castro, among others, expresses this thought when, in an early essay still much quoted, he speaks of *El castigo del discreto* as a "notable oddity."[1] The other idea, held by, for example, Menéndez Pidal[2] and Valdecasas,[3] is that instances of leniency toward errant wives and their seducers—or would-be seducers—may be found interspersed throughout the whole corpus of Lope's honor plays. Both of these notions are erroneous. Honor plays that dispense with harsh vengeance are not unique in Lope's theater, but neither are they of widespread occurrence. They are, rather, characteristic of, and concentrated in, the early period.

By avoiding vengeance, especially the "full" vengeance of assassination, the honor plays of the first period achieve a resolution that is, at least in some cases and in particular that of *Las ferias de Madrid,* genuinely comic. The plays of the middle-period have endings of a very different sort. Although fairly "happy" from the point of view of the protagonist, those dénouements—intense, bloody, and violent—are hardly comic. Not surprisingly, how to characterize them has been something of a problem for Spanish scholarship. My own suggestion is that they be termed "romancical," on the basis of their resemblance to narrative romance, fiction that deals with the conflict and death struggle of an all-virtuous hero and an enemy who would destroy him.

That the middle-period honor plays should have assimilated themselves more and more to romance, as I indicated in the discussion of *Los comendadores de Córdoba* (1596), *Peribáñez* (1605–1612, probably 1605–1608), and *Fuenteovejuna* (1611–1618, probably 1612–1614), is fascinating in view of the nature of the plays that preceded them and in view of the opposition to vengeance that Lope expressed in 1624. Largely responsible for this move toward romance were the political, economic, and social circumstances in Spain during the years around the turn of the sixteenth century.

In many ways, the experience most characteristic of the Spanish nation in those years was the experience of defeat. The situation was a new one for the majority of the Spanish people and one that they could not easily accept. In relation to those troubled times, the Golden Age theater functioned as what Kenneth Burke calls a "strategy,"[4] a strategy providing orientation and hope amidst all the swirling and disquieting developments. In the *Comedia,* audiences encountered characters doing what they, the people, needed to believe could still be done: meeting the specter of defeat and overcoming it through reliance on consecrated values. The triumph of the hero in ever greater measure was what the public came to see and celebrate, and the dramatists attempted to meet its expectations. Stemming from this compliance is the series of honor plays of Lope's middle period, plays in which the greatest possible threat to the integrity of the protagonist is met with the greatest possible resistance and ultimately vanquished.

In some basic sense, then, Lope's middle-period honor plays are an instance of an experienced showman's giving his public what it wants. That Lope should have catered to the taste of the audience in this fashion was held against him by many of his contemporaries, and continued to be held against him, by some, to the very end of the nineteenth century. What is more, Lope himself on occasion felt rather uneasy about it, if we are to judge by various of the dedications to his plays. The decision to accommodate the preferences of the public has in this century been warmly defended, however. Writing in 1935, Menéndez Pidal saw it as allied to Lope's determination to place Nature above Art,[5] and rather more recently, José F. Montesinos has found it to be central to Lope's discovery of what was in his time "a revolutionary principle in the history of literature, [the] principle . . . of the contingency, relativity and historical character of art."[6] There is, in any event, no real question of insincerity in the case of the middle-period honor plays. Lope's belief in the appropriateness of vengeance as a solution to conflicts of honor seems to have been far from unwavering, but there can be no doubt that he was engaged, and engaged fully, by the experiences of Peribáñez and the people of Fuenteovejuna. What those experiences signified to him, surely, was exactly what they signified to the public: the triumph of courage and heroism, the victory of good over evil, the affirmation of life in the face of death.

Just as intriguing as the approach to narrative romance manifested in the honor plays of the middle period is what may be called the retreat from romance observable in the honor plays of the last period. As I pointed out earlier, Lope all but ceased to write honor plays in this period, there being but two such plays that can be dated positively after 1620. At the same time, he altered in various ways the prevailing pattern of those honor plays he did write, *Porfiar hasta morir* (1624–1628) and *El castigo sin venganza* (dated manuscript: August 1, 1631), with the result that they emerge significantly changed in tonality. I have spoken of the altered tone at some length in the preceding chapter. What is lacking in it is the sense of good inevitably conquering evil, the spirit of triumph through heroism, the feeling of life asserting itself over death.

I do not propose here actually to account for this shift in tone. To do that would surely require more knowledge of Lope the man than we are able to command at a distance of more than three centuries. What I do wish to point out is that the modulation, the darkening, was not an isolated phenomenon, but rather symptomatic of a general change in Lope's theater. Critics have frequently observed that many of Lope's best-known, most sparkling comedies date from his declining years. Even more interesting, however, and this the critics have failed to note, is that these same comedies make up an unusually large percentage of the total number of plays that Lope wrote during the final period. Indeed, during this last period, Lope produced few plays of any sort besides comedies of various types and biblical and hagiographic plays. Conspicuously missing, then, from the last fifteen years or so of Lope's life are those plays celebrating Spanish history and Spanish heroism that loom so large in the earlier periods. There are, of course, a few exceptions. Those exceptions, however—*El caballero de Olmedo* (1615–1626, probably 1620–1625) is one—are of a type that tends to confirm rather than refute the shift I have been talking about.

Basically, what I am suggesting is that toward the end of his life Lope experienced an alteration in outlook, an alteration that took the form of increasing pessimism, and that revealed itself in his theater in a bilateral, though unified, development: on the one hand, a turning away from themes of heroism, and on the other, a turning toward comedy. Now it may at first seem surprising that an increasingly pessimistic vision should manifest itself in an increasingly greater interest in comedy, but there is really nothing paradoxical about this. Comedy in this case serves as a sort of refuge, an escape, as Henri Fluchère remarks in his discussion of Jacobean drama.[7] On the English stage, a kind of analogous development took place. Tragedy was pushed as far as it could go, and when it could be carried no further, the pessimism of the age sought release in pure wish fulfillment, in the unreal worlds of Shakespeare's late romances or the pastoral comedies of Beaumont and Fletcher.

Of course, there may still be some who believe Lope to have been incapable of great pessimism. We become so inured to the clichés of the manuals—and the manuals for a long time harped on Lope's supposed unceasing buoyancy, his zest for life—that it is only with the greatest difficulty, sometimes, that we are able to give them up. That Lope was not only open to pessimism but that this was, in fact, the mood that most characterized his later life has had, however, for many years now, the most unimpeachable documentation: Lope's own correspondence, published, beginning in 1935, by Agustín G. de Amezúa.[8] In these letters, as Amezúa points out, there is a strain of continuous sadness, a sadness that, as the years go by, converts itself into "a deep, absorbing, dense, and constant melancholy."⁹

Amezúa observes that Lope turned increasingly to Stoic doctrine as a source of consolation during his later, embittered years. Another consolation, evidently, was the writing of comedies, plays in whose closed, happy worlds Lope could seek refuge from the anxieties of the real world. These comedies, with their determined escapism, differ strongly as a group from a play like *El castigo sin venganza*. One among them, however, makes a particularly sharp contrast, for it is a play that features honor as a prominent motif and that could easily have ended tragically, like *El castigo sin venganza*, had not the dénouement been manipulated to become the expression of unadulterated wish fulfillment. That play is *La mayor virtud de un rey* (after August 12, 1634), and it is very probably the last work that Lope wrote for the theater.¹⁰ It is appropriate to conclude with a brief look at this piece, for although not itself an honor play, it shows in striking fashion how far Lope had moved since his early years in his treatment of the theme of honor.

The story of *La mayor virtud de un rey* is quickly told. Don Sancho de Mendoza, an elderly Castilian gentleman, leaves Spain after an unpleasant altercation at the court of the King and settles with his two daughters, Sol and Leonor, near Lisbon. Shortly afterward, the beautiful Sol catches the attention of Don Juan de Castro, chief valet to the King of Portugal, and the two young people are very soon deeply in love. At this point all would be well except that, having been earlier matched by the King to the Countess Teodora, Don Juan delays making known his intentions. The result of this delay is that Don Sancho becomes suspicious and, fearful for his honor, makes haste to return to Spain. Unhappily, before he is able to complete his preparations, Sol and Leonor are abducted by Don Juan. Don Sancho now has no recourse but to challenge Don Juan to a duel. His note of challenge, however, is intercepted by the King, who decides out of curiosity to take the place of Don Juan at the appointed rendezvous. Once there, the King is soon apprised of the scandalous in-

sult to Don Sancho's honor. His monarchical justice thereafter is swift. Disregarding his ties of special affection to Don
Juan, he orders him imprisoned and decrees that he shall be
beheaded. A bloody ending to the play now seems certain,
but suddenly the Countess Teodora steps forward to announce
that she has given up all claim to Don Juan. Her gesture
leaves the way open for Don Juan to marry Sol, and because
such a marriage meets both the King's standards of justice and
Don Sancho's need for redress, the piece ends happily after all.

Rennert and Castro long ago suspected that *La mayor
virtud de un rey* might have autobiographical overtones.[11]
More recently, Joseph H. Silverman has shown quite convincingly that the play is, in fact, nothing but an elaborate
fantasy in which Lope re-creates to his own satisfaction the
episode that so embittered the last days of his life, the elopement of his daughter Antonia Clara with Cristóbal Tenorio,
a protégé of the Count-Duke of Olivares.[12] In this fantasy
Lope is, of course, Don Sancho; Antonia Clara, Sol; Cristóbal,
Don Juan. Interestingly, at the beginning of the play the
relationships between the characters and their modes of behavior are quite true to life. Later, however, as Silverman has
demonstrated in detail, a wave of idealizing displacement sets
in, and the ending of the story is transformed completely. The
outcome of the real elopement-abduction was quite pathetic.
The legal action that Lope took to secure the return of his
daughter was totally fruitless, an outcome that could be expected in view of Tenorio's connections at court, and Antonia
Clara remained with her abductor until he suddenly abandoned her to marry a woman of higher station.

What engages the attention in *La mayor virtud de un rey,*
obviously, is that Lope has here reverted to the wish-fulfillment
dreaming that characterizes such early plays as *Las ferias de
Madrid.* Between the two plays, however, there has been a
lifetime of experience, and thus the sentimental polarities in
the later work are completely reversed. In *Las ferias de Madrid,* Lope's sympathies attached themselves exclusively to the
young lovers, Leandro and Violante; the husband of the latter, Patricio, is the villain of the piece, the blocking character,
and at the end of the play he is dispatched with no great

remorse for being an obstacle to the course of true love. In *La mayor virtud de un rey*, however, it is honor, not love, that matters most. Lope's sympathies here are primarily, if not exclusively, with the ostensible blocking character, Don Sancho. To be sure, there is in this play no real villain: at this point in his life, Lope was not disposed to divide mankind into distinct and separate camps of the good and the bad. The person who is the most culpable is, nevertheless, clearly the abductor. Don Juan is reviled by Sol, by Don Sancho, and by his King, and at the end he is saved from the punishment he has legally merited only by the generosity of others. Was Lope able to see the irony in this? One wonders. The heroes of our youth shade imperceptibly into the culprits of our old age, and the dreams of May are seldom formally discarded but instead are merely modulated into the reveries of December.

It is doubtful that Lope ever stands much in need of humanizing. Of the world's great writers, he is one of those who most unceasingly present themselves to the imagination as both human being and artist. Nevertheless, one cannot read *La mayor virtud de un rey* without one's sense of Lope the man being freshened and deepened. We hear his voice speaking between the lines throughout the play, and it speaks so forcefully that we are not surprised that it should materialize at the end. Here, through the person of Don Sancho, Lope quite literally takes his farewell of the theater, and his moving words may serve with equal appropriateness as our farewell to him:

> Aquí, senado,
> con mis fortunas acaba
> *La mayor virtud de un rey.*
> El poeta no se cansa
> de serviros, aunque ya
> le jubilaban las canas:
> tan agradecido está
> a las mercedes pasadas.
> Dadle aplauso, y a nosotros
> el perdón de nuestras faltas.
>
> (*Ac.N.*, XII, 648b)

Conclusion

Noble public, here ends, along with my adventures, *La mayor virtud de un rey*. Although his gray hairs have already earned him retirement, the poet does not weary of serving you, so grateful is he for past favors. Give him your applause, and to us, pardon for our failings.

Appendix: Tentative Chronology of the Honor Plays of Lope de Vega

ANYONE who attempts to compile a list of Lope's honor plays, or for that matter any other type of play written by him, must surmount two formidable difficulties. There is, first of all, the problem of sheer numbers. Among the extant plays, about three hundred and forty are considered by modern scholars to be fully authentic, and some familiarity with all of them is a prerequisite to the drawing up of any kind of catalogue. There is no easy way to acquire that familiarity, although the necessary wide reading may be supplemented by the plot summaries provided in such more or less comprehensive studies as those of Grillparzer, Schack, Schaeffer, and Hennigs.[1] Even after he has provided himself with the proper acquaintance of his materials, however, the would-be cataloguer must still wrestle with the question, especially troublesome in the case of the honor plays, of definition. Virtually all of Lope's plays deal in some fashion with honor. Where, then, is one to draw the line between those works in which honor is simply a present and recognized value and those which may appropriately be called honor plays?

Past precedent is not of great help in solving this dilemma. To be sure, the term "honor play" has traditionally been reserved for those plays in which male honor is shown to rest upon female chastity, those plays, in other words, in which the honor of an important male character has been jeopardized through an attack, actual or threatened, upon the purity of a young woman to whom he is united by familial ties. This limitation is not really very limiting, however, for it allows one, in theory at least, to group together plays as disparate in theme, tone, and action as *La francesilla, La corona merecida,* and *Peribáñez.*

If the term "honor play" is to have any usefulness at all, it must be more restrictive. The definition that seems most helpful is the one used in this book. According to it, an honor play is a play in which the dramatic interest centers upon the dishonor suffered by the protagonist as the result of the actions of the leading female character, or those of the antagonist, or both, and upon the efforts of the protagonist to recover his lost honor; its characteristic progression is from honor to dishonor to honor once again. Examined in the light of this definition, certain works that are sometimes designated honor plays, or associated with those plays, are seen clearly to lie outside the range of the type. These works fall into five more or less well-defined groups.

The first is comprised of those plays in which the female lead is the daughter or sister of the male whose honor is wounded and which resolve the honor grievance with a marriage. Examples here are numerous: *La francesilla* (dated manuscript: April 6, 1596), *El leal criado* (dated manuscript: June 24, 1594), *El enemigo engañado* (1590–1598, perhaps 1593–1598), *El vaquero de Moraña* (1599–1603), *El mayor imposible* (1615), *Pobreza no es vileza* (1613–1622, probably 1620–1622), *No son todos ruiseñores* (ca. 1630), and so on. In these plays, of course, the theme of honor is subordinate to that of love, and they are appropriately classified with the *comedias amorosas* or the *comedias de capa y espada*.

The second group of works properly excluded from the catalogue of honor plays is considerably smaller. It is made up of those pieces—*El caballero del milagro* (dated manuscript: November [December?] 30, 1593), *El rústico del cielo* (1605?), *El gran duque de Moscovia* (1606?), *El cuerdo en su casa* (1606–1612, probably 1606–1608), and one or two others—in which an honor conflict is avoided by virtue of the fact that the dishonored male is unaware of his injury or deceived about the nature of it.

The third group incarnates the common chivalresque motif of the calumniated queen. In this group, a queen, or empress, or lady of high nobility, is falsely accused of adultery but, because of her high station, not put immediately to death; at the end of the piece her innocence is definitively proved and her virtue is celebrated. Although honor is a prominent motif in these plays, their interest for the spectator derives less from it than from what Castro has called the "exaltation of the character of a woman."[2] These works, in other words, are the obverse of honor plays: whereas honor plays focus upon, and extol, the masculine value of honor, these focus upon, and extol, the corresponding feminine value of *vergüenza*. Among the many examples are *El nacimiento de Ursón y Valentín* (1588–1595), *El testimonio vengado* (1596–1603), *Los pleitos de Ingalaterra* (1598–1603), *El gallardo catalán* (1599–1603), *La discordia en los casados* (dated manuscript: August 2, 1611), and *El animal de Hungría* (1608–1612, probably 1611–1612).

The fourth group is like the third in that a husband is led wrongly to suspect the chastity and fidelity of his wife. But in the plays of this group—*En los indicios la culpa* (1596?–1603), *La inocente Laura* (1604–1608), *El más galán portugués* (1608–1613, probably 1610–1612), and *Los peligros de la ausencia* (1613–1620, probably 1615–1618), for example—the leading characters are not kings and queens but humble people. A further distinction is that in works of this type the husband usually initiates a vengeance, or thinks about exacting one. Fortunately, before the vengeance can be realized the wife is shown to be guiltless, and a happy ending is achieved.

The fifth and last group is composed of plays that embody the motif of the constant wife, such as *La corona merecida* (1603), *La batalla del honor* (dated manuscript: April 18, 1608), and *La firmeza en la desdicha* (1610–1612). The action in each case here is identical: a wife who is a paragon of virtue and a model of fidelity is pursued, to no avail, by a king or a prince. By the end of the play the would-be seducer, who has been spared the vengeance of the offended husband only because he is of royal blood, is made to see the error of his ways, and the play closes happily. As in the previous two groups of plays, the stress in these works is more on feminine than on masculine values.

With these exclusions made, only two further words of explanation are required before listing the works that do qualify as honor plays. First, the list that follows, although based upon that given by Fichter in his edition of *El castigo del discreto,* differs considerably from it, both because Fichter includes only plays of "conjugal honor," (thus omitting such works as *Fuenteovejuna* and *El robo de Dina,* which are, according to my criteria, undeniably honor plays); and because, at the same time, he admits to his list a number of pieces that, for reasons outlined above, seem to me better omitted. Second, I include only those plays that appear either in Table A ("Authentic Plays") or Table B ("Plays Probably by Lope") of the Morley-Bruerton *Cronología.* (As Morley and Bruerton explain, there is no reason for doubting Lope's authorship of the plays in Table B, and they have been

kept separate from those in Table A only because they were not
printed in "authentic" volumes.) Certain plays that appear in
Table C, "Doubtful Plays," are from my point of view full-fledged
honor plays, and two or three of these (the case of *El toledano
vengado* was mentioned earlier) are conceded by Morley and
Bruerton very probably to have been written, at least in some early
version, by Lope. But, for purposes of consistency, these plays are
not included in the following list.

Las ferias de Madrid: 1585–1588
Los embustes de Fabia: before 1596 (probably 1588–1595)
Carlos el perseguido: dated manuscript: November 2, 1590
La bella malmaridada: dated manuscript: December 17, 1596
Los comendadores de Córdoba: 1596
El desposorio encubierto: 1597–1603
El castigo del discreto: September, 1598–January, 1601
El piadoso veneciano: 1599–1608
La contienda de García de Paredes: dated manuscript: February
  15, 1600
El príncipe despeñado: dated manuscript: November 27, 1602
La desdichada Estefanía: dated manuscript: November 12, 1604
Peribáñez y el Comendador de Ocaña: 1605–1612 (probably
  1605–1608)
La victoria de la honra: 1609–1615 (probably 1609–1612)
La locura por la honra: 1610–1612
Fuenteovejuna: 1611–1618 (probably 1612–1614)
El robo de Dina: 1615–1622
Porfiar hasta morir: 1624–1628
El castigo sin venganza: dated manuscript: August 1, 1631

Abbreviations
Notes
Index

AJFS	*Australian Journal of French Studies*
AUMLA	*Journal of the Australasian Universities Language and Literature Association*
B.A.E.	Biblioteca de Autores Españoles
BCom	*Bulletin of the Comediantes*
BH	*Bulletin Hispanique*
BHS	*Bulletin of Hispanic Studies*
CA	*Cuadernos Americanos*
CHA	*Cuadernos Hispanoamericanos*
Clás. Ca.	Clásicos Castalia
Clás. Cast.	Clásicos Castellanos
Clás. Lit. Esp.	Clásicos de Literatura Española
CLS	*Comparative Literature Studies*
EFil	*Estudios Filológicos*
FMLS	*Forum for Modern Language Studies*
Hispanó	*Hispanófila*
HR	*Hispanic Review*
KRQ	*Kentucky Romance Quarterly*
MLN	*Modern Language Notes*
MLR	*Modern Language Review*
MP	*Modern Philology*
N.B.A.E.	Nueva Biblioteca de Autores Españoles
NRFH	*Nueva Revista de Filología Hispánica*
Publ. U.C.L.A. Lang. and Lit.	Publications of the University of California at Los Angeles in Languages and Literature
REH-PR	*Revista de Estudios Hispánicos* (Puerto Rico)
RenD	*Renaissance Drama*
RF	*Romanische Forschungen*
RFE	*Revista de Filología Española*
RFH	*Revista de Filología Hispánica*
RH	*Revue Hispanique*
RJ	*Romanistisches Jahrbuch*
RO	*Revista de Occidente*
RR	*Romanic Review*
SP	*Studies in Philology*
TDR	*Tulane Drama Review*
Teat. Ant. Esp.	Teatro Antiguo Español
TQ	*Texas Quarterly*

Notes

1. Introduction: Honor and Honor Plays

1. Francis Fergusson, *The Idea of a Theater* (Princeton, Princeton University Press, 1949).

2. Cf. Bruce W. Wardropper: "Dramatically speaking, there is little difference between a *comedia de capa y espada* and a *drama de honor* because the same devices and motivations are used in each. Both dramatic genres rely on concealment of motivation, on eavesdropping, on mistaken identity, on confusion of all kinds. But there is one essential difference between them, a difference which prizes them as far apart as comedy and tragedy. The *comedia de capa y espada* presents unmarried couples, consequently, love not honor, is the predominant motivation" ("Poetry and Drama in Calderón's *El médico de su honra*," *RR*, 49 [1958], 7).

3. See, for example, the publisher's blurb on the cover of Calderón's *The Surgeon of His Honor*, trans. Roy Campbell (Madison, University of Wisconsin Press, 1960).

4. Cf. the following passage from Lope's *La Dorotea*, ed. Edwin S. Morby, 2nd ed. (Madrid, Castalia, 1968), pp. 250–251:

IUL.—Vna cosa hallé leyendo el libro tercero de Xenofonte, que me causó admiración, no lexos deste propósito.

LUD.—Pues que tú la encareces, será notable.

IUL.—Díxole Armenio a Ciro que no matauan los maridos a sus mugeres, quando las hallauan con los adúlteros, por la culpa de la ofensa, sino por la rabia de que les huuiessen quitado el amor y puéstole en otro.

LUD.—Estraño pensamiento!

The motive of jealousy in the plays of Lope and his followers has been studied by Horst Baader in "Die Eifersucht in der spanischen *Comedia* des goldenen Zeitalters," *RF*, 74 (1962), 318–344.

5. See especially: Jenaro Artiles, "La idea de la venganza en el drama español del siglo XVII," *Segismundo,* nos. 5–6 (1967), 9–38;

Francisco Ayala, "Sobre el punto de honor castellano," *RO*, 2nd ser. no. 5 (August 1963), 151–174; Julio Caro Baroja, "Honour and Shame: A Historical Account of Several Conflicts," in *Honour and Shame: The Values of a Mediterranean Society*, ed. J. G. Péristiany (Chicago, University of Chicago Press, 1966), rpt. in Span. trans. in the author's *La ciudad y el campo* (Madrid and Barcelona, Alfaguara, 1966); Américo Castro, "Algunas observaciones acerca del concepto del honor en los siglos XVI y XVII," *Semblanzas y estudios españoles* (Princeton, privately published, 1956), earlier published in *RFE*, 3 (1916), 1–50, 357–386; Américo Castro, *De la edad conflictiva*, 2nd ed. (Madrid, Taurus, 1963); Gustavo Correa, "El doble aspecto de la honra en el teatro del siglo XVII," *HR*, 26 (1958), 99–107; William L. Fichter, "A Study of Conjugal Honor in [Lope de Vega's] Theater," introd. to his ed. of *El castigo del discreto* (New York, Instituto de las Españas, 1925); Harri Meier, "A honra no drama românico dos séculos XVI e XVII," in *Ensaios de filologia românica* (Lisbon, Ediçao da "Revista de Portugal," 1948); Ramón Menéndez Pidal, "Del honor en el teatro español," in *De Cervantes y Lope de Vega* (Buenos Aires, Espasa-Calpe Argentina, 1940), pp. 153–184; A. Rubió y Lluch, *El sentimiento del honor en el teatro de Calderón* (Barcelona, Vda. e Hijos de Subirana, 1882); Encarnación-Irene Serrano Martínez, *"Honneur" y "honor": su significación a través de las literaturas francesa y española* (Murcia, Universidad de Murcia, 1956); Alfonso García Valdecasas, *El hidalgo y el honor*, 2nd ed. (Madrid, Revista de Occidente, 1958); and Antonie Adrianus van Beysterveldt, *Répercussions du souci de la pureté de sang sur la conception de l'honneur dans la "Comedia Nueva" espagnole* (Leiden, Brill, 1966). See also Jenaro Artiles, "Bibliografía sobre el problema del honor y la honra en el drama español," in *Filología y crítica hispánica: Homenaje al Prof. Federico Sánchez Escribano*, ed. Alberto Porqueras Mayo and Carlos Rojas (Madrid, Ediciones Alcalá, 1969).

6. Salvador de Madariaga, *Englishmen, Frenchmen, Spaniards: An Essay in Comparative Psychology* (London, Oxford University Press, 1928). Madariaga characterizes each of the three peoples of whom he speaks by their adhesion to a particular value, the three values being fair play for the English: *droit* for the French; and *honor* for the Spanish.

7. Cf. the *coplas* of Fernán Pérez de Guzmán, "De honor y consciencia" (quoted in Bartolomé de Torres Naharro, *"Propalladia" and Other Works*, ed. Joseph E. Gillet, IV [Philadelphia, University of Pennsylvania Press, 1961], 198):

> La honor e la consciencia
> assi son entre si varias,
> tan discordes e contrarias
> por valor e por clemencia,
> que conuiene a la prudencia,

para que bien las discerna,
que con muy clara lucerna
mire la su differencia.

. . . .

La honor nunca consiente
vn punto contra su fama,
nin cura de aquella flama
del infierno muy ardiente;
con gesto alegre e plaziente
la consciencia el rostro offrece
al golpe, que assi paresce
que del primero non siente.

8. Kathleen Gouldson, "Three Studies in Golden Age Drama," in *Spanish Golden Age Poetry and Drama*, Liverpool Studies in Spanish Literature, 2nd ser., ed. E. Allison Peers (Liverpool, Institute of Hispanic Studies, 1946), p. 107.

9. The difference between "sense of honor" and "honor" is roughly the same as that which is sometimes made in Spanish between *honor* and *honra*. While both terms have the meaning of "honor," as that word is used throughout this study, *honor* has on occasion the additional meaning, denied to *honra* both by usage and by the Spanish Academy, of conscience, probity, rectitude, and so on. Thus, the first definition of *honor* given in the dictionary of the Academy is "cualidad moral que nos lleva al más severo cumplimiento de nuestros deberes respecto del prójimo y de nosotros mismos." It is essential to note, however, that the word *honor* is rarely used with this acceptation in the *Comedia*. There, the forms *honor* and *honra*, while not totally interchangeable, refer basically to the same value. The distinction is not so much between separate qualities as between differing ways in which one essential quality may be regarded. It is a question of perspective, as Américo Castro points out in his discussion of the words in *De la edad conflictiva,* pp. 66–78. Castro's analysis is lengthy and dense, but centers on the main point that *honor* is principally "[una] noción ideal y objetiva," while *honra* is "el funcionamiento de esa misma noción, vitalmente realizada en un proceso de vida. El honor *es*, pero la honra pertenece a alguien, actúa y se está moviendo en una vida" (p. 69). On the use of the terms *honor* and *honra* in the Spanish theater, see also Gillet, ed., "*Propalladia*," IV, 191–192, and van Beysterveldt, *Répercussions,* pp. 30–47.

10. The word *fama* is, to be sure, frequently employed in the *Comedia* as a synonym for "honor." When so used, however, context makes it apparent that what is being talked about is not fame in the usual sense of the word.

11. Cf. the following strophes from the *Libro de Apolonio* (quoted by María Rosa Lida de Malkiel in *La idea de la fama en la edad media castellana* [Mexico City and Buenos Aires, Fondo de Cultura Econó-

mica, 1952], p. 165), in which honor is clearly, although implicitly, distinguished from fame:

> Fijo, dixo el maestro, dizes me grant amor,
> nunca fijo a su padre podrie dezir meior;
> si tú esto fazes acabas gran honor,
> de quanto metges oy biuen tú eres el mejor.
>
> Nunca morrá tu nombre si tú esto fizieres,
> de mí aurás gran honrra mientre que tú visquieres;
> en tu vida aurás honrra, e después que murieres
> fablarán de tu seso varones e mugieres.

12. Castro, *De la edad conflictiva*, p. 154.

13. Citations of Lope's dramatic works are, unless otherwise indicated, from the so-called Academy edition, published in two series: *Obras de Lope de Vega*, ed. Marcelino Menéndez y Pelayo, 15 vols. (Madrid, Real Academia Española, 1890–1913); and *Obras de Lope de Vega (nueva edicion)*, ed. Emilio Cotarelo y Mori et al., 13 vols. (Madrid, Real Academia Española, 1916–1930). All quotations have been checked against authoritative modern editions, where they exist, and I have on occasion accepted alternative readings from those editions, just as I have consistently corrected the obvious misprints of the Academy editions and their sometimes awkward punctuation. The former emendations are acknowledged in the notes; the latter are not. As is well known, the two Academy series differ considerably in such respects as format and guiding editorial principles. The first series, for example, capitalizes the first letter of each verse and marks stanzaic divisions with indentations; the second series does neither. In the interest of consistency, I have followed throughout the practice of the second series in these matters. I have not, however, otherwise attempted to regularize the disparities between the two series. I use the abbreviation *Ac.* to indicate the first series, *Ac. N.* to indicate the second, and where I cite repeatedly from a particular play, I have usually given the volume number only once, with the first citation.

14. Passages similar to that quoted are not difficult to find in the *Comedia*. Castro reproduces several in his fundamental "Algunas observaciones," as does William L. Fichter in the introduction to his edition of Lope's *El castigo del discreto*. See also Ricardo del Arco y Garay, *La sociedad española en las obras dramáticas de Lope de Vega* (Madrid, Escelicer, 1942), pp. 441–462.

15. See, particularly, Frederick Bryson, *The Point of Honor in Sixteenth-Century Italy: An Aspect of the Life of the Gentleman* (Chicago, privately published, 1935); George Fenwick Jones, *Honor in German Literature* (Chapel Hill, University of North Carolina Press, 1959); and Curtis Brown Watson, *Shakespeare and the Renaissance Concept of Honor* (Princeton, Princeton University Press, 1960).

16. For a discussion of the term "shame culture," and a fascinating analysis of one such culture, see Ruth Benedict, *The Chrysanthemum and the Sword: Patterns of Japanese Culture* (1946; rpt. New York, Meridian-World, 1967).

17. Julian Pitt-Rivers, "Honour and Social Status," in *Honour and Shame,* p. 38. It is interesting to note that, as C. B. Watson points out, in the opinion of many Renaissance thinkers for an individual to feel or affect indifference toward society's evaluation of him was not simply an eccentricity but a sin tantamount to pride (see *Shakespeare and the Renaissance Concept of Honor,* pp. 67–68).

18. Aristotle, *Ethics,* Bk. VIII, Ch. xiv.

19. Thomas Hobbes, *Leviathan,* Pt. I, Ch. x.

20. Benedict, *The Chrysanthemum and the Sword,* pp. 212–218.

21. Those for whom Aristotle's words were a true expression of at least some part of their own thoughts on honor were the Humanists, the Erasmians, and men of similar persuasion (such as Cervantes and the anonymous author of *Lazarillo de Tormes*). They made up a small but outspoken minority in the sixteenth and early seventeenth centuries, asserting over and over that the only legitimate honor was that which resulted from virtue and attacking what León Hebreo in the *Diálogos de amor* called "El [honor] bastardo . . . el lisonjeador de la potencia" (quoted in Gillet, ed., "*Propalladia,*" IV, 194). See also Américo Castro, *El pensamiento de Cervantes* (Madrid, Hernando, 1925), pp. 366ff.

22. See Correa, "El doble aspecto de la honra en el teatro del siglo XVII."

23. Castro's documentation of this point in *De la edad conflictiva* is so thorough that it needs no buttressing, but there is a particularly interesting confirmation in an anonymous document of the Golden Age reproduced in Antonio Domínguez Ortiz, *La clase social de los conversos en Castilla en la edad moderna* (Madrid, Consejo Superior de Investigaciones Científicas, 1955), pp. 229–231. The relevant portion reads as follows: "En España ay dos generos de Noblezas. Una mayor, que es la Hidalguía, y otra menor, que es la limpieza, que llamamos Christianos viejos. Y aunque la primera de la Hidalguía es mas honrado de tenerla; pero muy mas afrentoso es faltar la segunda: porque en España mas estimamos a un hombre pechero y limpio que a un hidalgo que no es limpio."

Naturally, there were people in Spain who refused to believe that nobility of blood could count for less than purity. They were often precisely those whose distinguished ancestry had come under suspicion of "uncleanliness." Although this group was not notably vocal in its opinions, it is clear that it felt both disdainful toward, and threatened by, those who claimed indisputable purity. Some of this feeling comes through in Lope's rural plays, especially *Peribáñez* and *Fuenteovejuna,* where there is frequently an undercurrent of hostility in the conversation between the "unclean" noble and the "pure" peasants (see, for instance, the quotation on pp. 11–12 of this chapter).

24. See, among Castro's works, the following three books especially: *La realidad histórica de España,* 3rd ed. (Mexico City, Porrúa, 1966), *"Español," palabra extranjera: razones y motivos* (Madrid, Taurus, 1970), and *Los españoles: cómo llegaron a serlo* (Madrid, Taurus, 1965). The last is a revised edition of *Origen, ser y existir de los españoles* (Madrid, Taurus, 1959).

25. Cf. the following words of Lope de Rueda, quoted in Lida de Malkiel, *La idea de la fama,* p. 236n82: "En eso se aventajan los hombres de los hombres: en hacer más y valer más y sufrir más." The concept of *valer más* is examined in some detail in Caro Baroja, "Honour and Shame."

26. See *El Conde Lucanor,* XXV: "De lo que contescio al conde de Provencia commo fue librado de la prision por el consejo que le dio Saladin."

27. The notion that the honor of the man is affected by the purity of his female dependents is not, of course, peculiar to Spain. It is found, on occasion, in the literature of most Mediterranean countries, particularly in the Renaissance period, and it was not unknown in England (see the studies of Bryson, *The Point of Honor in Sixteeth-Century Italy,* and Watson, *Shakespeare and the Renaissance Concept of Honor,* passim; also E. M. Wilson, "Family Honour in the Plays of Shakespeare's Predecessors and Contemporaries," in *Essays and Studies, 1953* [London, John Murray, 1953]). It would seem, however, that in no other country—except, perhaps, Italy in the sixteenth century where, if we accept the suggestion of Burckhardt, the phenomenon reflects Spanish influence (*The Civilization of the Renaissance in Italy: An Essay* [London, Phaidon, 1960], p. 272)—has the honor of the male been so closely identified with the chastity of the women of his family.

28. See, for example, Wardropper, "Poetry and Drama," pp. 7–8. The explanation has the apparent authority of Golden Age authors behind it. See Miguel de Cervantes, *El ingenioso hidalgo Don Quixote de la Mancha,* ed. Francisco Rodríguez Marín, 7th ed., III, Clas. Cast., 8 (Madrid, Espasa-Calpe, 1962), 197–198), and Mateo Alemán, *Guzmán de Alfarache,* ed. Samuel Gili y Gaya, II, Clás. Cast., 83 (Madrid, La Lectura, 1927), 29.

29. See Ayala, "Sobre el punto de honor castellano," pp. 156–157.

30. Following the edition of Francisco López Estrada (*Fuente Ovejuna* [*dos comedias*], Clás. Ca., 10 [Madrid, Castalia, 1969]), I have here restored the reading of the *Dozena Parte.* The Academy edition amends at this point to "Cuando es mal / más tiñe que alimpia."

31. Since public opinion was thus the more or less exclusive arbiter of questions of honor and dishonor, it might seem to follow that an

insult dealt in private need be of no special concern to the individual. And no doubt in theory that was true. Such insults were rarely overlooked, however, because there was always a possibility that other people would somehow learn of the offense. Of course, an affront given without witnesses would also be avenged without witnesses. No man was interested in giving needless publicity to the wounding of his honor. Cf. Calderón's play *A secreto agravio, secreta venganza.*

32. See Fredson Bowers, *Elizabethan Revenge Tragedy, 1587–1642* (Princeton, Princeton University Press, 1940), pp. 3–8.

33. See Menéndez Pidal, "Del honor en el teatro español," pp. 159–162, and Correa, "El doble aspecto de la honra en el teatro del siglo XVII." The latter establishes a plausible relation between the social dimension of honor and its frequently noted ritualistic aspect: "Como imperativo de conducta la restauración de la honra implica un deber de carácter ritual y sacrosanto con el ofrecimiento de una víctima propiciatoria (el ofensor) a una oscura divinidad ofendida. Esta última no es otra que la sociedad misma, es decir, la peculiar estructura social que hace sentir su presencia a través del denso símbolo de la honra. La sociedad se santifica a sí misma y al santificarse confiere un matiz de religiosidad al símbolo que la expresa" (p. 105). The religiosity of honor is examined from a different point of view by Peter N. Dunn in "Honour and the Christian Background in Calderón," *BHS*, 37 (1960), 75–105, reprinted in Bruce W. Wardropper, ed., *Essays on the Theatre of Calderón* (New York, New York University Press, 1965).

34. As has been pointed out by Galo Sánchez, the laws and customs of the period did not simply permit the vengeance of the man whose wife had committed adultery, but actually had the effect of coercing him into the deed ("Datos jurídicos acerca de la venganza del honor," *RFE*, 4 [1917], 292–295). One of the documents discussed by Sánchez is the *Tractado muy probechoso, útil y necessario de los jueces y orden de los juicios y penas criminales* by Antonio de la Peña, a lawyer of Valladolid who had also served as a judge. In this work of about 1571, Peña considers, among other things, the punishments meted out to husbands who condone adultery. He writes as follows: "Lo que hoy en nuestro reyno se platica [*sic*] es que sacan al marido y a la muger caballeros en sendos asnos, él desnudo y delante y ella vestida un poco detrás con una restria de ajos en la mano; y en diciendo el verdugo 'quien tal haze que tal pague,' ella le da y açota con la restra de ajos; y ansí le vemos cada día executa esta pena, con algún destierro que se les da." Certain *fueros* of the time had provisions specifically exempting from chastisement those who took action against "complacent husbands" (see Sánchez, "Datos," pp. 294–295, and Artiles, "La idea de la venganza," pp. 14–17). Such laws do not appear to have existed in other European countries where, with the possible exception of Italy, the attitude toward vengeance

was decidedly more ambivalent. See Bowers, *Elizabethan Revenge Tragedy*, pp. 49–57, and Watson, *Shakespeare and the Renaissance Concept of Honor*, pp. 159–162.

35. Recently, the question has been asked—repeatedly—whether this approbation is genuine, that is, meant to be shared by the audience. The question seems not to have occurred to the critics and readers of earlier generations, who took it for granted that the dénuements of the plays were to be accepted at face value. The last few decades, however, have seen the emergence and increasing acceptance of a new school of thought about the endings of the honor plays. In the opinion of this revisionist school, the final scenes of the plays, while *seeming* to affirm the individual's acquiescence in the demands of honor, actually constitute a condemnation of that acquiescence. The interpretation depends on an ingenious and "ironic" reading of those scenes. Thus, in the instance of *El médico de su honra*, it is argued that the King's celebration of the deed of the hero, Gutierre, ordinarily in the Golden Age theater a reflection of the approval that the author expected his audience to feel, is here instead a kind of implicit criticism or reprobation. The argument rests primarily on the fact that the King in this case is the famous Peter I of Castile, sometimes called Pedro el Cruel. How, the revisionist critics ask, could the words of such a king be expected to have any kind of objective validity? But Peter is also known as Pedro el Justiciero, a point ignored for the most part by those critics. Furthermore, as A. Irvine Watson has shown, it is principally the just side of Peter that Calderón presents in the play ("Peter the Cruel or Peter the Just," *RJ*, 14 [1963], 322–346). Limitations of space prohibit here a full-scale consideration of the "new" interpretation of *El médico de su honra* and of Calderón's honor plays in general. I would like, however, to enter my basic agreement with Albert S. Gérard, who has written of the "ironic" readings of *El médico* as follows: "Apart from the fact that such large-scale ambiguity is most unlikely in seventeenth-century tragedy, there is an a priori reason for considering any such interpretations with a great deal of suspicion ... The structure of the Spanish *comedia* is based on a movement which carries it 'from order disturbed to order restored,' so that the development of the plot, and especially its *desenlace* is commanded by the principle of poetic justice. If Calderón had considered Gutierre as a criminal, he would in all likelihood have seen to it that he was suitably punished in the end ... But the medical metaphor of the title suggests that the theme of the play is really a restoration of order and that the principle of this order is honor as Gutierre himself understands it" ("The Loving Killers: The Rationale of Righteousness in Baroque Tragedy," *CLS*, 2 [1965], 220).

36. C. A. Jones, "*Honor* in Spanish Golden-Age Drama: Its Relation to Real Life and to Morals," *BHS*, 35 (1958), 206.

37. Ibid., p. 200.

38. On the dispute over the defensibility of vengeance see, particularly, Castro, "Algunas observaciones," pp. 350–354, 368–382.

39. The diary, the work of Mosén Juan Porcar, was published in 1934 under the title *Coses evengudes en la civtat y regne de Valencia.* Its contents have been summarized by Amédée Mas in *La caricature de la femme, du mariage et de l'amour dans l'oeuvre de Quevedo* (Paris, Ediciones Hispano-Americanas, 1957), pp. 348–352.

40. Margaret Wilson, *Spanish Drama of the Golden Age* (Oxford, Pergamon, 1969), p. 46.

41. Aubrey F. G. Bell, *Castilian Literature* (Oxford, Clarendon Press, 1938), p. 188. Cf. Charles Vincent Aubrun: "¿Cuáles son, pues, las relaciones del teatro con la realidad española del siglo XVII? La refleja y la deforma a la vez; ordena datos dispersos de la experiencia vivida en un mundo ficticio, al que propone como modelo o 'patrón' de la sociedad" (*La comedia española* [*1600–1680*], trans. Julio Lago Alonso [Madrid, Taurus, 1968], p. 11).

42. "Los casos de la honra son mejores, / porque mueven con fuerza a toda gente"

43. It should be noted that Jones's ideas on honor changed somewhat over the years. In addition to "*Honor* in Spanish Golden-Age Drama," see "Spanish Honour as Historical Phenomenon, Convention and Artistic Motive," *HR,* 33 (1965), 32–39.

2. *Early Plays: Comic Solutions to the Conflict of Honor*

1. The idea seems to derive from the influential, and in some ways still important, article of Donald C. Stuart, "Honor in the Spanish Drama," *RR,* 1 (1910), 247–258.

2. See Ramón Menéndez Pidal, "Del honor en el teatro español," in *De Cervantes y Lope de Vega* (Buenos Aires, Espasa-Calpe Argentina, 1940), pp. 165–169.

3. The work is thus dated by J. P. Wickersham Crawford in *Spanish Drama before Lope de Vega,* rev. ed. (Philadelphia, University of Pennsylvania Press, 1967). Joseph E. Gillet has affixed the more precise date of 1516 in his edition of Torres Naharro's "*Propalladia*" *and Other Works,* IV (Philadelphia, University of Pennsylvania Press, 1961), 476. Unless otherwise indicated, all datings of pre-Lopean plays in this chapter are from Crawford.

4. On the sixteenth- and seventeenth-century imitations of the *Celestina* see, especially, Marcelino Menéndez y Pelayo, *Orígenes de la novela,* III, N.B.A.E., 14 (Madrid, Bailly-Baillière, 1910), and María Rosa Lida de Malkiel, *La originalidad artística de "La Celestina"* (Buenos Aires, E.U.D.E.B.A., 1962), passim.

5. Crawford, *Spanish Drama before Lope de Vega,* esp. pp. 96–100.

6. See, for example, the *Comedia Tesorina* of Jayme de Güete

(ca. 1535?) and the *Comedia Tidea* (before 1550) of Francisco de las Natas.

7. *Teatro español del siglo XVI,* ed. Urban Cronan (Madrid, Sociedad de Bibliófilos Madrileños, 1913), p. 264.

8. Gillet, ed., *"Propalladia,"* IV, 520.

9. The matter is discussed in Américo Castro, *"La Celestina" como contienda literaria (castas y casticismos)* (Madrid, Revista de Occidente, 1965), pp. 67–92.

10. Menéndez y Pelayo, *Orígenes de la novela,* III, 52b.

11. See Alfredo Hermenegildo, *Los trágicos españoles del siglo XVI* (Madrid, Publicaciones de la Fundación Universitaria, 1961), and Othón Arróniz, *La influencia italiana en el nacimiento de la comedia española* (Madrid, Gredos, 1969).

12. *Obras sueltas,* ed. Conde de la Viñaza (Madrid, M. Tello, 1889), I, 246.

13. See Fredson Bowers, *Elizabethan Revenge Tragedy, 1587–1642* (Princeton, Princeton University Press, 1940), esp. pp. 279–281.

14. S. Griswold Morley and Courtney Bruerton, *Cronología de las comedias de Lope de Vega* (Madrid, Gredos, 1968). This is a revised edition of the authors' earlier *Chronology of Lope de Vega's "Comedias"* (New York, Modern Language Association of America, 1940).

15. I consider "fully authentic" only those plays that appear in either Table A or Table B of the Appendix to the Morley-Bruerton *Cronología.* See my Appendix.

16. See *El castigo del discreto,* ed. William L. Fichter (New York, Instituto de las Españas, 1925), pp. 17–27.

17. A manuscript in the so-called Gálvez collection indicates precisely when the play was finished: December 17, 1596. For a description of this collection, and an appreciation of the overwhelming support it gives to the Morley-Bruerton dating by versification, see Agustín G. de Amezúa, *Una colección manuscrita y desconocida de comedias de Lope de Vega Carpio* (Madrid, Real Academia Española, 1945).

18. See the prologue of Emilio Cotarelo y Mori to *Ac. N.,* III, xxv–xxvi.

19. *Novelas a la Señora Marcia Leonarda,* ed. John D. Fitz-Gerald and Leora A. Fitz-Gerald, in *RF,* 34 (1913–1915), 365–366. Emphasis mine.

20. It is interesting to note that in *La desdicha por la honra,* another of the *Novelas a la Señora Marcia Leonarda,* Lope appears to disassociate himself also from the doctrine of *limpieza.* The novella relates the adventures of Felisardo, a young Spaniard living in Italy at the beginning of the seventeenth century. Felisardo had always considered himself a *cristiano viejo,* but while in the service of the Viceroy of Sicily he learns, suddenly, that he is actually of *morisco* origin. He decides that he has no choice but to abandon the country

184

at once. He does not wish to leave his patron without some explanation, however, and thus he writes to the Viceroy, telling how he came to lose his honor. Shortly after, he receives from the Viceroy the following reply to his letter: "Felisardo: Vos me aueys seruido tan bien, y procedido tan honradamente en todas vuestras acciones, que me siento obligado a quereros y estimaros mucho; *en el nacer no merecen ni desmerecen los hombres, que no está en su mano: en las costumbres si, que ser buenas o malas corre por su cuenta.* Hazedme gusto de boluer a Sicilia, que os doy palabra, por vida de mis hijos, de hazer de vos mayor estimacion que hasta aqui, y tomar en mi honra qualquiera cosa que sucediere contra la vuestra; y no se yo porque aueis de estar corrido, siendo como soys cauallero, pues no lo está el Principe de Fez en Milan, siruiendo a su Magestad con vn habito de Santiago en los pechos . . . ; *porque la diferencia de las leyes no ofende la nobleza de la sangre,* y mas en los que ya tienen la verdadera, que es la nuestra, como vos la teneys, y confirmada por tantos años. Bolued, pues, Felisardo" (*Novelas,* pp. 323–324; emphasis mine).

In a typically stimulating article ("*La desdicha por la honra:* génesis y sentido de una novela de Lope," *NRFH,* 1 [1947], 13–42; rpt. in *Varia lección de clásicos españoles* [Madrid, Gredos, 1964]), Marcel Bataillon writes that Lope's sympathy for Felisardo in this story and his implied criticism of the revered value of *limpieza de sangre* might well have autobiographical implications. He suggests that Lope was himself lacking in *limpieza* or, what amounted to virtually the same thing as far as all practical consequences were concerned, that people felt that he was so lacking. In defense of his hypothesis, Bataillon marshalls a number of arguments, among them the fact that although Lope maneuvered for years to receive the habit of one of the great military orders, he was never given the coveted honor, and the fact that in the play *La villana de Getafe* (1610–1614), the hero, who bears a certain resemblance to Felisardo and who suffers dishonor as the result of lies about his ancestry, is called don Félix del Carpio and has, moreover, a manservant named Lope. Following up Bataillon's article, Diane J. Pamp demonstrates in a recent monograph that, although quite probably of pure *cristiano viejo* stock, Lope suffered all his adult life from rumors about his lineage, and that these rumors were the cause of the diatribes that appear in many of his works against those who indulge in libel and slander. See *Lope de Vega ante el problema de la limpieza de sangre* (Northampton, Mass., Smith College, 1968).

21. On Lope's life see the standard biography of Hugo A. Rennert and Américo Castro, *Vida de Lope de Vega (1562–1635)* (Madrid, Sucesores de Hernando, 1919; rpt. with additions and corrections by Fernando Lázaro Carreter, Salamanca, Anaya, 1968).

22. These plays are among those studied in Richard F. Glenn's perceptive article, "The Loss of Identity: Towards a Definition of the

Dialectic in Lope's Early Drama," *HR*, 41 (1973), 609–626. See also Richard W. Tyler, "False Accusation of Women in Plays 'Probably by Lope' de Vega," *BCom*, 17 (1965), 13–15.

23. Date from the revised edition of the Morley-Bruerton *Cronología*. Hereafter, unless otherwise indicated, all dates for Lope's plays are from this work.

24. The source of the plot of *Las ferias* has been a matter of some dispute. In "*Las ferias de Madrid* de Lope de Vega," *BH*, 57 (1955), 56–69, Courtney Bruerton advances the hypothesis that the play is based on a story of the Italian *novellista* Giovan Francesco Straparola. As Rinaldo Froldi has pointed out, however, Lope's play and the story of Straparola have little in common except the fact that in both there is a cuckolded husband who, through happenstance, learns of his dishonor from the very lips of his wife's seducer (see *Lope de Vega y la formación de la comedia* [Salamanca, Anaya, 1968], p. 142). In "The Comic Treatment of Conjugal Honor in Lope's *Las ferias de Madrid*," *HR*, 41 (1973), 33–42, Donald McGrady suggests a more plausible source. It is a versified story by the Licenciate Tamariz entitled *Novela de un estudiante y una dama*. The novella, which for many years existed only in manuscript, has recently been edited and published by McGrady himself. See Cristóbal de Tamariz, *Novelas en verso*, ed. Donald McGrady (Charlottesville, Biblioteca Siglo de Oro, 1974).

25. Emilio Cotarelo y Mori, ed., *Ac.N.*, V, xxviii.

26. Northrop Frye, *Anatomy of Criticism: Four Essays* (Princeton, Princeton University Press, 1957), p. 180.

27. Menéndez Pidal, "Del honor en el teatro español," p. 176.

28. See, however, McGrady, "The Comic Treatment of Conjugal Honor." Working independently, McGrady and I have arrived at conclusions about *Las ferias* that are in certain respects quite similar. The amount of overlap present in our two analyses is, however, minimal, for McGrady is interested primarily in the comic business of the play and I am interested primarily in its comic structure and characterizations.

29. Frye, *Anatomy*, p. 163. Frye's formulation is expressed in a slightly different fashion in *A Natural Perspective: The Development of Shakespearean Comedy and Romance* (New York, Columbia University Press, 1965), pp. 72ff.

30. In his obsessive jealousy of his wife, Patricio demonstrates the tendency of the blocking character to act "absurdly." Frye relates this type of absurdity to the Elizabethan theory of the "humor," and comments: "The humor's dramatic function is to express a state of what might be called ritual bondage. He is obsessed by his humor, and his function in the play is primarily to repeat his obsession. A sick man is not a humor, but a hypochondriac is, because, *qua* hypochondriac, he can never admit to good health, and can never do

anything inconsistent with the role that he has prescribed for himself" (*Anatomy,* p. 168). According to Henri Bergson, it is precisely the obsessive, rigid, mechanical behavior of the humors that makes them risible, for laughter is society's way of protecting itself against conduct it regards as dangerous by reason of being insufficiently flexible. See "Laughter," in *Comedy,* ed. Wylie Sypher (Garden City, N.Y., Doubleday, 1956), p. 150.

31. Fichter would seem to agree: "However immoral the ending of [*Las ferias de Madrid*] may seem to us, it must have appeared inevitable and just to the seventeenth century spectator, once the husband had dishonored the vacillating father by accusing him of connivance in the intrigue" (*El castigo del discreto,* p. 64).

32. On the ritual origin of comedy, see, especially, Francis Macdonald Cornford, *The Origin of Attic Comedy,* ed. Theodore H. Gaster (Garden City, N.Y., Doubleday, 1961) and Jane Ellen Harrison, *Themis: A Study of the Social Origins of Greek Religion* (1912; rpt. Cleveland, Meridian-World, 1962). On the origins of tragedy, also widely assumed to stem from ancient ritual, the fundamental study is Gilbert Murray's "Excursus on the Ritual Forms Preserved in Greek Tragedy," intercalated in Harrison's *Themis.* A useful introduction to the approach of the "Cambridge Anthropologists" to ancient drama is found in Gaster's preface to the Cornford volume. While basically sympathetic to the ideas of that school, Gaster points out the objections that have been raised to the extreme or too precise application of those ideas.

33. *Ac.,* VII, 551b. The play is *El vaquero de Moraña* (1599–1603). The idea here expressed was, of course, a commonplace in the *Comedia.* See Ernest H. Templin, *The Exculpation of "Yerros por Amores" in the Spanish Comedia,* Publ. U.C.L.A. Lang. and Lit., I, no. 1 (Berkeley, University of California Press, 1933).

34. For a brief account of what is now known about this affair, see the first part of Joaquín de Entrambasaguas's article "Los famosos 'Libelos contra unos cómicos,' de Lope de Vega," now reprinted with corrections in the author's *Estudios sobre Lope de Vega,* III (Madrid, Consejo Superior de Investigaciones Científicas, 1958), 7–74.

35. See Edwin S. Morby, "Persistence and Change in the Formation of *La Dorotea,*" *HR,* 18 (1950), 109–125, and 195–217, and the monumental work of Alan S. Trueblood, *Experience and Artistic Expression in Lope de Vega: The Making of "La Dorotea"* (Cambridge, Mass., Harvard University Press, 1974).

36. Froldi, *Lope de Vega y la formación de la comedia,* pp. 143–145.

3. Plays of the Middle Period: Vengeance Celebrated

1. For a justification of the date assigned see S. Griswold Morley and Courtney Bruerton, "*Addenda* to the Chronology of Lope de

Vega's *Comedias*," *HR*, 15 (1947), 57. Certain scholars have preferred to believe that the date of the play is earlier than that proposed by Morley and Bruerton. Among these is María Goyri de Menéndez Pidal. In her article "La Celia de Lope de Vega," *NRFH*, 4 (1950), 347–390, rpt. in *De Lope de Vega y del Romancero* (Zaragoza, Librería General, 1953), she argues for the date 1593, basing her case on the fact, among others, that a play with the title *Los comendadores* is known to have been produced in that year. It is, however, by no means necessary to assume that the play of 1593 and Lope's play, mentioned in the first *Peregrino* list and published in the second *Parte*, are one and the same, since it was not uncommon in the Golden Age for plays by different authors to carry identical or nearly identical titles. In their reply to María Goyri ("Lope de Vega, Celia, y *Los comendadores de Córdoba*," *NRFH*, 6 [1952], 57–68), Morley and Bruerton thus refuse to yield the point and, after weighing once again the relevant evidence, reaffirm 1596 as the date of composition. Their argument seems irrefutable.

2. In *El desposorio encubierto* (1597–1603), the husband decides to take no vengeance, the reason being that no one knows that he is married. I know of no other drama of the middle or late periods, whether honor play or not, in which a husband fails to take vengeance on a wife he is certain is guilty of an improper act or thought. Somewhat strangely, however, there are four plays in which guilty wives go unpunished, either because the husbands are unaware of their dishonor or because they have been led to believe that the truth is not what it seems. The four plays are: *El esclavo de Roma* (1596–1603), *El rústico del cielo* (1605?), *El santo negro Rosambuco* (before 1607), and *El cuerdo en su casa* (1606–1612, probably 1606–1608). The first play is a dramatization of the story of Androcles and the lion; the second and third are both *comedias de santos*. In all three pieces, honor is so unimportant an element that they are largely irrelevant here. The case of the last play, *El cuerdo en su casa*, is somewhat more interesting. Here, a guilty wife and her would-be seducer escape the punishment they deserve because the woman's rather foolish husband is persuaded that the man he saw in his house was actually a suitor of one of the servants. As William L. Fichter points out in his edition of *El castigo del discreto* (New York, Instituto de las Españas, 1925), p. 68, the play is reminiscent of such *entremeses* as Cervantes's *El viejo celoso*. It would be interesting to know how this farcical treatment of the theme of honor was received by the public of its time. We may suppose that it was not very popular, judging from the fact that Lope never again attempted a play of this type.

3. The relevant portions of these documents have been published by Emilio Cotarelo y Mori in his edition of the *Cancionero de Antón de Montoro* (Madrid, José Perales y Martínez, 1900), pp. 316–325,

and Marcelino Menéndez y Pelayo in the *Estudios sobre el teatro de Lope de Vega,* ed. Enrique Sánchez Reyes, V, Edición Nacional de las Obras Completas de Menéndez y Pelayo, 33 (Santander, Aldus, 1949), 249–285.

4. See Dámaso Alonso and José M. Blecua, *Antología de la poesía española: poesía de tipo tradicional* (Madrid, Gredos, 1956), pp. 227–228, and José María Alín, *El cancionero español de tipo tradicional* (Madrid, Taurus, 1968), p. 305.

5. See Margit Frenk Alatorre, "Un desconocido cantar de los Comendadores, fuente de Lope," in *Homenaje a William L. Fichter: Estudios sobre el teatro antiguo hispánico y otros ensayos,* ed. A. David Kossoff and José Amor y Vázquez (Madrid, Castalia, 1971).

6. Did Lope draw on still another source for *Los comendadores de Córdoba?* In his edition of the *Seiscientas apotegmas y otras obras en verso de Juan Rufo* (Madrid, Sociedad de Bibliófilos Españoles, 1923), Amezúa maintains that he did (see pp. lxxii–lxxxi). The source Amezúa designates is one of the several *casos* included in a curious and fascinating book known by several titles, principally *Libro de cosas notables que han sucedido en la ciudad de Córdoba, y a sus hijos en diversos tiempos.* So far as has been determined, the book remained unprinted until this century, when it was edited by Angel González Palencia (Madrid, Sociedad de Bibliófilos Españoles, 1949); none of the five known manuscript versions carries either the name of the author or the date of composition. A comparison of the *caso* from the *Libro de cosas notables* (no. 86 in the edition of González Palencia) with Lope's play, reveals that there are indeed remarkable similarities; in fact, the two authors tell the story of Fernán Alfonso, the Veinticuatro de Córdoba, in nearly identical fashion. At first glance Amezúa's thesis thus seems quite plausible. But there is need for caution. For numerous allusions in the *Libro* indicate that a substantial portion of the text, if not the entire book, was written some years after the composition of *Los comendadores de Córdoba.* The best guess, in fact, and the one made by González Palencia, is that the *Libro* dates from around 1618. In light of this it seems reasonable to conclude, as María Goyri de Menéndez Pidal has done ("La Celia de Lope de Vega," p. 369), that, rather than constituting a source of Lope's play, the anonymous *caso* is actually a paraphrase of the play.

7. Ed. G. de Amezúa, p. 207.

8. Ibid., pp. 202–203.

9. The fall from horseback is also a favored symbolic device in the plays of Calderón (see, particularly, Ángel Valbuena Briones, "Simbolismo: la caída del caballo," in *Perspectiva crítica de los dramas de Calderón* [Madrid, Ediciones Rialp, 1965], pp. 35–53; also Gwynne Edwards's edition of Calderón's *La hija del aire* [London, Tamesis, 1970], pp. xli–xlii, and Alan Soons, "The Convergence of Doctrine

and Symbol in *El médico de su honra,*" *RF,* 72 [1960], 371). In both Lope and Calderón, the fall is usually accepted by the characters themselves as a bad omen. Cf. *Peribáñez:* "Por mal agüero he tomado / que caiga el Comendador" (*Ac.,* X, 114a). The symbol of horse and rider is, I hardly need say, traditional in folklore. It has been analyzed at length by C. G. Jung in *Symbols of Transformation,* trans. R. F. C. Hull (New York, Harper, 1956), II, 274–282.

10. See A. A. Parker: "Spanish dramatic plots are constructed on the principle of poetic justice . . . In real life evil men may prosper and virtuous men may suffer. But in literature it was, in seventeenth-century Spain, considered fitting that wrongdoing should not go unpunished and that virtue should not remain unrewarded" ("The Approach to the Spanish Drama of the Golden Age," *TDR,* 4, no. 1 [1959], 44–45).

11. Menéndez y Pelayo annotates: "No es verso ni hace sentido. Acaso escribiría Lope: 'Tal es cojo, tal es ciego.' "

12. On the topos of the Theater of the World, so popular with artists and writers in the sixteenth and seventeenth centuries, see, especially, Jackson I. Cope, *The Theater and the Dream: From Metaphor to Form in Renaissance Drama* (Baltimore, Johns Hopkins Press, 1973); Frank J. Warnke, "The World as Theatre: Baroque Variations on a Traditional Topos," in *Festschrift für Edgar Mertner,* ed. Bernhard Fabian and Ulrich Suerbaum (Munich, Wilhelm Fink, 1969), rpt. in the author's *Versions of Baroque: European Literature in the Seventeenth Century* (New Haven, Yale University Press, 1972); and Emilio Orozco Díaz, *El teatro y la teatralidad del barroco* (Barcelona, Planeta, 1969).

13. Cf. Calderón's *El gran teatro del mundo,* where the "Autor" informs the players that to gain eternal salvation, one must enact one's role "con afecto, alma y acción" (*Autos sacramentales,* ed. Ángel Valbuena Prat, 4th ed., I, Clás. Cast., 69 [Madrid, Espasa-Calpe, 1958], 84).

14. See Leo Spitzer, " 'Soy quien soy,' " *NRFH,* 1 (1947), 113–127, and José Antonio Maravall, "Una interpretación histórico-social del teatro barroco," *CHA,* no. 235 (July 1969), 83–87.

15. R. B. Merriman, *The Rise of the Spanish Empire,* IV (New York, Macmillan, 1934), 552.

16. *Obras del Padre Juan de Mariana,* II, B.A.E., 31 (Madrid, Rivedeneyra, 1872), 462b. Cf. the following lament from *Guzmán de Alfarache:* "Ya estamos muy abatidos, porque los que nos han de honrar nos desfavorecen. El solo nombre español, que otro tiempo peleaba y con la reputación temblaba dél todo el mundo, ya por nuestros pecados la tenemos casi perdida. Estamos tan fallidos, que aun con las fuerzas no bastamos; pues los que fuimos somos y seremos" (ed. Samuel Gili y Gaya, II, Clás. Cast., 83 [Madrid, La Lectura, 1927], 144–145).

17. See J. H. Elliott, *Imperial Spain, 1469–1716* (New York, St. Martin's, 1964), pp. 283ff. For a discussion from a somewhat different point of view of the "inseguridad vital" of Spain during the years 1598–1620, see the interesting article of Pierre Vilar, "El tiempo del 'Quijote,'" in *Crecimiento y desarrollo* (Barcelona, Ediciones Ariel, 1964).

18. In my outline of the economic decline of Spain at the end of the sixteenth century, I have followed, for the most part, the standard account, Earl J. Hamilton, "The Decline of Spain," *Economic History Review,* 8 (1938), 168–179. Excellent brief analyses of that decline are also to be found in Elliott, *Imperial Spain;* Vilar, "El tiempo del 'Quijote'"; R. Trevor Davies, *The Golden Century of Spain, 1501–1621* (London, Macmillan, 1937); Jaime Vicens Vives, *Manual de historia económica de España* (Barcelona, Vicens Vives, 1959); John Lynch, *Spain under the Habsburgs,* 2 vols. (New York, Oxford University Press, 1964–1969); Antonio Domínguez Ortiz, *The Golden Age of Spain, 1516–1659* (New York, Basic Books, 1971); and Stanley G. Payne, *A History of Spain and Portugal* (Madison, University of Wisconsin Press, 1973), I, 267–330.

19. See Antonio Domínguez Ortiz, *La sociedad española en el siglo XVII,* I (Madrid, Consejo Superior de Investigaciones Científicas, 1963), 70.

20. See *Epistolario de Lope de Vega Carpio,* ed. Agustín G. de Amezúa, II ("Lope de Vega en sus cartas") (Madrid, Escelicer, 1940), 215ff.

21. Quoted in Jean H. Mariéjol, *Philip II: The First Modern King* (New York, Harper, 1933), p. 356; author's translation.

22. See Américo Castro, *De la edad conflictiva,* 2nd ed. (Madrid, Taurus, 1963); Antonio Domínguez Ortiz, *La clase social de los conversos en Castilla en la edad moderna* (Madrid, Consejo Superior de Investigaciones Científicas, 1955); Albert A. Sicroff, *Les controverses des status de "pureté de sang" en Espagne du XVᵉ au XVIIᵉ siècle* (Paris, Didier, 1960); and Julio Caro Baroja, *Los judíos en la España moderna y contemporánea* (Madrid, Arion, 1962), II, esp. 267–390. Briefer than the preceding studies, but notably illuminating on the situation of the New Christians in Golden Age Spain is Joseph H. Silverman, "Some Aspects of Literature and Life in the Golden Age of Spain," in *Estudios de literatura española ofrecidos a Marcos A. Morínigo* (Madrid, Insula, 1971), pp. 131–170.

23. See Castro, *De la edad conflictiva,* pp. 169–190.

24. See Sicroff, *Les controverses,* pp. 265–268, Domínguez Ortiz, *La clase social,* pp. 77–78, and Caro Baroja, *Los judíos,* II, 350–367.

25. Cf. Manuel Durán: "En esta forma el teatro de Lope se proponía alcanzar un triple objetivo: subrayar a través de la acción y la leyenda, los orígenes de la sociedad esspañola; proporcionar a esta sociedad una puerta de escape a las incertidumbres y las angustias del

presente al mostrar, a través de personajes con los que pudiera identi-
ficarse, que la acción—personal o colectiva—seguía siendo posible, por
lo menos en el mundo de la fantasía; y recordar a ese mismo público
que en algunas zonas del imperio español la acción—acción heroica—
seguía siendo posible . . . Lope debió comprender que la sociedad de su
tiempo exigía un teatro basado en la acción rápida y abundante *para
compensar* una realidad nacional cada vez más estancada, una creciente
frustración en la esfera internacional, un progresivo anquilosamiento
de las energías internas" ("Lope y el teatro de acción," *Hispanó,*
6, no. 3 [1963], 11; author's emphasis).

It would be well to point out that a sociological interpretation of
the *Comedia* is not, by itself, something new. Many years ago, for
example, Karl Vossler defined the Golden Age theater on the basis of
its relation to its audience. His analysis of that relation, however,
differs in important respects from that presented here, for he saw the
seventeenth-century stage primarily as an instrument with which the
people could take flight from a reality in danger of becoming meaning-
less: "La vida se refugia en la escena, huyendo, por decirlo así, de
su propria inanidad, y por allí verla, el pueblo afluye desbordante, por
gozar de su intensificación aparente y en ella embriagarse, aunque
sólo sea para no tener que negarla afuera, en la realidad" (*Lope de
Vega y su tiempo,* trans. R. de la Serna [Madrid, Revista de Occidente, 1933], p. 246). My position is that the *Comedia* was not a
means of fleeing from reality but a means of meeting it—not evasion,
but confrontation. Durán, apparently, would agree. The *Comedia,* he
writes, is "teatro que es, ante todo, reconocimiento y reconciliación.
Una sociedad se reconoce y se reconcilia con su destino" ("Lope y el
teatro de acción," p. 10).

26. In *The Origin of the Theater* (New York, Hill and Wang,
1961), Benjamin Hunninger maintains that modern drama is not
simply the figurative but the literal descendant of pagan drama. Dis-
carding the widely accepted notion (see O. B. Hardison, Jr., *Christian
Rite and Christian Drama in the Middle Ages: Essays in the Origin
and Early History of Modern Drama* [Baltimore, The Johns Hopkins
Press, 1965]) that the medieval theater grew out of the tropes of the
church liturgy, he affirms that it developed rather from the perfor-
mances given by the mimes, guardians of the ancient traditions.

In a recent series of articles, Charlotte Stern has elaborated a
theory on the origin of modern Spanish drama that offers striking
parallels with the ideas of Hunninger (see "Fray Iñigo de Mendoza
and Medieval Dramatic Ritual," *HR,* 33 [1965], 197–245; "Some New
Thoughts on the Early Spanish Drama," *BCom,* 18 [1966], 14–19;
"Juan del Encina's Carnival Eclogues and the Spanish Drama of the
Renaissance," *RenD,* 8 [1965], 181–195; and "The Early Spanish
Drama: From Medieval Ritual to Renaissance Art," *RenD,* n.s. 6
[1973], 177–201). While not denying that the liturgy of the church

may have played some part in its formation, Stern argues that the early sixteenth-century theater—that of Juan del Encina, Lucas Fernández, Gil Vicente, and their near contemporaries—evolved primarily out of medieval folk ritual and games. In support of her theory, Stern offers the following facts: the early sixteenth-century pieces are primarily festival or seasonal pieces; they seem frequently to be built on a prevailing mood or moods rather than a series of dramatic encounters; they often eschew dialogue in favor of such lyrical elements as songs and dances; they feature prominently the character of the simplistic shepherd. The first three of the foregoing seem to point to antecedents in rituals and ceremonies; the last mentioned proclaims ties to the rustic clown of medieval song, dance, and pantomime.

Stern's theory is provocative and plausible, particularly in view of the fact that recent research has tended to confirm the almost total lack of liturgical drama in Castile (see, especially, Richard B. Donovan, *The Liturgical Drama in Medieval Spain* [Toronto, Pontifical Institute of Medieval Studies, 1958]; N. D. Shergold, *A History of the Spanish Stage* [Oxford, Oxford University Press, 1967], pp. 1–84; and Humberto López Morales, *Tradición y creación en los orígenes del teatro castellano* [Madrid, Ediciones Alcalá, 1968], pp. 17–87). That the theory has important ramifications is indisputable, for as Stern writes, "early dramatic tradition in a traditionally-minded country like Spain undoubtedly has some bearing on the direction given later to the drama by Lope and his contemporaries" ("Some New Thoughts," p. 14). One implication of her argument is especially significant: that the seventeenth-century *Comedia* stems from an earlier drama "whose primary purpose was not to provide an aesthetic experience but to assure the emotional participation of the faithful" ("Fray Iñigo de Mendoza," p. 201).

27. This is not to deny that certain playwrights did on occasion dramatize points of view that were at least somewhat at variance with those held by the majority of their countrymen. Still, there has been a good deal of exaggeration of the part played by discrepant ideas in the *Comedia*. Generally speaking, the publicly expressed attitudes—as distinct from those held in private, about which in any case we know very little—of the Golden Age playwrights remained comfortably within the established ideological limits. Indeed, it could not easily have been otherwise, for the dramatists were largely dependent on the public for their livelihood, and the public, though troubled and uneasy, remained for the most part firm in its adherence to traditional ideas and values.

What most distinguishes the later dramatists of the seventeenth century from the earlier ones is not so much a divergent set of ideals (again I am speaking of ideals espoused publicly) as a notably different mode of expression. By comparison with the seemingly natural and spontaneous celebration of values in Lope, the celebration in Calderón, Moreto, and Rojas Zorrilla is formal, studied, and even artificial. These qualities have inevitably been related by scholars to the changed quality of life in the second two thirds of the century, which is to say, to the ever increasing gap between the world of illusion created on the stage and the real world beyond. See J. Rodríguez-Púertolas, "Alienación y realidad en Rojas Zorrilla," *BH,* 69 (1967), 325–346, and Charles Vincent Aubrun, *La comedia española (1600–1680),* trans. Julio Lago Alonso (Madrid, Taurus, 1968), pp. 66–73, 157–162, and 165–188.

28. Aubrun, *La comedia española,* p. 66.

29. José Hierro, "Algunos apectos del teatro del siglo de oro," *Bolívar,* no. 45 (December 1955), 872. An interpretation of the *Comedia* which is radically different from that proposed here has recently been offered by José Antonio Maravall (see "Una interpretación histórico-social del teatro barroco," *CHA,* no. 234 [June 1969], 621–649, and no. 235 [July 1969], 74–108, rpt. in *Teatro y literatura en la sociedad barroca* [Madrid, Seminario y Ediciones, 1972]). Maravall sees the *Comedia* not as an instrument of ritualistic celebration but rather as a tool of political propaganda designed to impose upon certain social groups, notably the peasants, a monarchical-seigneurial system of government. Maravall's interpretation is open to a number of objections, the most important of which is that there is no evidence whatsoever to support the notion that the *Comedia* was directed primarily toward the peasant class. In fact, as a number of recent studies have emphasized, the Golden Age theater was nurtured in a few relatively large cities and supported in large part by an urban population (see, particularly, Noël Salomon, *Recherches sur le thème paysan dans la "comedia" au temps de Lope de Vega* [Bordeaux, Féret & Fils, 1965], passim; R. O. Jones, "Poets and Peasants," in *Homenaje a William L. Fichter,* pp. 341–355; and Charles V. Aubrun, "Nouveau public, nouvelle comédie a Madrid au XVIIe siècle," in *Dramaturgie et société: rapports entre l'oeuvre théâtrale, son interprétation et son public aux XVIe et XVIIe siècles,* ed. Jean Jacquot with the collaboration of Elie Konigson and Marcel Oddon [Paris, Centre National de la Recherche Scientifique, 1968], I, 1–12).

30. I know this essay only through the résumé given in José Ortega y Gasset, *La deshumanización del arte e Ideas sobre la novela,* in *Obras completas,* 5th ed., III (Madrid, Revista de Occidente, 1962).

31. Ibid., p. 397.

32. My emphasis.

33. The most recent editor of the *Arte nuevo,* for example, comments on the range of meaning that "honra," as used in these lines, could sustain. She does not, however, consider the implications of the verbal phrase "mueven con fuerza." See *Arte nuevo de hacer comedias*

en este tiempo, ed. Juana de José Prades (Madrid, Consejo Superior de Investigaciones Científicas, 1971), pp. 214–218.

34. My definition of "myth" is that of most modern antropologists. See, for example, Jane Harrison: "a *mythos* to the Greek was primarily just a thing spoken, uttered by the *mouth*. Its antithesis or rather correlative is the thing done, enacted, the *ergon* or work . . . The primary meaning of myth in religion is just the same as in early literature; it is the spoken correlative of the acted rite, the thing done" (*Themis,* p. 328).

35. *Ac.,* VIII, 390a. The play is *El pleito de la honra,* long attributed to Lope but now regarded as of uncertain authorship by most authorities (see S. Griswold Morley and Courtney Bruerton, *Cronología de las comedias de Lope de Vega* [Madrid, Gredos, 1968], pp. 532–533). Other speeches from the Golden Age theater in which dishonor is equated with death are quoted in Fichter's edition of *El castigo del discreto,* p. 30, and Domingo Ricart, "El concepto de la honra en el teatro del Siglo de Oro y las ideas de Juan de Valdés," *Segismundo,* no. 1 (1965), 45–49. The notion that to be without honor is to be without life goes back in Spain at least to the time of the *Siete partidas:* "Ca segunt dixieron los antiguos que ficieron las leyes antiguas, dos yerros son como eguales, matar a home et enfamarlo de mal, porque el home después que es mal enfamado magüer non haya culpa, muerto es quanto al bien et a la honra deste mundo; et demás tal podría seer el enfamamiento, que mejor le seríe la muerte que la vida" (quoted in Jenaro Artiles, "La idea de la venganza en el drama español del siglo XVII," *Segismundo,* nos. 5–6 [1967], p. 11).

36. Maud Bodkin, *Archetypal Patterns in Poetry: Psychological Studies of Imagination* (1934; rpt. New York, Knopf, 1958), pp. 1–86.

37. See Northrop Frye, *Anatomy of Criticism: Four Essays* (Princeton, Princeton University Press, 1957), pp. 186–207.

38. Ibid., p. 187.

39. Lord Raglan, *The Hero: A Study in Tradition, Myth, and Drama* (1937; rpt. New York, Knopf, 1956), pp. 278–291.

40. On the use in ritual and ritual drama of the archetypal narrative of romance—what Raglan calls the "myth of the hero"—see also Joseph Campbell, *The Hero with a Thousand Faces* (1949; rpt. New York, Meridian, 1956), passim; Theodore H. Gaster, *Thespis: Ritual, Myth and Drama in the Ancient Near East* (1950; rpt. New York, Doubleday, 1961), passim; and Hardison, *Christian Rite and Christian Drama,* pp. 284–292.

41. The date of composition of *Peribáñez* is one of the most debated questions in the Lopean chronology and one to which there is still no definitive answer. For the issues involved, see, principally, Morley and Bruerton, *Cronología,* pp. 373–374, and also Noël Salomon "Toujours la date de 'Peribáñez y el Comendador de

Ocaña,'" in *Mélanges offerts à Marcel Bataillon* (Bordeaux, Féret & Fils, 1962), pp. 613–643.

42. See *Peribáñez y el Comendador de Ocaña; La dama boba*, ed. Alonso Zamora Vicente, Clás. Cast., 159 (Madrid, Espasa-Calpe, 1963), pp. xvii–xviii.

43. In *"La quinta de Florencia*, fuente de *Peribáñez*," NRFH, 4 (1950), 25–39, Courtney Bruerton argues that the real inspiration for *Peribáñez* was not the ballad alluded to but rather Lope's own play *La quinta de Florencia* (1599–1603), which is itself based on a story of Bandello. *La quinta de Florencia* has, however, little in common structurally with *Peribáñez*, and its thematic interest is very different: not masculine honor but feminine chastity and shame. It is thus not so much akin to the honor plays as to those plays, discussed briefly in the Appendix, that exalt the strength of character of women.

44. As Peter N. Dunn has pointed out, sonnets in Lope's plays often work in much the same manner. See "Some Uses of Sonnets in the Plays of Lope de Vega," BHS, 34 (1957), 213–222.

45. Edward M. Wilson, "Images et structure dans *Peribáñez*," BH, 51 (1949), 125–159, rpt. in Spanish trans. in *El teatro de Lope de Vega: artículos y estudios*, ed. José Francisco Gatti (Buenos Aires, E.U.D.E.B.A., 1962), pp. 50–90. See also Gustavo Correa, "El doble aspecto de la honra en *Peribáñez y el Comendador de Ocaña*," HR, 26 (1958), 188–199; Guillermo Araya, "Paralelismo antitético en 'Peribáñez y el comendador de Ocaña,'" EFil, no. 5 (1969), pp. 91–127; and Georges Güntert, "Relección del 'Peribáñez,'" RFE, 54 (1971), 37–52. The last-named adds to the discussion of the play the interesting point that the contrasts that Lope draws between the world of Peribáñez and that of the Comendador reflect Renaissance thinking not only on the opposition between *aldea* and *corte* (as others have noted) but also on that between *naturaleza* and *arte*. He emphasizes the fact that just as Peribáñez is, for a time, an uncertain examplar of *aldea* and *naturaleza*, so does the Comendador represent *corte* and *arte* in a less than perfect fashion. He shows, in other words, what happens when courtliness degenerates into mere mannerism and art into artificiality.

46. Wilson, "Images," p. 134.

47. In so saying, I sharply disagree with one of the most perceptive of the recent critics of *Peribáñez*, Guillermo Araya. In "Paralelismo antitético," Araya writes: "Toda la obra no consiste en otra cosa que en reiterar la pugna de dos clases de realidades en relación con las cuales puede existir plenamente una sola de ellas siempre que la otra se anule y desaparezca. Es decir, la 'capa pardilla' necesita eliminar a la 'guarnecida' para existir en plenitud" (p. 96). Whatever the historical truth of the second statement, I can find no indication, either in this play or in any other, that Lope subscribed to it. Indeed,

the evidence seems totally the contrary. In those plays that depict a conflict between nobles and peasants—*Peribáñez, Fuenteovejuna, El mejor alcalde, el rey*—Lope is manifestly careful not to ascribe that conflict to unreconcilable class differences. To have done otherwise would have been to assume, at least potentially, a revolutionary posture, and Lope was not a Jacobin. It is well, perhaps, to recall the words of Charles Vincent Aubrun and José F. Montesinos: "Les comedias où le poète nous propose des conflits de cette nature [i.e., between peasants and nobility] sont donc beaucoup moins révolutionnaires qu'il ne paraît de prime abord. On n'y démolit aucun système, on n'y discute aucun principe; au contraire, on s'y prononce avec emphase contre leurs corruptions occasionelles. S'il s'y trouve des rébellions et des assassinats, c'est que les victimes ont mérité ce châtiment en agissant contre l'institution même de la noblesse et contre ce qu'ils devaient au sang hérité" (Lope de Vega, *Peribáñez y el Comendador de Ocaña* [Paris, Hachette, 1943], p. xxxii).

48. At the beginning of the play, Bartolo, speaking for the peasants, refers to the Comendador as "mueso señor generoso" (112a); at the end of the play the King, not yet apprised of what has happened, calls Don Fadrique "[el] mejor soldado / que trujo roja cruz" (145b). Both statements are telling indications that the Comendador has qualities to be admired. Lope makes no effort to brush aside those qualities; but neither does he gloss over the fact that the Comendador fails lamentably to live up to them. It is bad enough that the Comendador should pervert the normal order of things by fixing his desire upon a peasant. But it is incomparably worse that he should attempt to take through trickery and force what he cannot win through persuasion, particularly in view of the fact that the woman concerned is his vassal. It is thus difficult to accept the view of J. Toledano, who sees the Comendador as "un hombre apasionado y nada más" ("Notas para una interpretación del *Peribáñez*," *Escorial*, 2nd ser. 20, no. 63 [1949], 743), or of Louis C. Pérez, who describes him as "merely another human being who is going through the test here on earth" ("Observations on Two Commanders in Lope de Vega," *Far Western Forum*, 1, no. 1 [1974], 83). The remarks of Toledano and Pérez serve as a useful corrective to the excessively harsh judgments of such earlier critics as Menéndez y Pelayo (see *Estudios*, V, 45) and John M. Hill and Mabel M. Harlan (see their anthology of *Cuatro comedias* [New York, Norton, 1941], p. 3). Nevertheless, they stand themselves in need of modification, for they seek to judge the Comendador by moral standards that are anachronistic both for the time of the action of the play and for Lope's own time.

Noël Salomon has recently advanced the interesting supposition that the characterization of the Comendador is, among other things, an oblique attack on Rodrigo Calderón, who received the title of Comendador de Ocaña in 1611 and who was at the presumed time of composition of the play a mortal enemy of Lope's patron, the Duke of Sessa. If this is so, it may account in part for the several references to impurity of blood that appear in the piece—the ancestry of Rodrigo Calderón was more than somewhat suspect—and be the key, as Salomon says, to "plus d'une allusion ambiguë de la fameuse 'tragicomedia'" (*Recherches*, p. 892). See also Salomon's "Toujours la date."

49. See, for example, pp. 114a, 128b, and 131a.

50. The first scene of *Peribáñez* has been discussed by a number of critics, most illuminatingly, perhaps, by Noël Salomon (*Recherches*, pp. 370–387), who calls attention to the reminiscences of the *Song of Songs* in the imagery of the scene, and by J. E. Varey ("La campagne dans de théâtre espagnol au XVIIe siècle," in *Dramaturgie et société*, I, 62–66), who speaks of the reinforcing role played here by music, frequently, although not always, in Lope a symbol of universal harmony. On this point, see also Victor Dixon, "The Symbolism of *Peribáñez*," *BHS*, 43 (1966), 11–24, and Leo Spitzer, "A Central Theme and Its Structural Equivalent in Lope's *Fuenteovejuna*," *HR*, 23 (1955), 274–292, rpt. in *Romanische Literaturstudien* (Tübingen, M. Niemeyer, 1959), pp. 760–777, and in Spanish trans. in *El teatro de Lope de Vega*, ed. Gatti, pp. 124–147. Spitzer's ideas are placed in a wider context in his well-known *Classical and Christian Ideas of World Harmony* (Baltimore, Johns Hopkins Press, 1963).

51. See Julian Pitt-Rivers *The People of the Sierra* (Chicago, University of Chicago Press, 1961), p. 169, and "Honour and Social Status," in *Honour and Shame: The Values of a Mediterranean Society*, ed. J. G. Péristiany (Chicago, University of Chicago Press, 1966), pp. 47–51.

52. In view of the fact that it was Peribáñez himself who requested it, the ceremony might also seem to be a second instance of presumption on his part, a second repudiation, so to speak, of the role to which he has been assigned on earth. It is doubtful, however, that Lope intended it to be seen in that light. It is true, of course, that immediately after the dubbing, Peribáñez adopts the abstract and rhetorical way of speaking characteristic of the Comendador. But he does so with a deep sense of irony ("¿No parece que ya os hablo / á lo grave y caballero?" he inquiries of Casilda [137b]), and he reverts to his own "voice" as soon as he has left Ocaña. Moreover, from the latter moment, the thought that he is now a knight seems never again to occur to him: as noted later in the text, even in his speech of exculpation before the King, he describes himself merely as "un hombre . . . de villana casta" (147a). Indeed, throughout the latter part of the play, Peribáñez appears obsessively, though no doubt unconsciously, determined to act the part of a simple peasant. We see this in the vengeance itself, as R. O. Jones has observed with acumen:

"Peribáñez returns to Ocaña on his *yegua* almost like a parody of a *caballero;* he climbs into his *corral* over a back wall, moralises on his sleeping chickens, geese, pigs and so on; hides (on hearing voices) in a *saca de harina,* from which he later steps forth to run the Comendador through: details which in themselves are almost comic. The insistence on unheroic detail (why does Peribáñez have to hide in a *saca de harina* of all things?) have [sic] a clear purpose: to manifest in objective form the unambitious peasant's attachment to his station" ("Poets and Peasants," p. 355).

53. Menéndez Pidal, "Del honor en el teatro español," pp. 173–174.

54. Alexey Almasov, "*Fuenteovejuna* y el honor villanesco en el teatro de Lope de Vega," *CHA,* nos. 161–162 (May–June 1963).

55. Salomon, *Recherches.*

56. See Jones, "Poets and Peasants," Maravall, "Una interpretación histórico-social," Aubrun, "Nouveau public, nouvelle comédie," and Manuel Tuñón de Lara, "La obra del Profesor Noël Salomon sobre los campesinos en las comedias de Lope de Vega," *CA,* 151, no. 2 (March–April 1967), 156–177.

57. See the preface to the 3rd ed. of *De la edad conflictiva* (Madrid, Taurus, 1972). Castro's study is fundamental for all the matters discussed in this paragraph. See also, for an application of Castro's ideas to *Peribáñez,* Guillermo Araya, "Paralelismo antitético," esp. pp. 108–122.

58. The Academy edition has "hidalgos casados." The reading "cansados" is found as early as the Barcelona printing of the *Quarta Parte* (1614), however, and is accepted by most modern editors. See Henri Mérimée, " 'Casados' ou 'cansados,' " *RFE,* 6 (1919), 61–63, and Hill and Harlan, eds., *Cuatro Comedias,* p. 168.

59. Cf. the passage from *Fuenteovejuna* cited in Chapter 1, pp. 11–12, and see Joseph H. Silverman, "Los 'hidalgos cansados' de Lope de Vega," in *Homenaje a William L. Fichter,* pp. 693–711.

60. See Maravall, "Una interpretación histórico-social," pp. 74–83.

61. See Carl Stephenson, *Medieval Feudalism* (1942; rpt. Ithaca, Cornell University Press, 1956), p. 20.

62. Alan Soons, "Towards an Interpretation of *El caballero de Olmedo,*" *RF,* 73 (1961), 165.

63. The symbolism of the statue and of Saint Roch is interpreted rather differently by Alison Turner in "The Dramatic Function of Imagery and Symbolism in *Peribáñez* and *El caballero de Olmedo,*" *Symposium,* 20 (1966), 174–186.

64. Wilson, "Images," esp. pp. 127–141.

65. There are interesting observations on the symbolism of the bull in Peribáñez, as well as other images, in Dixon, "The Symbolism of *Peribáñez.*" See also Varey, "La campagne dans le théâtre espagnol," pp. 62–66.

66. Bodkin, *Archetypal Patterns,* pp. 265–266.

67. Frye, *Anatomy*, pp. 187–188.

68. While not denying that Lope manufactured the plots of *Fuenteovejuna* chiefly out of raw material supplied by Rades, Duncan W. Moir suggests in a recent article that its writing was sparked by the perusal of an emblem-book published shortly before the play's presumed date of composition, Sebastián de Covarrubias Horozco's *Emblemas morales* (1610) (see "Lope de Vega's *Fuenteovejuna* and the *Emblemas morales* of Sebastián de Covarrubias Horozco [with a Few Remarks on *El villano en su rincón*]," in *Homenaje a William L. Fichter*, pp. 537–546). Moir's thesis is not totally convincing. To be sure, there is in the *Emblemas morales* an emblem illustrating the administration of justice, the poem-commentary on which makes explicit reference to the uprising in Fuenteovejuna. But the attitude toward the rebellion in the poem-commentary is the exact opposite of that projected by the play (Covarrubias is hostile; Lope is sympathetic). Moreover, the Fuenteovejuna incident seems to have been rather widely remembered, still, in the first decade of the seventeenth century (see Francisco López Estrada, ed., *Fuente Ovejuna* [*dos comedias*], Clás. Ca. 10 [Madrid, Castalia, 1969], pp. 19–20; also the same author's "*Fuente Ovejuna*" *en el teatro de Lope y de Monroy* [*Consideración critica de ambas obras*] [Seville, Universidad de Sevilla, 1965], pp. 83–98). There is thus no need to assume, as does Moir, that Lope's memory had to be jogged by any one particular allusion or account.

69. Menéndez y Pelayo, *Estudios*, V, 172.

70. The standard study of Lope's borrowings from Rades is Claude E. Anibal, "The Historical Elements of Lope de Vega's *Fuenteovejuna*," *PMLA*, 49 (1934), 657–718. Certain parts of Anibal's argument are now in need of rectification, however, in particular his idea that Rade's relation may be assumed to be historically accurate. See Salomon, *Recherches*, pp. 825–826; López Estrada, ed., *Fuente Ovejuna*, p. 16; and Manuel Cardenal Iracheta, "*Fuenteovejuna*," *Clavileño*, 2, no. 11 (1951), 20–26.

71. See Darnell H. Roaten and F. Sánchez y Escribano, *Wölfflin's Principles in Spanish Drama, 1500–1700* (New York, Hispanic Institute in the United States, 1952), pp. 96ff.; A. A. Parker, "Reflections on a New Definition of 'Baroque' Drama," *BHS*, 30 (1953), 144–146; G. W. Ribbans, "The Meaning and Structure of Lope's 'Fuenteovejuna,'" *BHS*, 31 (1954), 150–170; William C. McCrary, "*Fuenteovejuna*: Its Platonic Vision and Execution," *SP*, 58 (1961), 179–192; and J. B. Hall, "Theme and Structure in Lope's *Fuenteovejuna*," *FMLS*, 10 (1974), 57–66.

72. Diego Marín does not treat these plays as a separate category in *La intriga secundaria en el teatro de Lope de Vega* (Mexico City, Ediciones de Andrea, 1958).

73. Cf. William Empson on the functioning of the double plot in

certain of the more sophisticated Elizabethan plays: "Also the device sets your judgment free because you need not identify yourself firmly with any one of the characters (the drama of personality is liable to boil down to this); a situation is repeated for quite different characters, and this puts the main interest in the situation not the characters. Thus the effect of having two old men with ungrateful children, of different sorts, is to make us generalise the theme of Lear and feel that whole classes of children have become unfaithful, all nature is breaking up, as in the storm. The situation is made something valuable in itself, perhaps for reasons hardly realised; it can work on you like a myth" (*Some Versions of Pastoral* [Norfolk, Conn., New Directions, n.d.], p. 54).

74. Among them, Joaquín Casalduero, in "*Fuenteovejuna*," *RFH*, 5 (1943), 21–44, rpt. in the author's *Estudios sobre el teatro español*, 2nd ed. (Madrid, Gredos, 1967), pp. 13–46, and in Eng. trans. in *TDR*, 4 (1959), 83–107; and Bruce W. Wardropper, "*Fuente Ovejuna: El gusto* and *lo justo*," *SP*, 53 (1956), 159–171.

75. On the language of the peasants in this play, see Helga Hoock, *Lope de Vegas "Fuente Ovejuna" als Kunstwerk* (Würzburg, privately published, 1963), pp. 96ff., and Francisco López Estrada, "Los villanos filósofos y políticos (La configuración de 'Fuente Ovejuna' a través de los nombres y 'apellidos')," *CHA*, nos. 238–240 (October–December 1969), 522–523.

76. See Carlos Serrano, "Métaphore et idéologie: sur le tyran de 'Fuenteovejuna' de Lope de Véga (notes)," *Les Langues Néo-Latines*, no. 199 (1971), 32–35.

77. That the Comendador is, in fact, quite aware of the limits of his role is confirmed at several places in the text. To adduce but one example, there is the following speech from the end of Act I (540b):

> Pues, ¿la espalda ha de volver
> un hombre tan valeroso
> á un villano? ¡Tira, infame,
> tira, y guárdate, que rompo
> las leyes de caballero!

78. The motif of the hunter in *Fuenteovejuna* is examined by Javier Herrero in "The New Monarchy: A Structural Reinterpretation of *Fuenteovejuna*," *RHM*, 36 (1970–1971), 173–185. See also Pérez, "Observations on Two Commanders," pp. 76–80. Neither of these critics has noted the interesting point that in medieval art and literature the deer hunt was symbolic of the sex act. See Carl G. Jung et al., *Man and His Symbols* (Garden City, N.Y., Doubleday, 1964), p. 29.

79. Following nearly all modern editors, I have here restored the wording of the *Dozena Parte*. The Academy edition emends at this point to "que le echarais diligente."

80. See Raymond E. Barbera, "An Instance of Medieval Iconography in *Fuenteovejuna*," *RN*, 10 (1968), 160–162.

81. Ernst Robert Curtius, *European Literature and the Latin Middle Ages* (New York, Pantheon, 1953), p. 195.

82. The point is made by a number of critics. See, among other studies, Ribbans, "The Meaning and Structure"; McCrary, *"Fuenteovejuna"*; Spitzer, "A Central Theme"; López Estrada, "Los villanos filósofos"; and C. A. Soons, "Two Historical *Comedias* and the Question of *Manierismo*," *RF*, 73 (1961), 339–346.

83. Spitzer, "A Central Theme," pp. 275, 290.

84. Soons, "Two Historical *Comedias*," p. 340.

85. Lope's ironic treatment of the pastoral world cannot help reminding us of Cervantes's similar treatment in *Don Quijote* and *El coloquio de los perros*. In fact, Lope and Cervantes are but two among many authors in the seventeenth century who mock the pastoral myth. For them, as Bruce W. Wardropper points out, the pastoral "turns out to be an illusion because it deliberately precludes such genuine human concerns as politics" ("Comic Illusion: Lope de Vega's *El perro del hortelano*," *KRQ*, 14 [1967], 101). See also Juan Bautista Avalle-Arce, *La novela pastoril española* (Madrid, Revista de Occidente, 1959).

86. The most fully developed Platonic reading of the play is McCrary, *"Fuenteovejuna."* But several of McCrary's points were adumbrated in earlier studies, chiefly, Wardropper, "Fuente Ovejuna: *El gusto* and *lo justo*," and Spitzer, "A Central Theme."

87. Arnold G. Reichenberger, "The Uniqueness of the *Comedia*," *HR*, 27 (1959), 307.

88. The interdependence of *amor natural* and altruism in *Fuenteovejuna* has been discussed by Albert S. Gérard in "Self-Love in Lope de Vega's *Fuenteovejuna* and Corneille's *Tite et Bérénice*," *AJFS*, 4 (1967), 177–197.

89. See Menéndez y Pelayo, *Estudios*, V, 176–177.

90. See Antonio Gómez-Moriana, *Derecho de resistencia y tiranicidio* (Santiago de Compostela, Porto y Cía., 1968), esp. pp. 24, 69–71.

91. Ibid., pp. 54–58, 65–84. On the justification for rebellion in *Fuenteovejuna* see also Hall, "Theme and Structure," pp. 60–66, and Eduardo Forastieri Braschi, "*Fuenteovejuna* y la justificación," *REH-PR*, 2, nos. 1–4 (1972), 89–99.

92. I quote from Hall, "Theme and Structure," p. 62.

93. Additional examples are given ibid., pp. 63–64.

94. The Academy reading here ("Al palo aplica. / La espalda.") is nonsensical. I have punctuated in the manner of all modern editions.

95. Gómez-Moriana, *Derecho de resistencia*, pp. 71–72.

96. In "A Central Theme," Leo Spitzer discusses the ballad

(actually, the song is a combination of *romance* and *seguidilla*) at some length and with great ingenuity. He sees it primarily as "one of those warnings to the protagonists, customary in Lope's plays, issued by a chorus voicing popular opinion and therefore presented in the objective lyrical form of a folk-song" (pp. 280–281). His interpretation presupposes that the "niña en cabellos" of the song is a representation of Laurencia and takes it for granted that the young woman gives in to the "linces deseos" of the knight. If this is so, as Spitzer observes, "the subsequent moral victory of Laurencia (for she will not succumb to the Comendador) will appear all the greater precisely because *vox populi* had already anticipated her defeat" (p. 282). But as Francisco López Estrada has noted, the anonymous girl of the ballad is not necessarily meant to represent Laurencia ("La canción 'Al val de Fuente Ovejuna' de la comedia *Fuente Ovejuna*," in *Homenaje a William L. Fichter*, pp. 453–468). In fact, if we accept the explanation of the phrase "niña en cabellos" given by Covarrubias ("Niña en cabello, la donzella, porque en muchas partes traen a las donzellas en cabello, sin toca, cofia o covertura ninguna en la cabeça hasta que se casan" [*Tesoro de la Lengua Castellana o Española,* 1611, cited by López Estrada, p. 453]), it seems likely that she does not, for by this point in the play Laurencia is a married woman. Moreover, there is room to doubt that the "victory of evil appears here as having already happened" (Spitzer, "A Central Theme," p. 282). Surely, the song is, as far as it goes, ambiguous about the fate of the girl. I say as far as it goes, for the text conveys the distinct impression that the song remains unfinished, that its conclusion is prevented by the sudden appearance of the Comendador. If this is indeed the case, the ballad is for the audience essentially open-ended, and the dramatic tension of the scene is increased. It is normal, of course, for us to wonder how the song *would have* ended had the musicians had the opportunity to complete it. It seems to me at least as possible to imagine an ending that celebrated the victory of the girl over her attacker as one that reported her defeat. In that event, the song could much more appropriately be sung at the wedding of one of the village girls, serving, perhaps, as the expression of a collective wish-fulfillment fantasy for deliverance from the clutches of the Comendador. This fantasy, if such it is, is destroyed, like the wedding ceremony itself, by the Comendador's unexpected arrival. Once and for all, it would seem, reality intrudes upon the peasants' dream of evasion, and from now on it is reality with which they will have to deal.

97. Francis Fergusson, *The Idea of a Theater,* p. 113.

98. Casalduero, "*Fuenteovejuna,*" p. 44. In his recent article "The New Monarchy" Javier Herrero advocates at least a partial return to the "political" interpretation of *Fuenteovejuna*. Obviously, I am basically in sympathy with this approach. Herrero defines the political

statement of the play in a way that I find unacceptable, however. The work is, he says, "a glorification of the triumph of *absolute monarchy* over the forces [of] feudalism, of *anarchic aristocracy*" (p. 176; author's emphasis). Aside from the fact that this formulation sees the fall of Fernán Gómez as emblematic in a way for which the text offers little or no justification (cf. the remarks of Aubrun and Montesinos in note 47, above), it draws attention away from the feat of the villagers in order to throw into relief the role played by the Catholic monarchs. That role is, of course, not inconsequential. But surely the most important triumph in the play is not that of the King and Queen but that of the people of Fuenteovejuna, and it seems rather perverse to ignore or minimize the fact. All this is not to say that Lope had no interest in celebrating the notion of a powerful—if not absolute—monarchy. There are a number of plays, principally of the middle and late periods, that seem governed at least partly by that intent. *El villano en su rincón* (1611), despite its popular reputation as a work dedicated to singing the praises of country life and the natural dignity of all men, appears to be one such. Another is *El mejor alcalde, el rey* (1620–1623).

The latter is a most interesting work that is often grouped with such plays as *Peribáñez* and *Fuenteovejuna*. In reality, however, its thematic interests are quite different. Specifically, the theme of masculine honor is here moved to the periphery. We see this in the way in which the two men most affected by the abduction of Elvira, the peasant heroine, react to that deed. For Sancho, Elvira's betrothed, the kidnapping is a cause principally for jealousy; he is far less afflicted by feelings of dishonor, probably because, not yet being married to Elvira, he does not have the primary responsibility for her welfare and chastity. Nuño, Elvira's father, *does* experience an acute sense of dishonor, but he is convinced that there is little he and Sancho can do to secure the return of Elvira except to make an appeal to the humanity of Tello, the abductor. That appeal fails, for Tello is a haughty nobleman in the mold of Fernán Gómez. At this point Nuño suggests seeking the aid of the King. Henceforth, Alfonso, the King, plays an increasingly important part in the action, and as he does so, it becomes apparent that the play's real theme—as the title itself suggests—is the depth and breadth of the authority of the monarchy. The theme is driven home with the beheading of Tello at the end of the piece, an act that facilitates the marriage of Sancho and Elvira, yes, but that also exemplifies the nearly unlimited power of the King and the justice meted out to all those who, without reason, seek to undermine his rule. On this and other points, see the perspicacious article of José María Díez Borque, "Estructura social de la comedia de Lope: a propósito de 'El mejor alcalde, el rey,'" *Arbor*, 85, nos. 331–332 (1973), 121–134.

4. Late Plays: The Turn toward Tragedy

1. *Oresteia: Agamemnon, The Libation Bearers, The Eumenides,* trans. Richmond Lattimore (Chicago, University of Chicago Press, 1953), pp. 26–27.

2. A. C. Bradley, "Hegel's Theory of Tragedy," in *Oxford Lectures on Poetry* (1909; rpt. Bloomington, Indiana University Press, 1961), p. 88.

3. See A. A. Parker, "The Approach to the Spanish Drama," *TDR,* 4, no. 1 (1959), 42–59; "The Spanish Drama of the Golden Age: A Method of Analysis and Interpretation," in *The Great Playwrights,* ed. Eric Bentley (New York, Doubleday, 1970), I; "Towards a Definition of Calderonian Tragedy," *BHS,* 39 (1962), 222–237.

4. Parker, "The Approach to the Spanish Drama," p. 46. There are, of course, exceptions to the statement. As Willard F. King has recently suggested in the introduction to her edition and translation of Lope's *El caballero de Olmedo* (Lincoln, University of Nebraska Press, 1972), Don Alonso, the hero of that play, can more reasonably be considered a victim of destiny than of wrongdoing.

5. Northrop Frye, *Anatomy of Criticism: Four Essays* (Princeton, Princeton University Press, 1957), p. 208. Cf. Richard B. Sewall: "Above all, the source of tragic suffering is the sense, in the consciousness of tragic man, of simultaneous guilt and guiltlessness. Tillich called tragedy 'a mixture of guilt and necessity.' If tragic man could say, 'I sinned, therefore I suffer' or 'He (or They or God) sinned, therefore I suffer,' his problem would be resolved, and the peculiar poignancy of his suffering would be removed. If he felt himself entirely free or entirely determined, he would cease to be tragic. But he is neither—he is, in short, a paradox and mystery, the 'riddle of the world'" ("The Tragic Form," in *Tragedy: Modern Essays in Criticism,* ed. Laurence Michel and Richard B. Sewall [Englewood Cliffs, Prentice-Hall, 1963], p. 125).

6. John Jones, *On Aristotle and Greek Tragedy* (New York, Oxford University Press, 1962), p. 15.

7. Frye, *Anatomy,* p. 211.

8. I. A. Richards, *Principles of Literary Criticism* (1925; rpt. New York, Harcourt, Brace and World, 1961), p. 69.

9. Erich Auerbach, *Mimesis: The Representation of Reality in Western Literature,* trans. Willard Trask (Garden City, N.Y., Doubleday, 1957), p. 292. Cf. Margaret Wilson, *Spanish Drama of the Golden Age* (Oxford, Pergamon, 1969), p. 49: "Society represents the pattern of existence laid down for man by God, and is essentially good; but it can be corrupted by the sinfulness of individual men. When this happens it is society, not man, which finds itself in a truly dramatic situation. Society is the helpless victim of sin; where-

as for man, endowed with moral sense and free-will, the course is always clear. Here we see why the Spanish dramatists did not produce much great tragedy: unquestioningly accepting as they did the moral and theological teaching of their age, they found it difficult to imagine their heroes faced with a really tragic conflict. Dilemmas there might be, but none to which the established values did not provide an answer. *Sub specie aeternitatis,* all was well."

10. A particularly lucid exposition of the seventeenth-century Spanish conception of man and his attributes is Eugenio Frutos, *La filosofía de Calderón en sus autos sacramentales* (Zaragoza, Consejo Superior de Investigaciones Científicas, 1952), pp. 105–257.

11. The discussion of *La vida es sueño* that follows derives in significant measure from the excellent modern critical writing on this work. In particular, I have drawn on the articles of E. M. Wilson ("*La vida es sueño*," *Revista de la Universidad de Buenos Aires,* 3rd ser. 4, nos. 3–4 [1946], 61–78), A. E. Sloman ("The Structure of Calderón's *La vida es sueño*," *MLR,* 48 [1953], 293–300), Everett W. Hesse ("La concepción calderoniana del príncipe perfecto en *La vida es sueño*," *Clavileño,* 4, no. 20 [1953], 4–12), and William M. Whitby ("Rosaura's Role in the Structure of *La vida es sueño*," *HR,* 28 [1960], 16–27). All of these essays have been reprinted in *Critical Essays on the Theatre of Calderón,* ed. Bruce W. Wardropper (New York, New York University Press, 1965). A helpful, although intentionally partial, résumé of recent criticism of Calderón's play is contained in R. D. F. Pring-Mill, "Los calderonistas de habla inglesa y *La vida es sueño*: métodos del análisis temático-estructural," in *Litterae Hispanae et Lusitanae: Festschrift zum fünfzigjährigen Bestehen des Ibero-Amerikanischen Forschungsinstituts der Universität Hamburg,* ed. Hans Flasche (Munich, Max Hueber, 1968).

12. Aristotle, *Poetics,* Bk. II, Ch. xi.

13. I quote from the edition of Albert E. Sloman (Manchester, Manchester University Press, 1961).

14. Clifford Leech, *Shakespeare's Tragedies and Other Studies in Seventeenth Century Drama* (New York, Oxford University Press, 1950), p. 215.

15. Ernest H. Templin, *The Exculpation of "Yerros por Amores" in the Spanish Comedia,* Publ. U.C.L.A. Lang. and Lit., I, no. 1 (Berkeley, University of California Press, 1933), p. 33. Templin's study is a very useful introduction to the extremely important, and not yet sufficiently examined, topic of love in the *Comedia.* Helpful also is S. Serrano Poncela, "Amor y apetito en el teatro clásico español," *Asomante,* 9, no. 4 (1953), 46–62.

16. See the remarks of Federico Ruiz Morcuende in *Ac. N.,* X, xxxi–xxxiii.

17. In Lope's *La locura por la honra* (1610–1612), it is the father not of the antagonist but of the adulterous wife who expresses

explicit words of approval of the hero's vengeance. This was too much for the sensibility of Cotarelo y Mori, who declared the man's speech "[espantoso] en labios de un cristiano" (*Ac. N.*, VII, xiii). One wonders what Cotarelo would have thought of Calderón's *El pintor de su deshonra*, where *both* fathers, that of the slain rival as well as that of the assassinated wife, declare themselves satisfied with the fate of their children.

18. A play that, like *La victoria de la honra*, serves in some respects as a bridge between the middle-period plays and those of the late period is *El robo de Dina* (1615–1622), based on Genesis 34. Here, as in *Fuenteovejuna*, a story of abduction, rape, and vengeance is enacted in a rural setting that stands primarily for beauty, peace, harmony, and order. And here, as in the late plays, the agent of dishonor, Shechem, is characterized as a basically good person whose will and reason are subverted by passion. It is partly because he perceives Shechem's innate decency, partly because he believes that his daughter, Dinah, bears some responsibility for the fate that befalls her, that the patriarch Jacob feels compunction about taking revenge on Shechem. Dinah's brothers feel no such compunction, however, and thus Shechem is killed in the gruesome manner described in the Bible. At the end of the piece, an angel of the Lord appears to pronounce forgiveness for the deed, if not approval of it, and the play closes, like *La victoria de la honra*, with little feeling of tragedy. For a perspicacious study of this work see Edward Glaser, "Lope de Vega's *El robo de Dina*," *RJ*, 15 (1964), 315–334.

19. Marcelino Menéndez y Pelayo, *Estudios sobre el teatro de Lope de Vega*, ed. Enrique Sanchez Reyes, V, Edición Nacional de las obras completas de Menéndez y Pelayo, 33 (Santander, Aldus, 1949), 9–13.

20. Otis H. Green, *Spain and the Western Tradition*, I (Madison, University of Wisconsin Press, 1963), 237–240.

21. Here, as in all quotations from *Porfiar hasta morir*, the emphasis is mine.

22. J. Huizinga, *The Waning of the Middle Ages* (1924; rpt. Garden City, N.Y., Doubleday, 1956), esp. pp. 9–31.

23. Ibid., p. 10.

24. Denis de Rougemont, *Love in the Western World*, 2nd ed. (1940; rpt. Garden City, N.Y., Doubleday, 1957), p. 42.

25. Menéndez y Pelayo, *Estudios*, V, 19.

26. See Émile Gigas, "Études sur quelques *comedias* de Lope de Vega; III: *El castigo sin venganza*," *RH*, 53 (1921), 589–604, and the introduction by C. F. Adolfo van Dam to his edition of Lope's play (Groningen, P. Noordhoff, 1928). While acknowledging that Lope based his play primarily on the Spanish translation of Belleforest's adaptation of Bandello, Menéndez Pidal has argued, convincingly to my way of thinking, that he was also familiar with Bandello's

original text (see *"El castigo sin venganza,* un oscuro problema de honor,"* in *El padre Las Casas y Vitoria con otros temas de los siglos XVI y XVII* [Madrid, Espasa-Calpe, 1958], pp. 127–128). Less convincing is the hypothesis, advanced initially by Gigas, that Lope drew certain details of his story from Ferrarese local legend, presumably imported into Spain via Ganassa and other traveling Italian actors of the late sixteenth century. Useful summaries of the scholarly debate that has surrounded the question of Lope's relation to his sources in *El castigo sin venganza* may be found in two recent editions of the play, that of C. A. Jones (Oxford, Pergamon, 1966) and that of A. David Kossoff, Clás. Ca., 25 (Madrid, Castalia, 1970).

27. *El castigo sin venganza,* ed. van Dam, p. 71.

28. Ibid., p. 62.

29. Ibid., p. 82.

30. Edward M. Wilson, "Cuando Lope quiere, quiere," *CHA,* nos. 161–162 (May–June 1963), 265–298.

31. The imagery of darkness in this play has been studied from a point of view rather different from my own by C. B. Morris in "Lope de Vega's *El castigo sin venganza* and Poetic Tradition," *BHS,* 40 (1963), 69–78.

32. Maynard Mack, "The World of *Hamlet,"* in *Tragic Themes in Western Literature,* ed. Cleanth Brooks (New Haven, Yale University Press, 1955), p. 30.

33. See Frye, *Anatomy,* p. 214.

34. See Amado Alonso, "Lope de Vega y sus fuentes," *Thesaurus,* 8 (1952), 1–24.

35. The final scene of Act II, beginning with Federico's famous sonnet "¿Qué buscas, imposible pensamiento?" has been analyzed by Victor Dixon in *"El castigo sin venganza:* The Artistry of Lope de Vega,"* in *Studies in Spanish Literature of the Golden Age Presented to Edward M. Wilson,* ed. R. O. Jones (London, Tamesis, 1973), pp. 63–81. With a nice attention to both text and context, Dixon traces the shifting thoughts and emotions of this final scene, showing how Federico and Casandra first struggle to repress and deny their love, then acknowledge it with embarrassment and hesitation, and finally give themselves over completely to its irresistible force. On Federico's sonnet see also Peter N. Dunn, "Some Uses of Sonnets in the Plays of Lope de Vega," *BHS,* 34 (1957), 213–222; and on his much commented gloss, "Sin mí, sin vos y sin Dios," see, particularly, José María de Cossío, "El mote 'Sin mí, sin vos y sin Dios' glosado por Lope de Vega," *RFE,* 20 (1933), 397–400, and Rafael Lapesa, "Poesía de cancionero y poesía italianizante," in *De la Edad Media a nuestros días* (Madrid, Gredos, 1967), pp. 145–171.

36. The autograph reading. The Academy text reads "Y aunque muerto, estoy tal." Cf. the editions of C. A. Jones and David Kossoff.

37. At the end of the French translation of the work by C. le Senne and G. de Saix, there is an interesting epilogue spoken by Batín, the *gracioso*. Batín—here called Bettino—informs the audience that the play they have just seen was entitled by its author *Le châtiment sans vengeance:*

> Mais que beaucoup plus justement
> moi, l'humble Bettino, j'apelle
> *La vengeance sans châtiment*
> puisqu'elle unit dans la mort belle
> pour l'éternité deux amants.

(Quoted in Menéndez Pidal, *"El castigo sin venganza,"* p. 144.)

38. The idea was first advanced seriously by Harri Meier in his "A honra no drama românico dos séculos XVI e XVII," in *Ensaios de filologia românica* (Lisbon, Ediçao da "Revista de Portugal," 1948), though it did not gain wide currency until A. A. Parker published his thoughts on the play in "The Approach to the Spanish Drama."

39. Parker, "The Approach to the Spanish Drama," p. 50.

40. Aristotle, *Poetics*, Bk. II, Ch. xi. I quote from the translation of Thomas Twining in *Aristotle's Politics and Poetics*, trans. Benjamin Jowett and Thomas Twining (New York, Viking, 1957).

41. Herbert J. Muller, *The Spirit of Tragedy* (New York, Knopf, 1956), p. 7.

42. T. E. May, "Lope de Vega's *El castigo sin venganza:* The Idolatry of the Duke of Ferrara," *BHS,* 37 (1960), 154–182. May's view of the Duke is shared by at least one other scholar who has written on the play, Bruno Scarfe (see his "Concerning the Publication by Carlos Ortigoza-Vieya, *Aniquilamiento del móvil honor en 'Antíoco y Seleuco' de Moreto respecto 'El castigo sin venganza' de Lope,"* *AUMLA,* 34 [1970], 292–307). For the most part, however, critics have treated May's interpretation with a mixture of deference and wariness (see as examples the introduction by C. A. Jones to his edition of the play and the introduction by R. D. F. Pring-Mill to Lope de Vega, *Five Plays*, trans. Jill Booty [New York, Hill and Wang, 1961]). One commentator, the American A. David Kossoff, has expressed thoroughgoing disagreement (see his edition of the play, esp. pp. 28–30, but also pp. 343 and 358).

43. Emphasis mine.

44. Frye, *Anatomy*, p. 212.

45. As is well known, Hegel's ideas on tragedy were spread over several pages, and indeed, several volumes. They have, however, been conveniently summarized by A. C. Bradley in "Hegel's Theory of Tragedy."

46. Cf. Northrop Frye, *Fools of Time: Studies in Shakespearean Tragedy* (Toronto, University of Toronto Press, 1967): "In a tragic story there are plausible reasons why a character gets into a scapegoat

position, but they are never so plausible as to make the response of 'of course I should never have done that' relevant. Whatever the tragic hero has done, we are never so wise or virtuous that we cannot participate in the consequences of his fall with him" (p. 199).

47. William Troy, "Thoughts on Tragedy," in *Selected Essays,* ed. Stanley Edgar Hyman (New Brunswick, Rutgers University Press, 1967), p. 276. It is precisely the "inner principle of dissolution" that another critic of tragedy, Max Scheler, regards as the most characteristic feature of the tragic hero. See "On the Tragic," in *Tragedy: Modern Essays in Criticism,* p. 34.

48. These two lines, notably ambiguous, have been interpreted in widely varying ways by different commentators. The latest to offer readings are Victor Dixon and Alexander A. Parker, who defend their respective points of view in a joint article (*"El castigo sin venganza:* Two Lines, Two Interpretations," *MLN,* 85 [1970], 157–166). I find Dixon's interpretation marginally more convincing, and have adopted it in my translation.

49. Autograph reading. The Academy text here reads as follows:

> Aquí lo veré.
>
> *Éntrase Federico*
>
> Ya llega . . .
>
> Ya el Conde empuña la espada . . .
>
> Ejecutó mi justicia
>
> Quien ejecutó mi infamia.

50. Wilson, "Cuando Lope quiere, quiere," p. 295.

51. The parallels between the Duke and David, Federico and Absalom, are explored by A. David Kossoff in the introduction to his edition, pp. 30–32.

52. Autograph reading. The Academy text reads "muere en las venas helada."

53. See Albert S. Gérard, "The Loving Killers: The Rationale of Righteousness in Baroque Tragedy," *CLS,* 2 (1965), 215–218.

54. See in particular May, "Lope de Vega's *El castigo sin venganza,*" Scarfe, "Concerning the Publication."

55. Morris, "Lope de Vega's *El castigo sin venganza,*" p. 76.

56. See Herbert Weisinger, *Tragedy and the Paradox of the Fortunate Fall* (East Lansing, Michigan State University Press, 1953). The part played by the phase of perception in the "tragic rhythm" has been examined by a number of critics. See, among other studies, Francis Fergusson, *The Idea of a Theater* (Princeton, Princeton University Press, 1949); Kenneth Burke, *The Philosophy of Literary Form* (1941; rpt. New York, Knopf, 1957), and *A Grammar of Motives* (New York, Prentice-Hall, 1945); and Richard B. Sewall, *The Vision of Tragedy* (New Haven, Yale University Press, 1959).

57. See May, "Lope de Vega's *El castigo sin venganza,*" p. 173.

58. Alonso, "Lope de Vega y sus fuentes," p. 10.

59. Cf. Alfonso García Valdecasas, *El hidalgo y el honor,* 2nd ed. (Madrid, Revista de Occidente, 1958), p. 175.

60. Frye, *Anatomy,* p. 212.

5. Conclusion

1. Américo Castro, "Algunas observaciones acerca del concepto del honor en los siglos XVI y XVII," in *Semblanzas y estudios españoles* (Princeton, privately published, 1956), p. 366, rpt. from *RFE,* 3 (1916), 1–50 and 357–386.

2. Ramón Menéndez Pidal, "Del honor en el teatro español," in *De Cervantes y Lope de Vega* (Buenos Aires, Espasa-Calpe Argentina, 1940), pp. 175–178.

3. Alfonso García Valdecasas, *El hidalgo y el honor,* 2nd ed. (Madrid, Revista de Occidente, 1958), pp. 190–193.

4. Kenneth Burke, *The Philosophy of Literary Form* (1941; rpt. New York, Knopf, 1957), pp. 3–4 and passim.

5. Ramón Menéndez Pidal, "Lope de Vega: El arte nuevo y la nueva biografía," in *De Cervantes y Lope de Vega,* pp. 73–151.

6. José F. Montesinos, "La paradoja del 'Arte nuevo,'" *RO,* 2nd ser. 2, no. 15 (June 1964), 303, 328.

7. Henri Fluchère, *Shakespeare and the Elizabethans,* trans. Guy Hamilton (New York, Hill and Wang, 1956), esp. pp. 61–79.

8. *Epistolario de Lope de Vega,* ed. Agustín G. de Amezúa, 4 vols. (Madrid, 1935–1943).

9. *Epistolario,* ed. Amezúa, II ("Lope de Vega en sus cartas"), 271.

10. See Joseph H. Silverman, "Lope de Vega's Last Years and His Final Play, 'The Greatest Virtue of a King,'" *TQ,* 6, no. 1 (Spring 1963), 174–187. Morley and Bruerton date the play 1625–1636 on the basis of the versification, but Silverman's article provides persuasive reasons for adopting the date given in the text.

11. Hugo A. Rennert and Américo Castro, *Vida de Lope de Vega (1562–1635)* (1919; rpt. Salamanca, Anaya, 1968), pp. 323–324.

12. Silverman, "Lope de Vega's Last Years."

Appendix

1. Franz Grillparzer, *Studien zum spanischen Theater,* ed. August Sauer, Sämmtliche Werke, 17 (Stuttgart, J. G. Cotta, 1887); Adolf Friedrich von Schack, *Geschichte der dramatischen Literatur und Kunst in Spanien,* 3 vols. (Berlin, Duncker und Humblot, 1845–1846); Adolf Schaeffer, *Geschichte des spanischen Nationaldramas,* 2 vols. (Leipzig, F. A. Brockhaus, 1890); Wilhelm Hennigs, *Studien zu Lope de Vega Carpio: Eine Klassifikation seiner Comedias* (Göttingen, Vanderhoeck & Ruprecht, 1891).

2. Francisco de Rojas Zorrilla, *Cada qual lo que toca; La viña de Nabot,* ed. Américo Castro, Teat. Ant. Esp., 2 (Madrid, Centro de Estudios Históricos, 1917), p. 184.

Index

Works by Lope de Vega are listed by title.
All others will be found under their authors' names.

Aeschylus: *The Libation Bearers*, 113, 155; *Oresteia*, 113; *Prometheus Bound*, 156
Alemán, Mateo, 159; *Guzmán de Alfarache*, 56
Alfonso X: *Primera crónica general*, 17
Almasov, Alexey, 71
Alonso, Amado, 136, 156
Amezúa, Agustín G. de, 163, 164
Animal de Hungría, El, 171
Argensola, Lupercio Leonardo de, see Leonardo de Argensola, Lupercio
Aristotle, 7, 42–43, 98, 103, 114, 115, 116, 136, 141
Arte nuevo de hacer comedias en este tiempo, 15, 61
Aubrun, Charles Vincent, 60
Auerbach, Erich, 116
Autos sacramentales, 59
Ayala, Francisco, 9
Azorín (José Martínez Ruiz), 60

Bandello, Matteo, 24, 131, 156
Batalla del honor, La, 171
Beaumont, Sir Francis, 163
Bell, Aubrey F. G., 15
Bella malmaridada, La, 23, 25, 27, 160, 172
Belleforest, François de, 131–132, 156
Benavente, Jacinto, 159
Benedict, Ruth, 7

Beysterveldt, Antonie Adrianus van, vii
Bible, 10, 79; *John*, 81; *2 Samuel*, 153
Bodkin, Maud, 62, 81
Bradley, A. C., 114
Bruerton, Courtney, viii, ix, 23, 24, 35, 38, 171, 172
Burke, Kenneth, 161

Caballero del milagro, El, 170
Caballero de Olmedo, El, 66, 119, 163
Calderón de la Barca, Pedro, 13, 16; *El alcalde de Zalamea*, 72, 78; *Celos aun del aire matan*, 3; *El mayor monstruo los celos*, 3; *La vida es sueño*, 116–118
Campoamor, Ramón de, 159
Carlos el perseguido, 160, 172
Casalduero, Joaquín, 112
Castigo del discreto, El, vii, 23, 24–25, 160, 171, 172
Castigo sin venganza, El, vii, 118, 119, 131–158, 162, 164, 172; sources of, 131–132; motif of darkness in, 132–135; characterization of Federico and Casandra in, 135–141; characterization of the Duke in, 141–146; tragic resolution of, 146–158
Castro, Américo, vii, x, 5, 7, 8, 9, 16, 72, 160, 165, 170

Castro y Bellvís, Guillén de:
Las mocedades del Cid, 61
Cervantes y Saavedra, Miguel
de: *La Numancia,* 61
Comedias de capa y espada, 2,
18, 29, 118, 170
Comedy, 31–32, 33
Comendadores de Córdoba, Los,
5, 22, 38–54, 59, 61, 62, 63,
64, 65, 66, 68, 70, 76, 77,
83, 84, 85, 109, 113, 146,
161, 172; sources of, 39–41;
moral values in, 42–45; theme
of salvation through "aware-
ness" in, 42, 45–54; allegory
of the theater of the world in,
51–53; romancical structure of,
62–64
*Contienda de García de Paredes,
La,* 25, 172
Conversos (New Christians), 7–
8, 57. See also *Pureza de
sangre*
Corona merecida, La, 169, 171
Cotarelo y Mori, Emilio, 30, 33
Crawford, J. P. Wickersham, 18
Cuerdo en su casa, El, 170
Cueva, Juan de la: *El reto de
Zamora,* 61
Curtius, Ernst Robert, 95

Dante Alighieri, x
Desdichada Estefanía, La, 172
Desposorio encubierto, El, 160,
172
Discordia en los casados, La, 171

Eliot, T. S.: *Murder in the
Cathedral,* 156
Elliott, J. H., 55
Embustes de Fabia, Los, 160, 172
Encina, Juan del: *Égloga de tres
pastores,* 20
Enemigo engañado, El, 170
En los indicios la culpa, 171

Essex, Earl of, 55
Euripides, 131

Fergusson, Francis, 1, 111
Ferias de Madrid, Las, 23, 28–
37, 45, 118, 160, 165, 172;
plot of, 29–30; comic struc-
ture of, 32–33; theme of falsity
in, 33–34; autobiographical
overtones in, 35–37
Fernández, Sebastián: *Tragedia
Policiana,* 20
Fichter, William L., vii, 171
Firmeza en la desdicha, La, 171
Fletcher, John, 163
Fluchère, Henri, 163
Francesilla, La, 169, 170
Frazer, Sir James, *The Golden
Bough,* 33
Frenk Alatorre, Margit, 40
Froldi, Rinaldo, 36
Frye, Northrop, 30, 31, 33, 63,
64, 82, 114, 115, 136, 139,
147, 157
Fuenteovejuna, 11, 64, 65, 66,
70, 72, 82–112, 113, 119,
123, 146, 161, 162, 171, 172;
source of, 83–84; subplots in,
84–86; contrasting worlds in,
86–90; characterization of the
Comendador in, 90–94; mythic
overtones in, 94–97; theme of
natural love in, 97–102; theme
of tyranny in, 103–105; structure of, 105–109; ritualistic
scenes in, 109–112

Galán de la Membrilla, El, 11
Gallardo catalán, El, 171
Gérard, Albert S., 154
Gillet, Joseph E., 19
Gilman, Stephen, x
Goethe, Johann Wolfgang von,
149
Gómez-Moriana, Antonio, 102–
103, 109

Index

Góngora y Argote, Luis de, 159
Gran duque de Moscovia, El, 170
Granvela, Francisco Perrenot de, 36–37
Green, Otis H., 122, 123
Grillparzer, Franz, 169
Güete, Jayme de, *Comedia Vidriana,* 18–19, 20

Hechos de Garcilaso y moro Tarfe, Los, 27
Hegel, Georg Wilhelm Friedrich, 114, 148
Hennigs, Wilhelm, 169
Herrera, Fernando de, 159
Hierro, José, 60
Hijo de Reduán, El, 27
Hijo venturoso, El, 27
Hobbes, Thomas, 7
Hombría, 7, 8–9. *See also* "Imperative dimension of the person"
Honor: definition of, 4–6; bases of, 7–9; and female chastity, 9–12; and vengeance, 12–13; social dimension of, 13; and real life, 13–16; and peasants, 71–73
Honor plays: "action" of, 1; form of, 2–3; and analogous works, 2–3, 169–172; antecedents of, 17–23
Huizinga, J., 126

"Imperative dimension of the person," 9, 10, 13, 55
Inocente Laura, La, 171
Isabella I, 54

Jealousy, 3, 32
Jones, C. A., 14, 16
Juan Manuel, Don, 9, 89

Lattimore, Richmond, 113
Lazarillo de Tormes, La vida de (anonymous), 57

Leal criado, El, 170
Leech, Clifford, 118
Leonardo de Argensola, Lupercio, 22, 23; *Alejandra,* 21–22
Locura por la honra, La, 172
Love, 118–119

Mack, Maynard, 135
Madariaga, Salvador de, 4
Maravall, José Antonio, 52
Mariana, Juan de, 55
Martínez Ruiz, José, *see* Azorín
Más galán portugués, El, 171
May, T. E., 142, 153
Mayor imposible, El, 170
Mayor virtud de un rey, La: plot of, 164–165; autobiographical overtones in, 165–167
Molina, Luis de, 40
Mejor alcalde, el rey, El, 204
Menéndez Pidal, Ramón, vii, 17, 31, 71, 160, 161
Menéndez y Pelayo, Marcelino, viii, 102, 103, 122, 130
Merriman, R. B., 54
Milton, John: *Paradise Lost,* 157; *Samson Agonistes,* 156
Miró, Gabriel, 159
Molière, 31
Molina, Argote de, 122
Molina, Tirso de (Fray Gabriel Téllez): *El burlador de Sevilla,* 118
Montesinos, José F., viii, 162
Morley, S. Griswold, viii, ix, 23, 24, 35, 38, 171, 172
Morris, C. B., 155
Muller, Herbert J., 141, 142
Muñón, Sancho de: *Tragicomedia de Lisandro y Roselia,* 20–21
Myth: and ritual, 61; and the *Comedia,* 61–62; and romance, 62–65

Nacimiento de Ursón y Valentín, El, 28, 171

New Christians, see *Conversos*
No son todos ruiseñores, 170
Novelas a Marcia Leonarda, 25

Olivares, Count-Duke of, 165
Ortega y Gasset, José, 60
Ortiz, Agustín: *Comedia Radiana,*
    18,19,20
Osorio, Elena, 35–37

Parker, A. A., 114, 141
Pearce, Roy Harvey, x
Peligros de la ausencia, Los, 171
Pereda, José Maria de, 159
Pérez Galdós, Benito, 159
Peribáñez y el Comendador de
    Ocaña, vii, 25, 45, 64, 65–82,
    83, 84, 85, 86, 89, 94, 95,
    109, 111, 112, 113, 123, 133,
    146, 161, 162, 169, 172;
    sources of, 65–66; contrasting
    worlds in, 66–67; theme of
    "awareness" in, 67–68; ritual-
    istic scenes in, 68–76; struc-
    ture of, 76–78; imagery in,
    79–82
Philip II, 54, 55, 59
Philip III, 54
Piadoso veneciano, El, 172
Pitt-Rivers, Julian, 6, 70
Plato, 97–98
Plautus, 31
Pleitos de Ingalaterra, Los, 171
Pobreza no es vileza, 170
Poema de Mio Cid (anonymous),
    53
Poetic justice, 114, 132
Porfiar hasta morir, 118, 119,
    122–130, 131, 162, 172;
    source of, 122; courtly love
    and poetry in, 123–126; char-
    acterization of Macías in, 126–
    129; death of Macías in, 129–
    130
Príncipe despeñado, El, 172

Prudente venganza, La, 25–26
Pureza de sangre, 7–8, 10–12,
    72–73, 90

Quevedo y Villegas, Francisco de,
    55

Racine, Jean, 115; *Phèdre,* 43,
    133
Rades y Andrada, Fray Francisco
    de, 83, 103
Raglan, Lord, 65
Reichenberger, Arnold G., 98
Rennert, Hugo A., 165
Richards, I. A., 115
Ritual: and the *autos sacramen-*
    tales, 59; and the *Comedia,*
    60–61; and myth, 61; and
    romance, 65; and early Spanish
    drama, 192
Robo de Dina, El, 171, 172, 207
Rojas, Fernando de: *La Celestina,*
    18, 19, 20
Romance, 62–63
Romancero general (1600)
    (anonymous), 40
Rougemont, Denis de, 129, 130,
    136
Rueda, Lope de: *Cornudo y*
    contento, 23
Rufo, Juan, 40–42, 44, 49
Rústico del cielo, El, 170

Salomon, Noël, 71–72
Schack, Adolf Friedrich von, 169
Schaeffer, Adolf, 169
Seneca, 21
Serrano, Carlos, 92
Shakespeare, William, x, 68, 115,
    131, 163; *All's Well That*
    Ends Well, 30; *Hamlet,* 111,
    113, 132, 133, 149; *King*
    Lear, 146, 156; *Macbeth,* 133,
    146; *Othello,* 3, 154–155
Shame cultures, 6

Silverman, Joseph H., 165
Soons, Alan, 79, 97, 99
Sophocles, x, 131; *Antigone,*
149; *Oedipus Rex,* 146, 156
Spain, 1580–1621: military and
diplomatic setbacks of, 54–55;
economic difficulties of, 55–
57; social tensions in, 57–59.
See also *Conversos; Pureza de
sangre*
Spitzer, Leo, 52, 96, 97

Téllez, Fray Gabriel, *see* Molina,
Tirso de
Templin, Ernest H., 118
Tenorio, Cristóbal, 165
Terence, 31
Testimonio vengado, El, 171
Thomas Aquinas, St., 103, 104
Toledano vengado, El, 38, 172
Torres Naharro, Bartolomé de:
Comedia Ymenea, 17, 18, 19,
20
Tragedy, 113–115
Troy, William, 149

Valdecasas, Alfonso García, vii,
160
Vaquero de Moraña, El, 170
Vega, Antonio Clara de, 165
Vega Carpio, Lope Félix de: and
vengeance, 25–27; youthful
fantasies of, 27–28; and Elena
Osorio, 35–37; and the
theatrical public, 161–162;
final years of, 162–164; and
limpieza de sangre, 184–185
Vélez de Guevara, Luis: *La
serrana de la Vera,* 72
Victoria de la honra, La, 118,
119–122, 131, 172; characterizations in, 119–121; celebration of the hero in, 122
Virués, Cristóbal de, 22, 23;
Atila furioso, 21, 22; *La cruel
Casandra,* 21, 22

Wilson, Edward M., 67, 79, 133,
146, 153
World as a stage, topos of the,
51–52, 67–68, 89–90